STAGING DEMOCRACY

A volume in the NIU Series in

Slavic, East European, and Eurasian Studies
Edited by Christine D. Worobec

For a list of books in the series, visit our website at cornellpress.cornell.edu.

STAGING DEMOCRACY

POLITICAL
PERFORMANCE IN
UKRAINE, RUSSIA,
AND BEYOND

JESSICA PISANO

NORTHERN ILLINOIS UNIVERSITY PRESS
AN IMPRINT OF CORNELL UNIVERSITY PRESS
Ithaca and London

Copyright © 2022 by Cornell University

All rights reserved. Except for brief quotations in a review, this book, or parts thereof, must not be reproduced in any form without permission in writing from the publisher. For information, address Cornell University Press, Sage House, 512 East State Street, Ithaca, New York 14850. Visit our website at cornellpress.cornell.edu.

First published 2022 by Cornell University Press

Library of Congress Cataloging-in-Publication Data

Names: Pisano, Jessica, author.
Title: Staging democracy : political performance in Ukraine, Russia, and beyond / Jessica Pisano.
Description: Ithaca [New York] : Northern Illinois University Press, an imprint of Cornell University Press, 2022. | Series: NIU series in Slavic, East European, and Eurasian studies | Includes bibliographical references and index.
Identifiers: LCCN 2021040009 (print) | LCCN 2021040010 (ebook) | ISBN 9781501764066 (hardcover) | ISBN 9781501764202 (paperback) | ISBN 9781501764073 (ebook) | ISBN 9781501764080 (pdf)
Subjects: LCSH: Political culture—Ukraine. | Political culture—Russia (Federation) | Political participation—Economic aspects—Ukraine. | Political participation—Economic aspects—Russia (Federation) | Public relations and politics—Ukraine. | Public relations and politics—Russia (Federation)
Classification: LCC JA75.7 .P57 2022 (print) | LCC JA75.7 (ebook) | DDC 320.9—dc23
LC record available at https://lccn.loc.gov/2021040009
LC ebook record available at https://lccn.loc.gov/2021040010

For those who want to preserve democracy

I am afraid that the term "dictatorship," regardless of how intelligible it may otherwise be, tends to obscure rather than clarify the real nature of power in this system.

Václav Havel, "Power of the Powerless"

# Contents

Preface   ix

Introduction: Performances of Democracy   1

1. Researching Political Theater   18
2. History of the Form   31
3. Setting the Stage   51
4. Staging Performances   70
5. Improvisation   90
6. Meanings of Participation   113
7. States of Ambiguity   136

   Conclusion: A New Social Contract   161

Notes   181
Index   229

 PREFACE

As this book went to press, the Russian Federation launched a full-scale war on Ukraine. Within a week as many as a million Ukrainian women and children had fled to other European countries. Many other millions of Ukrainian people of all ages and ethnicities took up arms and words, laying down body and soul for their freedom: to fight for their lives, to protect their democracy, and to rule their own land. As Russia's war reverberates around the globe, this book means to clarify the nature of the political regime that gave rise to it.

* * *

The argument of this book was born on the New Haven line, on the train home to New York after a memorial service for sociologist and political scientist Juan Linz. Soon after, a world away, as violence broke out in the Ukrainian capital against people protesting government malfeasance, another political scientist and dedicated teacher, Robert Dahl, also would pass. Linz and Dahl, great thinkers about authoritarianism and democracy, helped shape the intellectual agenda of generations of scholars and policy makers.

The world Linz and Dahl knew, described, and so compellingly theorized has shifted beyond recognition. Understanding democracy and authoritarianism is as urgent as ever, but the unstable terrain between them has left many people wondering how to think about and categorize politics: even established democracies are producing politics that do not seem very democratic at all, while repressive regimes build modern transportation and communications infrastructure, foster efficient service systems, and encourage government responsiveness.

Political scientists have invented words for regimes in the middle of the democracy-authoritarianism spectrum, as the competitive authoritarianism political scientists Lucan Way and Steven Levitsky have described in *Competitive Authoritarianism: Hybrid Regimes after the Cold War* (Cambridge: Cambridge University Press, 2012). But changes in many countries, including established democracies, have left us struggling for vocabulary even to discuss the topic. Today's regimes do not necessarily share the features of the governments and societies from which they sprang. Sometimes described as hybrids, they may instead be variants: entities with novel properties. We need additional conceptual tools for thinking about politics. That need includes how to parse shifts that involve economic as well as political change—without falling back on other twentieth-century concepts like fascism which, as political scientist Marlene Laruelle reminds us in *Is Russia Fascist? Unraveling Propaganda East and West* (Ithaca, NY: Cornell University Press, 2021), sometimes may be more useful in the practice of politics than for its analysis. This book is an effort to engage with those needs, to contribute to an analytical apparatus that will allow us to view political change more clearly and discover what new avenues for understanding may open before us. It suggests a new vocabulary and set of concepts and shows how they help us understand phenomena that otherwise may seem beyond our grasp.

When I began researching this book two decades ago, Vladimir Putin had just come to power in Russia, and Ukraine seemed to be swinging pendulum-like between something like democracy, with an active and engaged citizenry, and a political order that felt like authoritarianism. In Ukraine, national politics changed dramatically from one presidential administration to the next. One group of politicians, when they were in power, implemented a liberal economic and political agenda, fostering European alliances and focusing on Ukrainian national identity. The other group blackmailed political opponents, built political machines, gutted scientific institutions, and appeased the Kremlin. When the latter group was out of office, the party seemed to recede from national politics, but really its cadres were busy building its agenda and support in the provinces for the next elections. Through it all, newspapers and television told Ukrainians that they were a divided, polarized nation.

Some Ukrainian politicians did more to uphold democratic standards than others, but all were part of the same web of relationships linking industry and government in backroom deals that excluded most of their constituents. In his book *Patronal Politics* (New York: Cambridge University Press, 2015), the political scientist Henry Hale would later explain this political back and forth by focusing on the effects of exchange networks among political elites who didn't necessarily share the same ideas but who knew and traded favors with each other. Hale had figured out how this worked for political elites. I wanted to know how it worked for everyone else.

At the time, I looked at those networks from vantage points far from the national capital. The people I knew were farmers and factory workers, tractor drivers, land surveyors, and local functionaries who made their lives in and around a region along Ukraine's border with Russia and on the other side of the country, along Ukraine's border with the European Union. They kept a sharp eye on Russia and the money for Ukrainian infrastructure that flowed from Moscow. But even though Ukrainian national politics seemed to move to and fro, the basic challenges they faced as they tried to make a living and educate their children did not change very much from year to year. Instead, what changed for them was whether or not their bosses or suppliers or teachers pressured them to support politicians. Those demands usually arrived when the second group of politicians was in power, the ones who thought more of their personal relationships with Moscow than with their allies in the West.

When those calls and visits and meetings came, people had to promise to vote for someone, or get other people to vote for someone, or take a bus to go demonstrate on a city square somewhere, or show up and smile and talk about how well things were going when a delegation from the regional capital pulled up in front of the local town hall. Their job was to pretend to care, to make it look like they and all those they supervised were exercising their civic right to express their political preferences.

At first, people in Ukraine who supported the Party of Regions—the party that American political operator and Trump consigliere Paul Manafort worked for and that was organizing the most paid demonstrations—seemed to do so by default. The personal qualities of Viktor Yanukovych, the party's leader and Ukraine's future prime minister and president, were not appealing to them. But many felt both ignored by and condescended to by the pro-democracy politicians and their compatriots who supported them.

For people watching from the audience, without a view behind the scenes, for a while it all looked more or less like democracy as usual. But on stage, at paid demonstrations and when people went to vote at their boss's request, something else was happening. People were starting to think about politics differently. They used to think programmatically, voting for politicians according to their ideas. Now they were just picking sides. They were buying into whole ways of thinking and seeing, an Alice in Wonderland state of mind where the world on the other side of the mirror made no sense at all.

In the following years, Russia's aggression against Ukraine would pull some Party of Regions supporters into Moscow's orbit. It would alienate many more. The war made fervent Ukrainian patriots of Russian-speaking Ukrainians, killing thousands and displacing more than a million and a half people in its first years and rending families and friendships across the post-Soviet world. Sunflower fields abused by monoculture in a region where I researched my book, *The Post-Soviet Potemkin Village* (New York: Cambridge University Press, 2008), would have their share of nitrogen, fertilized by blood and bone.

All this had an impact on the material I eventually decided to use in this book. As of this writing, Ukraine and Russia remain locked in a protracted yet undeclared war. It is hard to see how it will end, or to know how people will come to view this period years from now. Amid a politics in which the future of the past is uncertain, I made choices about privileging certain types of evidence over others. I describe my methods in detail in chapter 1. The proliferation of coercion and violence in the region has made me circumspect about identifying all my sources. It is difficult to say what local punishments might one day be meted out to those who decide to reveal the compliance of their superiors or the participation of their neighbors. I wrote with this in mind, relying on published evidence where I could and using my accrued knowledge of local context to interpret it. This is what is needed to do this kind of work, and to forge what I hope is a responsible path through the moral labyrinth that is research among real people with real lives and hopes.

STAGING DEMOCRACY

Introduction
Performances of Democracy

In June 1996, on the eve of the first—and arguably last—competitive presidential elections in Russia, with the country still mired in the economic and social tumult that had followed the dissolution of the Soviet empire, a rash of writing spread across the walls of buildings in the southwestern rust belt city of Voronezh. The inscriptions were visible on large roadside cement pipes near the outskirts of the city, on buildings along major bus routes, and on the doors, gates, and walls of less traveled streets in the urban center.

The graffiti commented on electoral politics. It appeared to express the artists' preferences for presidential candidates. One prominent inscription, scrawled across the side of an apartment building, read, "If you want severe hunger, cast your vote for the sickle and hammer." On the walls of an underground passageway where young adults copied homemade paeans to the late Kurt Cobain onto the walls, a misspelled tag referred to the Communist Party candidate: "Zyuganov is a bastard with a capital B." Nearby, others targeted President Boris Yeltsin, changing the "Ye" in Yeltsin to a swastika to read, "Yeltsin is the butcher of communism." One accused Yeltsin of economic crimes: "Not one vote for Yeltsin the thief." And another supported General Alexander Lebed: "Where there's Lebed, there's truth and order." Playing on the meaning of Lebed's family name, "swan," someone else had added, "And what about where there's a duck?"

If similar inscriptions had appeared in postindustrial neighborhoods elsewhere in the world—on walls in Youngstown, Ohio, in Sheffield, England, or in Germany's Ruhrgebiet—onlookers might have understood them as a kind of civic engagement or personalization: here were young people using their own medium to engage in political debate.[1] For some, street art expresses freedom and creativity, a rejection of conventional social norms and an effort to reclaim public space for social critique.[2] Seen through this lens, the street artists of Voronezh expressed youthful ebullience, even resistance to the constraints of the previous, communist order.

In Russia's heartland, another interpretation dominated press coverage and local discussions about the graffiti. This interpretation cast the writing as Soviet reminiscence, a mere spin on the visual propaganda that had saturated public space during decades of communist rule.[3] A humor magazine published by students at Voronezh State University made the point. In one cartoon, an elderly woman trundled by a fence enclosing two buildings. Slogans atop the buildings read, "Put the decisions of the first punk congress into practice!" and "Yegor, you are wrong!" The latter addressed either Yegor Ligachev and his famous criticism of Boris Yeltsin ("Boris, you are wrong") or Yegor Gaidar, the former prime minister and architect of Russia's shock therapy in the early 1990s. On the fence, someone had scrawled "Glory to the Communist Party of the Soviet Union." The woman, leaning on her cane and looking at the fence in disapproval, says, "Hooligan!"[4]

The joke was that despite the ideological reversal that accompanied the end of Soviet power, the form of communication—here, slogans on buildings—looked just like the authoritative discourse of late socialism.[5] And as anthropologist Alexei Yurchak has argued, in late socialism, form had been the entire point.[6]

Neither interpretation of the graffiti—individual expression or authoritative discourse—captured the actual origin of the writing on Voronezh walls. In an effort to target youth constituencies, competing political parties had organized production of the graffiti. The artists were cash-strapped university students struggling to pay for food amid rapidly rising prices. Local branch offices of candidates' campaigns, including that of incumbent president Boris Yeltsin, had hired them to go out at night with paint and brushes. Campaign workers had instructed the students to create speech acts that were meant to look like mild transgressions—even though in fact they were coordinated by some of the same power structures operating official party politics.[7]

The artifice of electoral graffiti in Voronezh heralded the proliferation, by the dawn of the twenty-first century, of performances now ubiquitous across territory formerly governed by the Soviet Union: choreographed elections, elite-directed social movements, mass demonstrations outwardly resembling grassroots mobilization, and smaller dramatizations.[8] To their audiences, these performances look like practices traditionally associated with liberal democratic society. For many of their participants, another logic governs, one that generates other forms of meaning, community, and fealty toward the organizers.

The slogan of the Yeltsin campaign in 1996 was "Vote or lose" (*Golosui ili proigraesh'*). Addressing itself personally and informally to voters, the slogan meant to remind them of the dangers of a return to communism as the incumbent president battled Gennadii Zyuganov, leader of the Communist Party of the Russian Federation. The slogan also neatly captured the political economy that would drive political participation in the decades to come and would slowly prompt a shift in the meanings people associated with their participation in elections and street demonstrations.

Political parties in both Russia and Ukraine would gain voters by taking things and holding them hostage in return for participation in shows of support: people's access to their livelihoods or their pensions, their access to critical infrastructure, their access to services, and their children's access to education. Across Russia and Ukraine as well as the broader region, many people would mobilize because if they did not, local authorities would remove their access to things they believed were theirs to keep, and on which they had come to rely. Yeltsin's campaign slogan carried a hint of that future: Vote for us, or lose everything.

Performing Democracy

This book is about performances of democratic politics in Russia and Ukraine: why people take part in such performances, how they are related to economic change, and how they affect the meanings that attach to political participation. While scholarship written in English about Eastern Europe and Eurasia often focuses on voluntarism and resistance, this book homes in on dramatic performances that express support for existing political orders. We can think of these as command performances, theater performed for the king.[9] By focusing on local political economies of performance, this book shows how millions of people are called to participate in political theater and how their participation changes how they think about politics.

But where is the line between political theater and ordinary politics?[10] Sociologists and political philosophers have long theorized the role of performance in everyday life, and descriptions of politics as theater begin with Plato's *Laws* and Aristotle's *Poetics*. Democratic popular movements worldwide use spectacle to advance political arguments. In the worlds of the anthropologists Clifford Geertz or Georges Balandier, all of politics is theater.[11] This book takes all politics to include theatrical elements, but it focuses on dramas that unfold at appointed times and places, involve specific people, and have identifiable beginnings and ends. These dramas have a *metteur en scène*, a director or directors who select the cast, block the play on the stage, and oversee the production. Some people are onstage, while others are in the audience.

The performances in this book can be distinguished from their democratic homologues—what people in liberal societies might like to think of as the "real thing," but which also can be viewed as theater, albeit of a different sort—by the perceptions and motivations of their participants, and by the meanings those participants find in the play.

Some see command performances as fraudulent versions of democratic institutions, imagining politics as divisible into genuine and ersatz versions.[12] This book argues that political theater is best understood not as mere imitation, a pale mirror of democratic institutions, but as a political practice with its own set of meanings. Even as they portray democratic contestation, command performances encode, express, and advance a real politics that is different from the ideal their form purports to represent.

In Russia, today's command performances remind some people of Soviet-era pageantry, but that too is part of the theater.[13] In "The Kingdom of Political Imitation," published in the Russian newspaper *Vedomosti* in 2014, political scientist Ekaterina Schulmann suggested that today's "Stalin moustaches are also stick-ons."[14] Twenty-first-century performances do borrow their stagecraft and dramaturgy from Soviet-era repertoires, recalling another time. But their underlying political economy is anchored in market economies, the product of an alchemy of privatization, deregulation, and risk shift.

The economic conditions for the proliferation of political theater arose amid a global shift from socialism in the East and welfare capitalism in the West to neoliberal capitalism almost everywhere. In Russia and Ukraine, markets have made many people more economically insecure than Soviet-era systems had, and the privatization and enclosure campaigns of the 1990s in both countries ultimately led to more, not less dependence on local political and economic elites.[15] Governments and ruling parties now use that dependence to pressure people to participate in command performances. And the enclosure and erosion or disappearance of public-sector services and common-pool resources within which people formerly had been able to carve out spaces of subsistence and freedom offer new opportunities for political coercion and state expansion.

This material story helps us understand the changing social contract underlying the political phenomena that observers often gloss as illiberalism or populism. Where command performances proliferate and leaders talk about "our people," they refer not merely to people who support them at the polls: they mean a political community nested within the population. The contours of this imagined community of supporters are mainly defined not by people's ethnic identity or adherence to ideology, but by their participation in an exchange.

In that exchange, people trade political participation—going out onto a public square to demonstrate in support of the government, or showing up to vote in elections without choice—for mitigation of economic risk. If you support the leader, you get to keep your government job. If you support the leader, no one raids your business or shuts it down because of supposed fire or other safety inspection issues. If you support the leader, your kid keeps his place in kindergarten, your university professor gives you a passing grade, your village gets a gas line. Because some leaders favor the use of nationalist rhetoric, divisions between those who support them and those who do not might seem to be identity based, but at their source, they depend on economy.

Taken as a systemic politics, the tactics used in political theater can pose a potential threat to almost all aspects of certain people's daily material existence: their livelihoods, their children's future, their home life. Political theater involves the conversion of goods and services people previously regarded as entitlements into privileges—privileges that they then receive in return for loyalty and participation in political performance. This exchange transforms relations between state and society, politicizing the responsibilities of the state toward citizens: the state assumes obligations not toward the entire population, but only toward those who support incumbent politicians or parties of power—political parties that act on behalf of executive-branch politicians. In this, we can see the seeds of so-called populist logics of governance.

Over time, popular participation in the exchange networks underlying command performances generates boundaries within political communities. The practice of political theater gives rise to distinct epistemic groups that cohere around particular understandings of what it means to participate in politics. This can harden borders within political communities, destabilize perceptions of politics, and produce fuzziness at the edges of the state. By studying the stagecraft and stage management of command performances, we can observe how and why this happens.

Thinking across Regime Types

Some might wonder what Russia and Ukraine are doing in the same book about politics in the early twenty-first century. After the dissolution of the Soviet Union, Russia and Ukraine followed different paths, designing their institutions of governance differently at both the federal level or national level, and in their regions.[16] Those trajectories contributed to key differences in the nature and behavior of the policing apparatus in each country and the numbers of party organizations involved in politics. Today, most people view the two countries as embodying distinct regime types: independent Ukraine is widely seen as an unconsolidated democracy, while most outside observers describe Russia under Vladimir Putin as an authoritarian regime.

Yet despite deep and consequent differences in the two countries' politics—differences that led Ukrainian president Volodymyr Zelensky to remark of the two countries in 2019 that "only one thing remains 'in common,' and that is the state border"[17]—much of the stagecraft and stage management widely used in Ukraine in command performances is also widely used in Russia. Political theater and its underlying political economy cut across regime types. This has been the case even as in Ukraine there have been multiple enactments of the script onstage at the same time, as some opposition parties leverage many of the same tactics as the party of power, while in Russia, there is only one enactment, and one relevant party.[18] Differences in national context are not a barrier to understanding. Instead, they help show how and why political theater can develop in diverse political settings.

If political theater can exist in both democracies and autocracies, what are its boundary conditions? The performances of political theater in this book emerge when and where political elites believe they need to be seen, whether by international audiences or domestic players on the stage, as supportive of liberal democratic forms of governance—or at least responsive to citizens' needs and concerns. Political theater may be present in regimes whose leaders are seen as populist or illiberal, but it does not necessarily require the presence of a charismatic leader. Rather, it depends on local networks and improvisation, and the cooperation of participants.

While the performances described in this book may look to some like a variation on authoritarianism, political theater works because of economic insecurity. And although elements of contemporary dramaturgy have roots in the Soviet past, the conditions that make economic pressure possible, luring people onto the stage, are not unique to post-Soviet space. Instead, they are typical of middle-income countries throughout the world. The tools of political theater used in Russia and Ukraine can be used effectively anywhere the welfare state is waning, the social contract is shifting to place risk on individuals rather than society as a whole, and where politicians have—or can create—the means to politicize bureaucracies.

Since traditional regime-type concepts do not fully illuminate the politics that these productions express or produce, this book temporarily brackets generalizations about the concentration of power, the rule of law, and the extent of freedom upon which traditional regime-type designations depend. Setting aside those categories to focus on the stagecraft and stage management of command performances, the contours of a different story emerge. That story has less to do with the tools of authoritarian control as it is traditionally understood than with an increasingly global shift in how states construe their responsibilities to individuals and individuals understand their responsibilities to states. Economic arrangements and relationships are at the heart of the complex stage management of contemporary political theater.

Decades of scholarship about Russia and Ukraine situated these countries in a post-Soviet or postsocialist world in which polities have achieved greater or lesser degrees of political freedom and market development for their populations.[19] This book analyzes their politics in the contemporary capitalist order, in which economic insecurity has destabilized democratic governance and birthed new forms of politics worldwide.[20]

The performances in this book are widely recognized as such in both Ukraine and Russia. "Political theater" captures in the English language a genus of phenomena found in the Russophone world. The Russian language describes these phenomena with a rich vocabulary that includes "window dressing" (*pokazukha*), "mimicry" (*imitatsiia*—a loan word from English,[21] in contrast to the Russian *podrazhanie*), and "Potemkin villages" (*Potemkinskie derevni*),[22] among others.[23] We can think of political theater as example of what anthropology, borrowing from psychoanalysis, refers to as an experience-near concept,[24] what ethnographers call an emic category, a variation on a name that people give to their own experiences.

Relatives of political theater can be found elsewhere.[25] In Lusophone Africa and Brazil, people speak of laws that are "só para inglês ver," or "just for the English to see," originally in reference to nineteenth-century pro forma Portuguese efforts to stamp out the slave trade in the face of British criticism.[26] In Francophone Africa, Emmanuel Terray wrote of *le climatiseur* (air conditioning) and *la véranda*,[27] a reference to the politics that takes place behind the scenes and the visible, formal institutions of politics. Journalism and scholarly research in and about Latin America long has referred to *la fachada democrática*, the democratic façade. And in politics in the United States, even before the era of presidential carnival-barker kayfabe, or portrayal of theater as reality, the sociologist Edward Walker documented how Astroturf lobbyists paid PR firms to create campaigns that resemble grassroots political movements,[28] while the political scientist Alexander Hertel-Fernandez wrote about how major corporations in the United States engaged in large-scale mobilization of their employees, inciting them to vote for particular policy initiatives or risk retribution in the workplace.[29]

How Does Political Theater Work?

The sites of the portrayals analyzed in this book include electoral contests and social movements involving multiple economic, social, and political institutions. They range from miniature dramatizations to impress delegations from the capital, to large-scale mobilizations at the national level. To visualize one version of what political theater can look like, let us imagine an example from Russia in the summer of 2020. The government introduced a referendum to amend the constitution permitting the current president to remain in place for additional terms. This was not a question to the population with a cliffhanger finish, the way a controversial ballot measure might be in certain jurisdictions. In this case, the outcome was understood by all in advance: a clear demonstration of support by the population, regardless of how they might think or feel. This demonstration is an example of political theater. But who stages the play, and how does it work?

The president of the country may act as dramaturge, selecting the script. The story is simple: changes to the constitution allow the president to stay in power and expand his control over the judiciary. The script also proposes some modifications to protect the minimum wage and pensions. The country debates the question in newspapers, on television, and in special meetings convened for this purpose. Then, in a grand finale, an overwhelming majority of the population votes to approve the changes.

The president's chief ideologist directs the play. He sits in the *theatron*, viewing the action from the audience's perspective. Like any director, he does not go backstage and does not know for certain exactly what is happening there. His job is to select the cast and block the play: Which regions should most resoundingly vote to approve the measures? Where should cheering extras stand on the vast stage that is the country's territory?

Meanwhile, the stage managers, mid-level functionaries in the capital and the provinces, busily call "Places!": they telephone local leaders—district-level functionaries, heads of schools and hospitals, directors of industrial farms and enterprises, and many others—to tell them when they and their extras should appear onstage.[30] Those local leaders in turn inform the extras—their employees and subordinates—of scene changes and anything else they need to know to participate in the show. The extras generally comply, understanding that their livelihoods may depend on it.

The audience includes journalists, members of the international community, and others. The president sits in a box seat, watching the proceedings, though occasionally he joins the cast. Most of the audience understands that they have come to watch a show, though at times some may be so carried away by the realism of the performance that they forget themselves. As they view the drama unfolding on the stage, members of the audience may not notice that early in the first act, some of the extras, being careful not to make any noise, have slipped off the stage and are exiting the theater through a side door. Such attrition is common in political theater. Less frequently, someone might shout "fire," only to exit the theater in the security guards' firm embrace.

In Russia and Ukraine, participants in political drama include both individuals who see themselves as partaking in a charade and individuals for whom the charade *is* politics. Both are aware of an understanding in their societies that the activity in question is a performance. For both, the meanings that attach to these performances are more than the sum of the exchange relationships that are part of the stagecraft of political drama.

Like the Voronezh graffiti, which when viewed through different interpretive lenses could be seen to express two entirely different politics, incommensurable interpretations of political participation can, and often do, grow out of the practice of political theater. Narratives associated with these divergent interpretations both reflect and structure popular perceptions of politics. Over time, political communities living on the same territory can come to live, speak, and consume information in parallel worlds whose boundaries are defined by their interpretation of the meaning of official performances.

Putting the Pieces Together

Observers of politics from social scientists to fiction writers generally tell three stories about political theater in Russia and Ukraine. Each of these stories illuminates important aspects of politics, yet each leaves key questions unanswered. These stories cohere around regime hybridity, clientelism, and dramaturgy. This book brings these approaches together, examines how they operate locally, and shows how a combination of perspectives can illuminate aspects of politics we did not previously see.

The account that political scientists most frequently provide of performances of democratic institutions suggests that they may be evidence of regime hybridity.[31] This approach locates political systems with high degrees of theatricality somewhere in between democracy and authoritarianism, using political freedom and inclusiveness as key criteria. This interpretation usually brackets questions surrounding the meanings people assign to elections, demonstrations, or other forms of political participation. Regime type concepts—democracy, authoritarianism, and their hybrid cousins—are useful tools for thinking about how power is enacted: they simplify analysis across large numbers of countries, help us name and identify distinctive institutional pathways and rules at the national level, provide conceptual poles for analyses of political transitions, and suggest fruitful lines for comparative inquiry along a number of vectors.[32]

At the same time, regime types also lead us to imagine state-society relationships as homogeneous across territory and coextensive with state boundaries. Countries are democracies or autocracies, or something in between, even when life within them varies radically for different people. Using only regime types to categorize countries' politics, we may miss intermittent, episodic, or cyclical changes in the extent and ways in which state institutions control society.[33] Hybridity alone does not help us see or explain variation of people's experience of the state within polities.

Regime types as a tool for analyzing politics also can obscure important ideas about political change at the national level. When we presume that autocracies resemble other autocracies and that democracies resemble, or are at least comparable with, other democracies, we may tend not to think about comparisons across different types of regimes. In the case of Russia and Ukraine, this can make salient features of political orders shared across regime types—in this case, conditions propitious for the production of political theater—invisible. We need regime types for thinking about politics, but we also need conceptual tools like political theater to allow us to think outside the regime type box.

A second approach takes up relationships between democracy and the economy to focus on clientelism.[34] This concept can explain some of the underlying political economy of performances of democracy, but it stops short of providing a full vision of the phenomena. Clientelism without dramaturgy does not account for the symbolic politics that develop out of the practice of political theater. The lens of clientelism permits us to see and analyze relationships between voters and party and state representatives, but we need the theatrical metaphor to see how contemporary performances are related to Soviet-era dramatic forms and how command performances affect how people think about participation.

Further, to understand the meaning and value of exchanges for the people who participate in them, we need to place exchanges in their local contexts of complex ongoing relationships in which people inhabit multiple roles. Some people participate in performances in direct response to an exchange as clients or brokers, but sometimes they enter the stage for other reasons entirely.[35] Translating that complexity into political concepts, this book uses the more varied terminology of theater production to describe people's roles.

A third story scholars and writers tell about command performances views post-Soviet politics in its ensemble as dramaturgy. Its main *dramatis personae* are political technologists. This story's narrative arc can be traced from Viktor Pelevin's novelistic treatment of marketing and politics in *Generation "P,"* through Andrew Wilson's account of political technologists' craft in *Virtual Politics*, to Peter Pomerantsev's journalistic explorations of Putin's Russia as a cultural field where truth and facts are unsettled categories.[36] To these may be added accounts of spectacle and dissimulation in contemporary Eurasia,[37] many of which draw on the work of the anthropologist Alexei Yurchak, who emphasized a state-led shift away from literal and toward performative meaning in late Soviet culture.[38] In some of these accounts, the action that unfolds upon the media stage drives political life, and people are spectators, not actors. The economic motivations driving societal mobilization in command performances are incidental to these story lines. But political theater is not only the product of political technologists' fancy and does not only involve or concern political elites. And the reasons that entice people onto the stage are tangible and concrete. To understand political theater, we also need the political economy story.

What Kind of Theater Is Political Theater?

Now let's get back to our sheep. Most of the performances in this book follow a theatrical tradition whose story line appeals to our emotions and sends us back for more. To understand the conventions of this form is to understand how political theater influences audiences and why politicians might want to use it.

The German playwright Bertolt Brecht, in his 1930 notes, "The Modern Theater Is the Epic Theater," contrasted two varieties of theater whose form we inherit from the ancients. These are dramatic theater, whose conventions descend from Aristotle, and epic theater, rooted in Plato's texts.[39] In Brecht's formulation, dramatic theater guides the audience through a narrative arc that brings the viewer from point A to point B. The play fills the viewer with emotions and sensations. It creates pleasure and resolution through catharsis. Losing herself in the drama, the spectator has the impression of sharing in the experience unfolding on the stage.

As the spectator is swept along, there is little room for emancipatory or transformational politics that might break the momentum and make her stop and think about the state of the world or her society. For this reason, Aristotelian form offers a convenient model for politicians who stand to benefit from the reproduction of status quo politics. Parties of power usually prefer it.

The other sort, modern or epic theater, is usually favored by opposition movements.[40] It offers something different. It means to prompt social reflection about contemporary problems, challenging the audience and provoking viewers to action.[41] In this type of theater, the spectator is an observer situated outside the action. She does not identify with the characters. Brecht called this *Verfremdungseffekt*, or alienation effect. It is something like what Russian formalist poets in the early twentieth century called *ostranenie*, or defamiliarization.[42] In epic theater, the dramaturge denaturalizes the spectator's environment, pushing her to face the meaning of the action on the stage.

Both dramatic and epic theater can be found in politics in Russia and Ukraine. State-led performances usually follow Aristotelian conventions. Chapter 7 addresses the emotionality that typifies those performances. Sometimes political incumbents pretend to be underdogs, as in the Voronezh graffiti, and draw on epic theater. Until the liberal populist showman Volodymyr Zelensky adopted Aristotelian theatrical forms to campaign for and govern as president of Ukraine, organized critique in Russia and Ukraine tended to adopt epic forms.[43]

This book focuses on pro-regime dramatic political theater, but it keeps epic political theater and the theatricality of democratic oppositional politics in mind. Analysis of only one of these approaches to politics without acknowledgment of the other's existence would mean losing sight of a perspective necessary for understanding the whole. For ease of reading, throughout this book the term "political theater" refers to the Aristotelian, dramatic form, and "command performance" and "political theater" appear interchangeably.

In their form, performances of political theater might seem to bear a family resemblance to the phantasms of capitalist reproduction that Jean

Baudrillard described as simulacra, or the Soviet "hyperreality" about which the literary theorist Mikhail Epstein has written.[44] But in dramatic political theater, the signified—liberal democratic institutions—do exist elsewhere, and they do interact with the signifier, command performances of such institutions.[45]

The Slavicist Thomas Seifrid has written that in Russia, simulacra could be understood as imaginary, rather than illusion, and as aspirational, rather than deceptive. In Seifrid's view, a simulacrum was not "sham culture suspended over reality's absence" but instead a creative response to "fabricated signs that it appropriates, magpie-like, from abroad—sustained by a hope in the referent's eventual advent."[46] In contrast to Baudrillard's simulacra, political theater is meaningful, its internal logic coherent, its appeal to elites possible only insofar as its referents exist somewhere in the world, whether in material form or in people's imaginations.

Finally, some books that use performance as a lens suggest that people perform behaviors and identities for others while reserving some other version of their selves for their private worlds. The sociologist Erving Goffman described this phenomenon as a "front and back stage" on which people create and maintain images of themselves for others.[47] A related idea, the notion that oppressed people will support the state in public but privately disagree, appears in scholarship about dissimulation in authoritarian culture.[48] The political scientist Lisa Wedeen described spectacle in Syria in this way: people act "as if" they believed fictions promoted by the regime, all the while holding their own opinions.[49] These approaches to performance issue from a historical moment in which the notion of a neat distinction between public and private worlds reverberates through social, political, and economic institutions, in everything from gender identity to the structure of labor markets.[50]

Unlike some of this literature, this book's theatrical metaphor does not presuppose a neat separation between public and private selves. It does not even presuppose a particular kind of political subject. The theatrical metaphor in this book does not illuminate processes of subjectification. It can help us understand what politics can come to mean to participants, but it does not presume to show us what kind of person enters the stage.[51] The analysis here focuses less on the subject herself than on her surrounding context. In this way, it is unlike the metaphor present in Goffman's dramaturgical analyses or in work about authoritarian regimes. Instead, this book presumes a changing political subject with varying relationships to others.

This leaves open the possibility of dynamic relationships between public and private worlds, and between state and society. Such an approach can help us denaturalize the concepts of state and society as discrete, stable categories of analysis and instead begin to interrogate how their meanings and relationship may change over time.⁵²

Political Theater and the State

A decade into the rule of Vladimir Putin, an exasperated Russian journalist commenting on deteriorating public heating infrastructure voiced a complaint common at the time: "the complete helplessness of authorities to organize anything other than window-dressing."⁵³ In both Russia and Ukraine, state institutions neither exercise a monopoly on violence throughout national territory nor hold a unique claim on citizens' fiscal obligation.⁵⁴ Instead, a network of actors wearing multiple hats—bureaucrats with one foot in business, and regional and national business magnates with ties to governing institutions—participate in controlling and extracting tribute from the population.⁵⁵

In colloquial Russian and Ukrainian, references to the administrative state are relatively uncommon. Instead of *gosudarstvo* (in Russian) or *derzhava* (in Ukrainian), people usually invoke a diffuse and abstract form like *vlast'* or *vlada*—power, rule, the authorities—or *sistema*, a backroom system of governance that includes networks of state and business interests that make or influence key decisions in both countries.⁵⁶

With few exceptions, ambiguity in the everyday practice, identity, and boundaries of state interests in Russia and its neighbors has not yet been widely reflected in theorization about the nature of the contemporary state.⁵⁷ The literature on postsocialism has acknowledged the imbrication of business and politics, as scholars ask whether and to what extent the state has captured business, and subsequently, whether and to what extent business has captured the state.⁵⁸

But even amid explicit recognition of interlaced state and business interests, we usually continue to talk about state, business, and society as if they were discrete things with clear boundaries, rather than ever-shifting constellations of political, economic, and social actors.⁵⁹ A clear separation between the concepts of state and society is fundamental to most social scientific analysis. But a strict analytical distinction between state representatives and profit seekers does not adequately reflect the realities of individuals who serve a variety of interests in both the traditional administrative state and in industry.⁶⁰ And in contemporary Russian and Ukrainian politics, that clear separation may obscure important aspects of how political theater works.

In 1991, the political theorist Timothy Mitchell called on scholars to analyze the "detailed political processes through which the uncertain yet powerful distinction between state and society is produced."⁶¹ Some recent research in political science and anthropology has turned a critical eye toward standard understandings of the state, treating the state as cultural artifact, a site of interaction,⁶² and an assemblage to be deconstructed "to shake a stable sense of just what this state is."⁶³ This study takes the state to be a thing in the world whose description requires recalibration, and a category we need to keep in order to think clearly about people's participation in politics. It acknowledges the administrative state in the traditional sense but interrogates its reach through analysis of individuals' experiences with state agents. It examines political theater to better understand sources of variation in people's experiences with government and the ways that variation may shape perceptions of regime legitimacy.⁶⁴

Scholars have addressed reasons why politicians may orchestrate spectacle, as well as some of the mechanisms that encourage or compel regional elites to do so.⁶⁵ Their motives often are political. But command performances involve people at every level of society. Mid-level bureaucrats risk losing their jobs and access to privileges if they do not comply with—or at least appear to comply with—supervisors' commands to produce simulations.⁶⁶ The nature and extent of their exposure to pressure are determined by their place in an administrative state apparatus. The political scientist Bryn Rosenfeld has shown that this kind of dependence can make middle-class people less interested in democracy.⁶⁷ Meanwhile, managers of private enterprises face pressure to mobilize employees for political theater or risk losing state subsidies and advantageous tax arrangements, exposure to additional regulation or seizure, or investigation.⁶⁸ All this is possible because of vertical pressure exerted through bureaucracies in the executive branch. To communicate directions to the stage, politicians need the administrative institutions of the state. Political theater relies on things only government can offer: vertical and horizontal bureaucratic cooperation and, in Russia and Ukraine, the organizational resources of incumbent political parties.⁶⁹

Since the turn of the millennium, sites of recruitment for participation in political theater in Russia and Ukraine have been places where people live, work, and study, where they go to heal, and where they are punished.⁷⁰ Political theater is possible thanks to the cooperation of numerous private and public-sector individuals who may have little or no obvious or explicit connection to any state or party apparatus, but whose positions periodically draw them into acting as the stagehands and stage managers of political theater. From the point of view of those they may ask to participate in political theater, the face of power is local and personal. Often, the precise form political theater may take is decided locally, subject to the improvisations of individuals who must deliver players to the stage using resources and levers already at hand. Political leaders' strategists may act as dramaturges for political theater, but those who ensure compliance on the ground are everyday citizens staffing state and social institutions. They are the people I sometimes call "state agents" in this book.

The following chapters examine twenty-first-century stage management of performances of dramatic political theater in Ukraine and Russia at the local level. They analyze the economic relationships used to produce these performances, including both the everyday household economies of people who participate and broader, accompanying societal changes. Examining this backstage and onstage action in paid and prodded elections and demonstrations, we can see the work such performances do, including how political theater can at once change what the state is and expand its reach in contemporary capitalism.

Plan of the Book

The opening chapters of the book introduce the history and context for the development of twenty-first-century political theater. Chapter 1 discusses the research for this book. Chapter 2 examines the relationship between contemporary political theater and the Soviet past. Analyzing a televised confrontation between a young cardiologist and Vladimir Putin in 2011, the chapter shows that continuity of form, not ideology, links contemporary political theater with the authoritarian spectacles of the Soviet era. Chapter 3 looks to the 1990s, showing how broken supply chains, privatization, and state withdrawal set the stage for large-scale productions of political theater in twenty-first-century Ukraine and Russia. It argues that the rupture of the late twentieth-century Soviet social contract shaped the repertoire of tactics that later became available to the stagehands of political theater.

The middle chapters of the book analyze in situ the local economic compacts that draw people into command performances. They show how the practice of political theater brought the state back into every sphere of life in communities across Russia and Ukraine. Chapter 4 focuses on threats of collective punishment around the turn of the millennium in two border regions of Ukraine whose populations supported parties of power at the ballot box. The chapter draws on research in a center of industry, large-scale agriculture, and education on the Russian border, and a cluster of smallholder farming villages on the border with European Union member states. In the following decade, as local property relations and the organization of economic production shifted, people's vulnerability to local authorities' tools of persuasion and coercion also changed. What emerged from those changes were new forms of political stagecraft that affected some people while leaving others relatively untouched. Chapter 5 highlights that variation, closely examining people's interactions with local authorities over the course of a decade in villages in a southwestern border region of Ukraine.

Chapters 6 and 7 examine the political consequences of command performances. Analyzing an incident on Ukraine's Euromaidan, chapter 6 argues that over time, command performances change the meaning and salience of politics for people drawn into such performances. Chapter 7 shows what happens when democratic institutions and regime-led political theater unfold in the same time and place. It examines a significant recent episode in Russian associational life, the development of a nationwide popular movement commemorating family losses in World War II called Immortal Regiment. The chapter argues that performances of political theater destabilize perceptions of political participation and produce doubt. Unlike Soviet politics that sought to stamp out multivalent interpretation (*mnogoznachnost'*), political theater thrives on ambiguity: no longer an instrument of its disenchantment, irony is a tool of state power.[71]

The book concludes with three arguments. It shows why Hayekian solutions to lessen state regulation of the economy would not eliminate the conditions that make command performances possible. Highlighting the recent adoption of similar dramaturgical forms in American politics, it suggests political theater in Eastern Europe may prefigure political effects of precarity in capitalism amid economic crisis elsewhere. Finally, it shows that the dislocation of clear boundaries between political and economic authority can reverberate in a blurring of boundaries between state and society, with implications for the future of politics.

 CHAPTER 1

Researching Political Theater

On a wintry day in early March 1953, as thousands in Moscow publicly mourned the death of Stalin, Anna Vladimirovna decided to go to the cinema. The theater was open to the public, but for the next forty years she would tell no one where she had been that day.[1] The film showing in her hometown in the Russian Far East was a cinematic adaptation of Vasilii Azhaev's novel, *Far from Moscow*, a paean to wartime oil pipeline workers in Siberia under Nazi bombardment. In her telling, that afternoon at the movies had been an act of neither defiance nor celebration. Instead, it had been an expression of indifference—indifference made possible by the nine time zones that separated her city from the capital.

If nineteenth-century Russian provincial characters familiar to readers from Chekhov's stories were, as the Slavicist Anne Lounsbery describes them, "wholly defined by a painful awareness of their distance from a center," Anna Vladimirovna cut a different sort of provincial figure, one who might be at home in the stories of Chekhov's lesser-known contemporary, Russian writer Nikolai Leskov.[2] Her secret, a secret she guarded until the Soviet Union ended, was that she did not really care what happened in Moscow.

That governments are less effective in their margins than in their metropoles has long been a widely shared perception among scholars of empire—even as scholars also have acknowledged that nations, and empires, are made in their peripheries.[3] Far from mid-twentieth-century eastern Siberia, the

American historian Jill Lepore wrote of James Alexander, an early eighteenth-century lawyer in New York, that "he saw himself as a defender of the rule of law in a world that, because of its very great distance from England, had come to be ruled by men."[4]

Scholars often study politics in national capitals or regional centers, imagining that things work in similar ways in the rest of the country or region in question. The political scientist and sociologist Stein Rokkan called this "whole-nation bias" the fallacy that "best known places" are representative of a state as a whole.[5] These contradictory suppositions—that national and regional capitals are synecdoche, and that states might be relatively less effective in peripheries than in the center—infuse much analysis of politics.

This leaves us with some questions. How do observations about political theater in the center hold up in places far from the reach of the capital? Does politicians' ability to mobilize people for participation diminish far from capital cities? In political theater, where economic opportunity and political coercion are linked, can people who live at the edges of states, where cross-border labor market possibilities offer independence from local economies, avoid participation? Does distance protect people in peripheries from pressures that rouse their compatriots in capital cities to participation in command performances?

In Ukraine and Russia, the answer to these questions, most often, is no. Even if national capitals may not be of great interest to people in the periphery, the politics of the center reach them nonetheless. Importantly, what happens in the margins also directly affects the center.

In coming to this determination, the research for this book included performances of political theater in far-flung borderland towns, in provincial cities, in villages, and in capital cities. In Ukraine, research included the capital Kyiv but spanned the length and breadth of the country: from towns and villages in the southwestern region of Zakarpattia, neighbors to European Union member states Romania, Hungary, Slovakia, and Poland, to the eastern provincial capital and towns and villages of Kharkiv region, which borders the Russian region of Belgorod to the north and the Donbas to the southeast. In Russia, research began in the 1990s in cities, towns, and villages in Voronezh region, whose southern reaches touch the Ukrainian breakaway region of Luhansk, as well as in Moscow and Saint Petersburg and its environs. A brief period of research along the Sino-Russian border included the fluvial border city of Blagoveshchensk, which faces northern Heilongjiang Province in China to the south. Research for this book also included multiple visits to cities and towns on the Crimean Peninsula in years prior to the imposition of Russian rule in 2014.

These places lie at the westernmost, easternmost, and southernmost reaches of the former Soviet Union. They capture a wide variety of ethnic and other demographic variation. They include places surrounded by postsocialist territory and regions that share boundaries with the European Union. The project expressly did not involve the kind of research wherein the researcher chooses a set of cases based on a certain kind of variation and then sets about explaining that variation, or wherein the researcher attempts to determine how and why a phenomenon is more present in one case than in another. Instead, the mix of regions and regional economies that appear here show whether and to what extent the range of mechanisms that produce political theater may be uniform across a particular territory, and what that might tell us about the regularity of individuals' experience with command performances. They expose the spatial politics of political theater.

To understand how and why some people cooperate in performances of democracy, and how those performances can change the ways people think about political participation, I spent two decades researching and thinking about political theater in Russia and Ukraine. Before writing this book, I had spent years listening carefully to people who make a life from the land and how they felt about the changes national politics had made in their lives. Many of their concerns never made it into books, much less into the policy agendas of the politicians who represented them. I already knew that the view from the audience was dramatically different from the view from the stage. What I needed to figure out was how to go about researching the performance.

One of the challenges was that where political theater is prevalent, semantic fields are populated by things that are meant to look like other things. For example, across Eastern Europe, struggling opposition parties seeking to improve their own visibility use a tactic known among political technologists as "victim of the regime." People working for a political party put up posters, then deface their own posters, creating the impression that their party is important enough to elicit censorship. Distinguishing between deliberate attempts to deceive and the sort of political participation that fits more squarely within traditions of liberal democracy is not always a straightforward matter. Without evidence gathered close to the source, there may be little way of knowing whether what we observe might best be understood as theater—much less any opportunity to discern how the performance had been staged.[6]

In Russia and Ukraine, political theater is an open secret: it is not hidden, but it is not fully observable through high-altitude research. Research that looks at performances of democracy from a distance or only during the performances themselves can tell us certain things about the nature of political theater and its underlying political or moral economies. But it also might miss important contextual details, or even whether what is happening is theater at all. This may be one reason why, although the post-Soviet versions of the performances described in this book have been in wide use in Ukraine and Russia since 1999, it was fifteen years before the publication of the first survey-based research about workplace-based electoral manipulation in Russia.[7]

Even up close, it can be hard to tell why people participate in political theater. Performances always include a mix of people responding to different of motivations: economic incentives, emotions, peer pressure. Political participation, including participation in political theater, is bound up in complicated ways with people's political convictions, and exposure to mechanisms of persuasion is often contingent on factors that may have little to do with people's political beliefs. If we think of mass grassroots demonstrations of the type one tends to encounter in liberal democracies, people show up for a variety of reasons: conviction, frustration, excitement, entertainment, a desire to accompany a friend or to court a lover. Political theater also draws people who may not have much choice about participating, people who really want to participate, or both. People might participate because everyone around them is doing so, because they are accustomed to participating, or they may be uncertain themselves about why they participate.[8]

As a result, the fact that someone shows up to wave a flag or cast a paid-for ballot or participates in some other show of support for a politician may tell observers little about how that person thinks about politics. Some people understand their participation as consistent with or constituting their political preferences. Others experience a deep tension between their preferences and the preferences they are expected to perform. And still others participate but do not give that tension much thought or mind. People coerced onto the stage might still sincerely approve of political leaders: pressure does not preclude the possibility that a person might gladly have participated in its absence.[9]

To fully account for the links between context and action, I needed to be able both to listen to people's accounts of their participation and to observe that participation. In other words, sorting out the action onstage required access to backstage.[10]

I set out to observe the stage places-calls of political theater: the moments in which people received threats from a supervisor at work, money from a local party representative, or intimations from a daycare or kindergarten administrator about the need to support a certain political candidate to keep their child's place. I wanted to understand how those moments related to other things in their lives, how those contexts shaped their decisions about political participation, and what they thought political participation meant.

To research this book, I spent extended periods of time with my interlocutors. I continued to listen to how they felt about politics, but mainly I tried to focus on understanding the contexts in which they lived: What were the main challenges they faced in the day to day? Who made decisions, big and small, that affected them and their families? How did pressure to participate in political theater fit into the other exchanges in which they participated in their daily lives?

Back in North America, access to information about the performances discussed in this book improved as social media made the details of local realities more accessible to a global community. But descriptions in social media often reflected the perspectives of the young or the relatively well-off. Those who reported their experiences often focused on obvious coercion rather than the more widespread winks, nods, and understandings that accompany the production of political spectacle and are woven into the fabric of everyday economic life. A long-term commitment to researching performances at close range became more, not less exigent as new media made certain types of information more widely and immediately available, and as social media became crowded with more and less reliably sourced information.

Russia and Ukraine are large and diverse countries. When post-Soviet command performances began to proliferate in Russia and Ukraine near the turn of the millennium, I was in eastern Ukraine studying responses to land privatization. Over the following two decades, as I sought to understand the economic context of political theater in a variety of regional contexts, I visited capital cities, towns and villages of border regions in Russia's southwest, Ukraine's east and southwest, Crimea, and, briefly, the Russian Far East, on the border with China's Heilongjiang Province. I spent extended periods along Ukraine's border with European Union member states while conducting research for this and another project.

Most years, I spent time in one country or the other, with a preponderance of research in Ukraine, including several months every year between 2007 and 2012, and intense, shorter periods of research in 2014 as Ukraine entered a time of war and economic crisis. Conditions of political repression can pose methodological dilemmas for researchers, and there were fewer barriers to sustained on-the-record discussion about participation in political theater in Ukraine than there were in Russia.[11] In Ukraine, this was especially the case during the periods immediately following the so-called Orange Revolution and Euromaidan, when many people felt a reprieve from the local grip of parties of power and were willing to discuss their experiences more openly.

Political theater is a top-down phenomenon, but its stage managers use discretion and improvisation at the local level to run performances. Stage directions are rarely written down, and because of the nature of the threats that directors and stage managers use to elicit people's participation, people can be hesitant to talk about their involvement. As human beings tend to do regarding the details of their lives, people participating in political theater may normalize their involvement such that there is nothing remarkable to report: this is simply what we do. I needed a ground-level view that included sustained engagement with people over topics unrelated to politics to reveal the extent of the imbrication of dramaturgy in people's lives.

My research focused on people's daily experiences. The sociologist Matthew Desmond, writing about poverty and eviction in Milwaukee during the Great Recession, describes ethnography as "what you do when you try understand people by allowing their lives to mold your own as fully and genuinely as possible."[12] This is what I tried to do as I participated in community life. In rural areas, I attended church services, weddings, and funerals, annual village festivals, and family celebrations; spent time in village libraries, schools, and pubs, and shopping in village stores; traveled to town for health and dental care; visited cemeteries with those who tended their relatives' graves; helped young people with their studies; and many other activities.

I participated in meetings and events that are part of the stagecraft of political theater, but I also took part in the different kinds of work that were part of people's everyday routines. In villages, conversations took place around shared tasks: working in gardens, fetching water from wells, washing laundry or dishes in the metal tubs that many people still use in their rural courtyards or kitchen outbuildings, repairing bicycles, pressing grapes, carrying boxes of vegetables for market, shopping for automobile parts at outdoor markets, canning fruit, pouring tea for visiting farmers, and on one occasion, installing new windows in a village homestead. We talked about political theater, but work, not politics, was the point.

I watched the action onstage from the wings, and I also talked with a wide variety of people to understand how they interpreted political theater. These included state officials, members of civic associations and election monitoring organizations, heads of private and state enterprises, head doctors and health care practitioners, school principals and teachers, and many others.

I spoke with people who were the object of attempts to persuade them to participate in political theater and the people responsible for persuading them.

In both countries, I talked with government officials at the district and village council level, representatives of civic organizations focused on issues from veterans' rights to service provision for victims of domestic violence, people who worked in universities, schools, and other public institutions. I sought out conversations in rural and urban households, at border crossings and on long-distance ground transportation, and in places where people were on vacation. In touristic locations in southwestern Ukraine and Crimea, where people from all over Russia and the former Soviet world went to relax and improve their health, people had time on their hands and an active interest in discussion.

Sometimes I observed people's interactions directly. This could mean listening as local functionaries instructed public school teachers on how to vote, or as mid-level regional bureaucrats told heads of agricultural enterprises they had better deliver votes if they wanted diesel for the harvest. Other times, it meant discreetly staying out of the way as a villager worked out the details of a quid pro quo with a local party agent. In those cases, the people present knew that I was there and that I was a foreign researcher learning about how things worked.

Conversations about some sensitive subjects for this book took place in kitchens and in other protected spaces. In eastern Ukraine and in trips across the border into Russia around the turn of the millennium, many conversations could happen because I had a car. That vehicle was one of those protected spaces.

Conducting research along the Ukraine-Russia border at that time, I drove to villages and former collective farms in outlying districts. I would get up early to retrieve my Soviet-model 4x4—a vehicle capable of handling unpaved rural roads in most weather—from a forest of outdoor corrugated metal garages in the north of the city of Kharkiv. That garage offered opportunities for conversation with people I would not otherwise have encountered. In winter months, after reconnecting the vehicle battery, I began the day talking with other drivers as we all waited for the engines to warm. During the ensuing two- to four-hour drive across lunar landscapes of potholed asphalt and dirt roads, the need to buy gas, negotiate frequent stops by ubiquitous traffic police officers, and occasionally conduct minor vehicle repairs put me into contact with a broad spectrum of people beyond those immediately involved in my sphere of research interest.

Once out of the city, I crossed paths with others who told their stories. Public transportation outside the city was limited and expensive, and I often stopped and gave rides to people, usually elders, who otherwise planned to walk several kilometers to their destinations. Once, in a trip beyond the boundaries of the region, I transported and listened to a pair of traffic police for a hundred kilometers after they flagged me down and insisted on a ride to the nearest district center. On some trips to outlying districts, district-level functionaries I knew well accompanied me and used the occasion to talk. Their mandates frequently required on-site work in the region, but their budgets did not always include funds for gasoline.

These trips, as well as trips in the Russian countryside around Voronezh, revealed local logics of power and status that otherwise might not be evident. When I gave a lift to a male farmer or functionary, a verbal struggle sometimes ensued as my passenger would try to persuade me to let him drive my vehicle. At that time in rural places, when people saw a woman driving with a man in the passenger seat, they assumed the man must not be sober—otherwise, the logic went, why would the woman take the wheel? Sometimes we settled on a compromise. I would drive us out to the destination, but shortly before arrival we would change places, ensuring my passenger did not unfairly acquire a reputation as a drunk.

Away from offices and known communities with embedded hierarchies, rides in my vehicle were occasions for freer conversation than ordinarily would have been possible. Inside, people who avoided talking about politics with me in other situations shared their views. In each case, the enclosed space, the favor of providing transportation, and the strangeness of a foreign researcher serving as their chauffeur provided a context in which many people were willing to discuss local politics with a greater degree of openness—and to complain about the meetings and threats that had become regular parts of their lives.

Several years later, research in southwestern Ukraine included an entirely different set of conditions and interpersonal dynamics. There, in a village close to the highly policed border of the European Union, I stayed with my family on the homestead of a middle-aged widow. Over the course of eleven years of my research trips to that area, border crossings between Ukraine and the European Union slowly became occasions for friendly exchange, as guards and customs agents came to know us as part of the local mosaic and understood our trips as visits not requiring explanation or even, on some occasions, appropriate documentation. In and around that village, we walked, rode one-speed Belarusian bicycles, and took local buses and suburban trains, each of which brought its own conversations and exposure to local gossip. Anchored in a particular village, as a guest in the home of a particular individual with her own local networks and history of relationships and interests, I was an outsider with affective and linguistic ties that happened to resemble those of some others living in the area—with all of their attendant advantages and complications.

In the southwest, a part of Ukraine with a substantial Hungarian-speaking minority, at first I communicated with Magyars in Ukrainian and Russian. As the years passed and my command of Hungarian improved, those research conversations took place in Hungarian.

Multilingualism mattered in this environment. The content of people's stories often depended on the language they used to talk about their experiences. For example, in the summer of 2014, a number of Ukrainian-speaking villagers sought me out for private conversation in Ukrainian. In those conversations, they spoke of things about which they previously had remained mainly silent—things they formerly had insisted happened elsewhere, but not in their community: the local mechanics and specificities of vote buying, draft dodging, and other subjects.

As word of those conversations made its way around that village, Magyars who for years had insisted to me that they spoke only Hungarian approached speaking near-fluent Ukrainian. In that language, they recounted stories they had never before told in my presence. In that post-Maidan moment, Ukrainian had become the language of critique of the previous regime. What had been, and remained, a taboo subject in the Hungarian language could be discussed freely by switching into Ukrainian, illuminating the precise paths of political operatives in the villages and townships of Ukraine's southwest.

Not only language but also variation in my own social position as a researcher shaped the content of conversations and opportunities to process information. Some years I conducted research solo and talked with everyone in more or less equal measure. Other times my male partner and I conducted research together. Alone, I would participate for hours in animated conversation, always contributing actively to group discussions lest I be mistaken for a state informant. With my partner, I was able to focus on listening and preparing my questions while others often ignored my presence and directed their comments to him.

A female social identity offered other advantages for this project. Political theater often happens when local politicians and functionaries pressure people by threatening their access to things like spots in day care or preschool or health care for ailing family members, or when they offer food in return for votes. These often were areas of responsibility assumed by women. In rural spaces especially, groups of women would pull me aside to exchange confidences and to recount news of events that were directly on-topic for the project. Research during pregnancy and later with a young child in tow further opened these conversations, as women talked local politics while they offered advice about every aspect of family life.

Long-term field research in small communities means that one's every movement and comment are noticed and interpreted, and that news of conversations circulates faster than a researcher's feet can move. In summer and fall, breaks from that intensity came with trips south. In Crimea, conversations spanned a decade, including weeks in the coastal cities of Sevastopol and Yalta, in the smaller seaside resort settlements of Yevpatoria and Alushta, and in shorter visits to inland farms and settlements around Bakhchiysarai. In those settings, communal meals, waiting rooms, and beachside locations were occasions for conversations with workers and pensioners from cities and villages throughout Ukraine and Russia who had come to the peninsula on long, subsidized vacations for rest and health. Near Yalta, in the relaxed ambiance of a summertime colony far from national capitals, Ukrainian employees and Russian clients of a sanatorium that had served party elites during the Soviet period spoke of ways in which their experiences of elections had become embedded in health care systems in their countries. Similar conversations were possible during stays in the town of Beregszász (Berehove) in southwestern Ukraine, where a Soviet-era swimming pool built on thermal springs draws tourists on a budget from throughout the Russian-speaking world.

A brief period of research in the Russian Far East complemented extended periods in Ukraine and European Russia. In February 2010, we traveled to the banks of the Amur River, where northern Heilongjiang Province and the Chinese city of Heihe meet the Russian city of Blagoveshchensk. There, conversations with members of the local chapter of an organization of veterans of the Soviet war in Afghanistan, university students, petty merchants and traders, and the foot soldiers of cross-border commerce—middle-aged women and men who drag suitcases of consumer goods across a border crossing that, at that time, involved riding a bus across the frozen river—helped illuminate similarities and differences between quotidian experiences of engagement with the state seven time zones from the borderlands with the European Union.

A chapter focusing on the 1990s draws on research in Russia and Ukraine during that decade. Then, the specificities of economic calamity had been local. People in different places experienced the dissolution of the Soviet Union and its aftermath in distinct ways: ration coupons in Leningrad, water rationing in Voronezh, electricity outages in eastern Ukraine; relative plenty on a former collective farm with its own canning facilities, and privation on a neighboring enterprise whose chairman had not had the forethought to develop any form of food processing. Conversations throughout that decade form the backbone of this work's understanding of the challenges people faced at that time of radical economic change. Those conversations took place mainly in large cities and small towns and villages of Russia's southwest, particularly in southern districts of the Voronezh region and the area between Lipetsk and Voronezh, and in towns and villages in regions along Ukraine's border with Russia.

Some of the descriptions in this book are direct observations, while others draw on other people's narratives. In some cases, I could confirm their accounts either through direct observation or comparison of multiple independent narratives. For example, when official written documentation confirmed that an elected official did something, I report it as fact. Otherwise, I note that that a particular person "was said" to have done something. I report information my interlocutors identify as gossip as such in the text. Other accounts play a different role. Some claims that I could not independently verify figure in the text because they were significant for my interlocutors in their processes of meaning-making. I identify these explicitly in the text.

Where possible, I tried to confirm my interlocutors' narratives through direct observation. In local political economies of political theater, the devil is in the details. External validation was possible with extended on-site observation. For example, in one context, villagers recounted that a local latifundist hired only Roma men for day labor in his fields. I report this preference for workers in the text as fact rather than hearsay because for months I observed each morning as men from a Romani settlement assembled by the village pub to be picked up by the landowner's van. Or, when I heard complaints that heavy day-shopper foot traffic near a border crossing had led local residents to sell their cows because they were unable to bring them back from pasture for midday milking, I could report complaint as fact because I had watched over a period of weeks as dwindling numbers of cows retuned to the village in the evening, walking in visible discomfort with udders overfull.

Over time, changes in both Ukraine and Russia dampened some people's enthusiasm for discussing certain aspects of their participation in command performances. While the existence of command performances had become better known internationally, in some settings it had become locally risky to discuss them in any detail. This situation became particularly acute by the summer of 2014 in conversations with people in Ukraine who had been displaced from territory claimed by the Donetsk People's Republic. At the time, no one could be certain just how far the armed conflict would widen, nor what constituencies would eventually find themselves at the business end of victors' justice.

In political theater, tools of political coercion are embedded in existing social and economic hierarchies. Risk is local, and people may have practical reasons to have concerns about speaking in detail to a researcher about practices everyone knows exist. The same dynamics that allowed paymasters to use wages and benefits to compel particular electoral behavior also discouraged discussion of mechanics of coercion with outsiders. Especially in rural areas, people perceived a risk if they broke ranks to talk about local pressure. The logic of command performances included the possibility of economic retribution. As a result, some people were reluctant to discuss the meetings and other venues and mechanisms through which their supervisors and other figures of authority applied pressure.

These concerns inform the way I use ethnographic research in this book. In some cases, I quote conversations and interviews. In other instances, field research provides context or aids in interpreting phenomena already documented by others. Where possible, I refer to local published sources to document the existence of phenomena widely known within Ukrainian and Russian society. These include a variety of textual and visual sources: traditional and electronic media, including articles from regional and local newspapers, radio and television broadcasts and call-in shows, social media and other internet-based communication, and secondary sources published in the region.

Sometimes I draw on political satire and other forms of humor to make a point.[13] Where political environments made it difficult to quantify participation in political theater, televised jokes about command performances could offer a sense of the breadth of the phenomenon. Humor that doesn't resonate with its audience doesn't make it onto the screen of a private broadcasting company. The comedy troupe Studio Kvartal-95, led by Volodymyr Zelensky before he became president of Ukraine, often parodied political theater in their skits. I refer to their political laughter-through-tears in the book.

In recent years, some books about politics have focused on the anger, resentment, or fear some people feel in the face of economic loss that leads them to show up for a certain kind of politician.[14] In Polish politics, the sociologist David Ost connected anger arising from economic change with the rise of illiberalism,[15] while in the United States, the political scientist Katherine J. Cramer focused on the role of rural resentment in the class politics of conservative Wisconsin in the years leading up to the 2016 US presidential elections.[16] Other widely read works of nonfiction traced complex interplays of emotion and material concerns, attributing support for electoral revolutions to antisystemic masses who are angry, distrustful, and impatient for something different—and accepting of demagogues who promise change.[17]

Strong emotions can accompany support for certain political leaders, but in the case of political theater, it may not be necessary to plumb those depths. While emotions may be corollaries of political behavior, why people participate in political theater is a material story, one that has to do with the connection between how people are situated in market economies and what kinds of choices are available to them in politics.[18]

Conducting research for this book, I assumed most people were basically rational beings who think carefully about their choices. This is a work of political ethnography, and I was doing participant-observation research, but this approach dovetails with the assumptions and expectations of more conventional frameworks for studying politics. Far from obscuring the full range of human agency, a focus on the material conditions of people's lives can show what options are open to people and some of the reasons why they do what they do. The answers, and the implications of those answers, may surprise some observers. Eventually, they may even surprise politicians.

 CHAPTER 2

History of the Form

In mid-December 2010, Russian prime minister Vladimir Putin held one of his call-in shows during which citizens from all over Russia could phone the studio to ask him questions. For several hours, he would answer those questions on live television. Putin had begun this annual tradition nearly a decade before, as president of the Russian Federation, and he would continue it after he reassumed the presidency two years later.

That year, something unusual happened. A young cardiology intern from the town of Ivanovo confronted the prime minister, describing a scene instantly recognized across the country: "Vladimir Vladimirovich," he said, "in November you were in our town on a working visit. You were evaluating the development of health care in the region. So, I think to date there has never been such window dressing [*pokazukha*] in our town. Hospitals quickly were prepared for your visit, and a lot of equipment was temporarily brought into the regional hospital for your visit and brought out afterward." The doctor went on to say that employees had been given fake slips showing their salaries were more than twice what they were in reality, real patients had been driven from their beds, and hospital workers had been recruited to dress up as patients and lie in the beds as the prime minister's entourage passed through the wing.[1]

As the doctor spoke, the moderator for the studio audience, Maria Sittel'—a newscaster on state television familiar to Russian viewers—grew visibly uncomfortable. When the doctor finished speaking, the studio audience broke into applause, prompting the apparently nonplussed Putin to ask, "I don't understand what you're applauding—the artfulness of the local leader or the physician's courage." The young people on whom the camera trained at that moment responded in unison, "the courage." Putin then responded at length to the question and assured the audience that the matter would be investigated.

It later became apparent that the hospital had not been the only theatrical space in the call-in show. Preparations for Putin's visit to the Ivanovo regional hospital were only part of the performance. Theater was a basic mechanism of communication not only in the events described in the doctor's phone call, but also in the organization and presentation of the televised phone call itself. As media commentary on the event revealed in the days and weeks that followed, both the hospital visit and the phone call itself had been staged. The orchestration of the entire episode meant to provide an illusion of openness and responsiveness on the part of the Putin government.

What had happened during the show? Its organizers had ensured that from the audience's perspective, the doctor's phone call appeared both serendipitous and anonymous. During the show, toll-free telephone numbers and addresses for text messages flashed across the screen, producing an impression that a lucky caller could reach the premier simply by dialing or texting. During the call, Sittel' identified the caller as "a cardiologist from Ivanovo." The doctor did not introduce himself, and the premier noted that he had not caught the caller's name.

It subsequently emerged that, suggestions to the contrary by members of the Ivanovo regional government and some national media notwithstanding, the cardiologist from Ivanovo was a real person, he had a name, and the show's organizers had known about him in advance. The doctor's name was Ivan Khrenov. That his last name carries obscene connotations in Russian slang could not have been lost on the viewing public, and it was not lost on those who subsequently sought to use derision as a political tool to discredit the young doctor.

In media investigations of Khrenov, it further came to light that the young doctor had not himself dialed the call center. Rather, as he later explained in a televised interview, after receiving his parents' blessing, he had submitted a letter in advance to the prime minister. That letter had been chosen from among about two million others to be presented, perhaps, to Putin. Several days before the show, a technician had arrived at the family's apartment to verify that his phone line was working properly. Khrenov wondered if the technician had been from the FSB, the federal security service.

During the show, the television studio had called Khrenov. That Khrenov had managed to reach Putin and ask such a question was no accident, but part of the theater. A reporter from the Russian daily newspaper *Izvestiia* wrote, "Everyone accepts the rules of the game, and even the truth-lover Khrenov has no way of leaping across the barrier if not for a higher will."[2] But the staging of the phone call differed in important respects from the performance in the Ivanovo hospital. The phone call revealed an economic reality: the situation for Russian health care is not as rosy as it may appear. The illusion of the phone call concealed a political reality: ordinary people cannot, in fact, simply get through to the prime minister's line with a confrontational question.

In the aftermath of the call, Russian media space filled with discussion of the cardiologist's phone call to Putin. Over the days that followed, the call became a subject of jokes and heated debates on television shows, radio debates, blogosphere commentary, Twitter, and YouTube. It seemed that everywhere one turned in Russian media and virtual space, Khrenov's call was the focus of discussion.

The response of the Ivanovo regional administration was swift. Local politicians immediately questioned the veracity and reliability of the doctor's narrative, and television and newspapers dissected the elements of his story to identify factual errors or find any way to discredit him. The speaker of the regional assembly, Sergei Pakhomov, suggested that "competent organs" should deal with the doctor,[3] and the local prosecutor called him in. On television and in print media, rumors flew that Khrenov would be fired. The head doctor of the Ivanovo regional hospital called the phone call a "provocation."[4]

Several days afterward, Khrenov received a call that the prime minister's press secretary later confirmed to have come from the prime minister himself. Putin reportedly offered the doctor his protection,[5] reassuring him, "We won't leave you in the lurch. We'll help you, we know the whole situation. Don't worry."[6] Some ultimately came to see the episode as a public relations coup for Putin. In the end, the premier came across as a sympathetic character supporting an honest doctor who had dared to tell on dishonest local bureaucrats.

This was not the first time such an event had occurred, an ordinary person publicly voicing a broad social complaint to Vladimir Putin and, in so doing, receiving his sympathy—and a redirection of responsibility toward mid-level professionals or bureaucrats. Three years earlier, at a February 2008 press conference, a female university student who appeared to be either extremely nervous or under the influence of a controlled substance had asked Putin about stipends for students. She argued, "Students have to work, and that affects how we study. So we work, we earn money, we give [money] to teachers—those are the kinds of specialists we produce." Putin met the student's frank recognition of bribes to educators, a widely known and discussed social phenomenon related to low teachers' salaries, with joking complicity. He drily asked, "What are you saying about teachers?" The audience responded with laughter.[7]

As official media and virtual space responded to the cardiologist's truth-telling with furious but short-lived debates about the nature of the event that had transpired and the guilt of the young doctor, the question of the influence of the Soviet past played a starring role. For many who followed the story, the cardiologist's account of preparations for the prime minister's visit to Ivanovo, the hospital's mise-en-scène, and certain elements of the reactions to it evoked elements of the Soviet past. What was that past, and how did people understand it? What was its relationship to today's performances of political theater? Why did the open revelation of performance provoke neither surprise nor outrage, but recognition and mirth? And what do those responses reveal about contemporary politics?

A Little Hack Work

The doctor's call drew on Soviet-era political repertoires. The ritual of a leader's visit to a provincial institution and the upstanding citizen's denunciation of corrupt local officials were among its clearest evocations. The Soviet past, and memories of that past, were present in Khrenov's story in numerous, interlinking, and complex ways. The past was there as reminiscence, as palimpsest, and as self-conscious political theater. As a performance, it was Soviet in form, but it expressed the anxieties of a neoliberal economic present. The call unfolded in the context of a performance of responsiveness meant to reassure the Russian public of the liberal politics of an increasingly authoritarian regime.

For viewers of a certain age, elements of the call-in show struck a familiar chord. A few days afterward, the Moscow daily *Moskovskii komsomolets* described the liturgy in which the Ivanovo hospital staff had participated as "local physicians awaiting the leader [*vozhd'*]."[8] This referred to Soviet repertoires of political behavior and the performances of economic development that had been the stock-in-trade of Soviet-era delegations' visits to enterprises of any sort. Delegations of public officials hailing from local municipalities, regional capitals, Moscow, and other countries viewed rehearsed demonstrations of productivity, all furnished with props showcasing achievements, real and imaginary, of agriculture or industry.

In contrast to other signature practices of the era, like the informal networks of exchange about which people hid their participation even from themselves,[9] participants in those visits recognized such events as performances. Model farms, factory production lines, schools, stores, and many other institutions had been staples of Soviet-era performance, meant to present successful results and attract resources and praise while disguising failure and deflecting punishment. Soviet officialdom openly acknowledged the phenomenon, criticizing some such performances as efforts to conceal less than full and enthusiastic participation in state projects.

The Soviet period had produced many variations on such performances: the Soviet constitution had enshrined freedom of speech on paper, even as legislative institutions failed to protect it in fact, and Soviet formal institutions were alienated from politics and economics in practice in almost every area of life. Firm-level incentives developed by economic planners in Moscow led company managers to misrepresent both production levels and input needs, leading eventually to the incorporation of distortions in the plan itself.[10] Consumers managed to circumvent official shortages through complex interpersonal exchanges.[11] And on factory shop floors, professional pushers (*tolkachi*) managed disruption in supply chains.[12]

Recognition of such performances as theater suffuses Soviet-era cultural commentary and contemporary Russian literature. In his 1988 satirical letter to the general secretary, comic Mikhail Zadornov described preparations in an unnamed Soviet city in advance of the leader's visit: Streets with newly constructed underground pedestrian passageways are illuminated, paved, and vacuumed. Stores fill with foods that had long ago disappeared. A bridge finally is completed. Trees have their leaves painted green. The city monuments are washed with shampoo manufactured in Yugoslavia. Kindergartens and day cares are opened in the dachas of local leaders. Telephone lines cut decades ago by retreating German occupying troops are reestablished. Aerial spraying of crops recommences. Petitioners ask the general secretary to let slip the word that he will visit again so that local leaders will "once again be obligated to do something for the people."[13]

Russian surrealist writer Viktor Pelevin, in his satirical post-Soviet novel *Omon Ra*, highlighted the trope by elevating its absurdity. Performance saturates his protagonist's phantasmagoric world. Aspiring cosmonauts are subjected to double amputations in order to squeeze into and pilot space vessels that officially are unmanned. People don fragmentation vests to dress as bears and boars as they entertain hunting expeditions of party elite. And ground-shaking tests of nuclear warheads are simulations produced by two million political prisoners ordered to jump up and down simultaneously.[14]

The Ivanovo hospital visit and the prime minister's call-in show contained elements that resonated with practices associated with both Soviet and more remote pasts. But are such mises-en-scène merely practices carried over from the Soviet period? Elements of Soviet artifice present in today's performances may seem like continuities—unconscious reproductions of past practices—but the appearance of continuity can itself be part of the staging. In the absence of open acknowledgment of political strategies and tactics, how is it possible to distinguish palimpsests from theater?

The appearance of similar forms across different periods is not in itself prima facie evidence of continuity. Morphological similarity does not mean that today's and yesterday's performances are, to use the language of evolutionary biology, homologous structures, or structures with a common origin. Instead, phenotypical similarities between contemporary and historical political, economic, and social phenomena can belie underlying shifts that have taken place. Interpreting elements of the past or formal similitude as persistence can mean misreading the field in which actors move. It may seem that political actors are simply repeating the past, even as they incorporate new practices in the service of entirely novel aims.

An example from Putin-era politics crystallizes the epistemological and methodological challenge of differentiating persistence from deliberate performance of Soviet repertoires. To the extent that political and social actors have chosen Soviet vocabularies to communicate meaning in episodes in the present, those vocabularies have tended to date from a particular period in Soviet history. The "Brezhnevization" of the Putin government has meant evocation of a time in which the practice of aspirational imitation dominated certain aspects of Soviet society. A late Soviet joke cited by historian Anna Krylova refers to this period as a time when, confronted with a stalled train, officials "would have started rocking the train and announcing train stations in order to create the illusion of movement."[15]

In 2011, Brezhnev-era politics came to dominate public discourse after Vladimir Putin's press secretary, Dmitrii Peskov, commented on the usefulness of the period in a widely discussed television interview.[16] Likewise, in a series of performances the same year, comedian Mikhail Zadornov, wearing a Pioneer neckerchief "to put everyone in a good mood," referred to parallels between the Brezhnev and Putin eras: "I'll suggest the next sentence in a whisper, because otherwise they'll cut it out, but such that only he who can hear it, will hear it. In a whisper: they say that the stenographers of the

United Russia congress did a little hack work—they took the material from the twenty-fifth congress of the CPSU and simply changed the last names where necessary. They'll kick me out of the Pioneers after that phrase."[17] There may be evident similarities between the two periods, but did contemporary politicians evoke the 1960s and 1970s because governance in the current period happened to remind them of those days? Or did politicians wish to improve perceptions of contemporary realities by association, evoking the nostalgia some people feel for those years?[18] Is this broadly agreed upon resemblance a case of persistence, or a performance of elements of that period for political gain?

Historical legacies, understood as persistent institutional effects, do seem real and observable in many areas of post-Soviet politics, economics, and society. However, it is also the case that not all apparent legacies derive from the meaningful and unconscious integration of elements of the past into present practices. Not all legacies are true palimpsests. Instead, some apparent continuity in the form of command performances is the product of deliberate political maneuvering in the present. Political actors write the past onto the surface of the present, integrating elements of earlier historical experience into their organizational and symbolic repertoires to enhance their legitimacy and to consolidate power over political and material resources. From there, they pursue agendas and behaviors that may share little in common with the pasts they have invoked. In a sense, such institutions and practices exhibit continuity of form as they incorporate elements of the past, but above all they, too, are theater.

Nothing Seems Serious or Real

Command performance may have seemed ubiquitous in Soviet-era politics and economic life, but Russian tropes of imitation and pretense hardly originated in the Soviet world. In 2010, Vladimir Putin's call-in show drew upon not only Soviet, but also Russian imperial repertoires. As the young doctor's story unfolded in the week following the broadcast, its details came increasingly to resemble a central trope in imperial history. There, selfish boyars—played here by twenty-first-century power-hungry bureaucrats (*chinovniki*)—insulate the benevolent tsar from knowledge of what troubles the country.

Khrenov's letter to Putin followed the form of an appeal to the autocrat. The author presumes that the information contained therein is unknown to the leader. He suggests confidence that, once informed, the leader will take action. In such an appeal, trouble comes from the regional authorities and not from the tsar himself. Putin, by contrast, is Khrenov's protector. Even Khrenov's mother reproduced conventions of this genre, telling a journalist, "If they're really going to drive him out, of course he'll appeal to Putin. Maybe he'll go to Moscow."[19]

Scholars have identified artifice, and the cultural anxiety that accompanies it, as endemic in Russia since well before the Petrine era. At the same time, outside observers who lacked the knowledge necessary to understand what they were seeing sometimes described as mere artifice things that reminded them of, but were not identical to, something more familiar. Some artifice was deliberate. In fourteenth- to sixteenth-century Muscovy, as Nancy Shields Kollmann describes it, a meticulously maintained illiberal façade depicted a sovereign autocrat. Behind that façade, a system of kinship-based informal power sharing, a "highly articulated political infrastructure," discouraged competition among boyars and stemmed political instability.[20]

The resonance that Kollmann's vision of Muscovite autocracy might find in contemporary politics is evident not only in the production of political theater, but also in the scholarly discourse that surrounds it. Foreign observers of Muscovite politics tended to focus on more readily observable realms of law and institutional design than the practice of power. As Kollmann notes, historian Marshall Poe found that the idea of "Muscovy as a despotic state" originated in the narratives of sixteenth- and seventeenth-century travelers hailing from farther west on the European continent. The lenses through which they regarded Muscovite politics were colored by their own education as much as, Kollmann wrote, "their familiarity with the practices of Muscovite autocratic power." Such approaches to understanding Russian statehood, Poe argued, continued through the nineteenth and twentieth centuries.[21] In other words, while the trope of despotism suffused accounts of politics in Russia, that trope may have been as revelatory of the attitudes of observers as the behavior of the observed.

If "Russian despotism" persisted as a central trope into twentieth-century historiography, artifice was dimly present in most scholarly treatments of Russian politics—even if it formed an integral part of political realities not only of Muscovy, but also of imperial Russia.[22] Writing of the latter period, Thomas Seifrid identifies the Petrine era, with its superficial imposition of the urban aesthetics and quotidian practices of Europe, as the temporal origin of Russia's politics of illusion.[23] In his analysis of illusion in works of Russian literature, architecture, and geometry, Seifrid writes that

> Russian culture does seem to be distinguished by a set of practices that work toward producing the sign or façade of something in anticipation

HISTORY OF THE FORM   39

of obtaining its referent, only to stop there; and for this activity often to be state-sponsored or -directed and to be linked somehow with the working out of national identity, because the nature or direction of "Russia" is somehow bound up in the façade that has been produced. As a result, Russian culture is also typified by a kind of reflective anxiety over this kind of practice.[24]

As Seifrid notes, variations on this theme suffuse politics in the following decades. The spectacle of miniaturized reproduction of foreign spaces on the country estates of Catherine's time,[25] together with the reputed Potemkin village facades of the empress's travels in Crimea, extended this semiotic practice.

But Muscovite facades and their relatives two centuries later under Peter I and Catherine are different from the productions of twenty- and twenty-first-century politics. In Petrine-era discourse, the tsar's creations, including his capital city, had been construed as constructed out of nothing. In Seifrid's account, Peter I "had insisted that behind its façade stood a void. The proper analogy," Seifrid argues, "was therefore not a palimpsest but a mask."[26] Elements of Petrine political culture suggested narratives of original creation and meant to establish the sovereign's legitimacy through discursive obliteration of existing cultural forms. These included Pushkin's evocation of the book of Genesis in his lyrical representation of Petersburg, the capital city built "on the shore of wasteland waves" (*na beregu pustynnykh voln*), or the tsar's use of "Peter the First."[27] The production of a political narrative in which the sovereign represents the beginning of history, rather than its continuation, is a discursive move hardly unique to Peter: in Russia, it resurfaces in Soviet presentations of history.

But a radical break from and negation of the past is not part of the repertory of contemporary political actors. In today's political theater, there is no semiotic restructuring of political ontology, no alignment of historical time with the life of the state or sovereign. Rather, the contemporary sovereign's "eternal legitimacy"[28] is anchored elsewhere, in the theater of apparently democratic politics. There, repeated performances of elections and other institutions in which the public acts as both audience and participant confer a type of legitimacy on political leaders.

In the nineteenth-century literary and political imagination, tropes of artifice and performance resurface, most famously in Nikolai Gogol's play *The Inspector General* (*Revizor*) and with greatest present resonance in his novel *Dead Souls* (*Mertvye dushi*), in which Gogol's protagonist Chichikov schemes to raise money by purchasing recently deceased serfs, thus ridding landowners of a tax burden, and then using their names as collateral. The political and economic gambit that that novel describes seems directly to foreshadow twenty-first-century electoral practices: Gogol's language is widely used today to describe the practice of using "dead souls" at the ballot box. In one contemporary variation on this trope, the souls in question may not be permanently departed: in a typical example in an election in eastern Ukraine in 2004, the souls in question were simply away on contract labor in Russia, and stand-ins were bused in to vote in their stead.[29]

Foreign and native intellectuals alike had noted the role and prevalence of superficial political change in Russia. Those observers, sometimes writing from metropolitan perspectives more informed by elite politics than by inside knowledge of the rural cultures in which most inhabitants of the empire's territories lived, called attention to thin shifts in a discursive skin seemingly stretched across supposed contradictions and chaos. Mikhail Epstein, in his reading of the "progression from 'imitation' to 'simulation'" in Russian history,[30] noted the presence of this trope in traditions as disparate as those represented by Slavophile Ivan Aksakov and French aristocrat Marquis de Custine. Epstein summarizes, "The ostentatious, fraudulent nature of the civilization begets external, superficial forms, devoid of both genuine European and intrinsic Russian contents, and remains a tsardom of names and outward appearances."[31]

Writing in reaction to political liberalization in the second half of the nineteenth century, Ivan Aksakov had observed, "It is as if we had everything, but as a matter of fact there is nothing or very little. Everything chez nous exists as if; nothing seems serious, real, but has the appearance of something temporary, counterfeit, done for show . . . everything was fulfilled according to the law, everything was liberalized according to form and the model given, but the fruits engendered, as the government-recognized necessity for reforms proves, are the most useless!"[32] Meanwhile, in a travelogue filled with the kinds of observations that a few decades later would come to typify colonial discourses of civilizational missions in the Southern Hemisphere, the Marquis de Custine penned a critique that crystallized "Europe" as the normative model for Russia: "Russians have only names for everything, but nothing in reality. Russia is a country for facades. Russia is an empire of catalogues: if one runs through the titles, everything seems beautiful. But . . . open the book and you discover there is nothing in it. . . . How many cities and roads exist only as projects. Well, the entire nation in essence, is nothing but a placard stuck over Europe."[33] The persistence of such commentary across time, and the realities that prompted it, could be seen as an indication of continuity in the production of the politics of spectacle. It might even arouse suspicion that there may be something endemic in Russian traditions of governmentality fostering the reproduction of artifice. Or, as certain nineteenth-century references to the phenomenon suggest, apparent recurrence may merely point to a punctuated equilibrium: in moments of initiative or incipient social transformation, early change appears shallow, and reform formal.

Traces of apparent artifice remaining in the historical record may be artifacts of a social order in which critics of reform were themselves ill-positioned to observe the underlying, real-life dynamics of imitative politics. Foreign observers entered Russia burdened with a theoretical apparatus that led them to view local political realities through the lens of an imagined Europe, their point of reference for the real.[34] As in the case of the "despotic rule" of early Muscovy, continuity over time in the presence of artifice in the documentary record indicates persistence of a trope. It cannot necessarily be presumed to indicate persistence of the signified itself. It is possible that the reproduction across time of narratives of despotism and fakery may tell us as much about those who propagate the narrative as about the lives of those who participate in artifice and give it meaning.

Whatever the explanation, what continuity can be observed in a long historical trajectory of political theater resides in what is most observable: the form of the performance. The actions and reasons driving the performance, however, are another story altogether.

2 X 2 = 4

In the days that followed Khrenov's telephone call to the prime minister, parody was an important tool for those who commented on the episode. Political and cultural figures selected and performed elements of Soviet culture to achieve a particular end—namely, to discredit the young cardiologist.

A few days after the call, a popular musical parody and morning show on the nationally syndicated radio station Car Radio (Avtoradio) made Khrenov the subject of a song. The show was *Murzilki International*, named for a children's literature and art magazine published throughout most of the Soviet period and into the present day. The show's parodies, which match Oleg Lomovoi's lyrics about current events to the music of well-known songs, do not draw exclusively, or even primarily, on Soviet-era music. Instead, the group sings to the tunes of Russian folk songs and contemporary Russian, European, and American popular performers such as the Russian band Accident (Neschastnyi sluchai), singer Alla Pugacheva, the Swedish group Ace of Base, Terence Trent D'Arby, and Metallica.[35] The song about the call-in show drew explicitly on numerous musical, gestural, and verbal tropes associated with the Soviet past as *Murzilki* described, contextualized, and commented on Khrenov's action.

Murzilki used Soviet tropes not to create an illusion of historical continuity, but to ridicule the young doctor. The Soviet past furnished the tools with which to critique the present. The parody used children's vocabularies of the late Soviet period to mock and discredit Khrenov and, by association, everyone who had appreciated the content of his phone call to Putin. Their parody began with a Pioneer salute: "Dress to Khrenov, the country's [Young] Pioneer!" (Ravniaisia na Khrenova, pioner strany!). The tone of the song was facetious. Its refrain hailed the doctor as honest and brave, observing how quickly he achieved fame—and played on his surname, calling Khrenov a "f#@%ing cardiologist."[36]

The critique embedded in the musical rendition of the doctor's truth-telling carried serious overtones. In this interpretation, Khrenov was not a brave individualist but rather a friend of power. The song used Soviet-era language associated with snitches to level that accusation. The doctor "informed" (*nastuchal*). He "reported the facts" (*fakty soobshchal*). Khrenov's critique is cast as an appeal from within the system, using the language of the system. It is not an attempt to overturn the system.

This impression deepened in the song's third stanza, which used contemporary prison slang to describe Putin "arranging" the "wise guy" who would seek to deceive. The parody's musical accompaniment contrasted with the prison and security overtones of its lyrics. The verse is set to the music of a Soviet-era children's song about multiplication tables, "Two times two is four" (Dvazhdy dva — chetyre).[37] Against its background, Khrenov's zeal appears naïve and idealistic. Even more than an informant, Khrenov is a tattletale. The lyrics portray a person perplexed by what an honest person can do with corruption all around. The answer: go tell Putin.

In their sarcasm, the lyrics suggested that resistance is futile. Normal behavior meant participating in the charade. Telling the truth only makes the speaker look naïve and foolish. Other comments about Khrenov's phone call followed a similar pattern. They drew on Soviet tropes to critique Khrenov's action, expressing not so much solidarity with the local functionaries who directed the performance in Ivanovo, but dissatisfaction with the fact that Khrenov broke ranks.

The idea that Khrenov enacted a Soviet heroic children's trope in the service of a political regime could be found elsewhere in media space. Writing in the daily *Komsomol'skaia pravda*, Evgeniia Suprycheva dryly observed, "The glory of Pavlik Morozov has been eclipsed. A new hero is on the stage: a cardiologist, that same guy who gave up, wholesale, all of the functionaries of his native Ivanovo."³⁸ Khrenov took up a central role in an enactment of a Soviet morality tale: the son who turns on (and in) his father to maintain his fidelity to the values of the communist state.

The use of the Pavlik Morozov trope is curious: Khrenov's loyalty appeared to lie with the people around him who were struggling to make ends meet, rather than with an ideology promulgated by the state. However, Suprycheva's "clever boy" (*soobrazitel'nyi mal'chik*) Khrenov is the object of derision not because he challenges the performance of the central state, but because he is viewed as complicit in it. If regional authorities publicly smeared Khrenov after the phone call, referring to the young doctor as "psychologically unstable" (*nevmeniaemyi*), parts of the national media moved to discredit him with implicit accusations of "acting Soviet"—specifically, being a good communist. Khrenov's own words likewise may have contributed to this perception: in a televised interview, he attempted to legitimize one of his arguments by making reference to a statement by Stalin.³⁹

Such critiques, while using Soviet characters and vocabularies of morality to make a point, approached the Soviet past as a disparate set of tools with which to comment on the present. Amid a wide variety of possible shared social metaphors that could have been used to interpret the situation, and given the eclectic and sometimes contradictory character of the references people used to comment on it, critiques of Khrenov's actions reflected not mere reproduction of Soviet discourse, but rather deliberate, and ironic, recycling. In these examples, the Soviet period functioned not so much as a constraint framing present action as a reservoir of usable pasts.

It's Everywhere in Our Country

After the call-in show, the doctor had wondered publicly about what had caused such reaction from members of the regional administration: "I didn't reveal any horrible secrets. I simply described window-dressing that constantly is going on here and there. Everyone admits to me: they say, well, we know about that, it's common knowledge. So why did the functionaries react so sharply to those words?"⁴⁰ The young doctor was not alone in the view that he "didn't reveal any secrets." When the hosts of a radio show asked callers about a milder version of the phenomena the doctor had described—namely, whether they adjust figures or reports for their bosses' sake when evaluators come—one Muscovite responded rapidly, "It's an absurd question. It's everywhere in our country."⁴¹

Others in Russian media agreed. In a December 2010 episode of Roman Gerasimov's Channel 5 live political talk show *Open Studio (Otkrytaia studiia)*,

Gerasimov noted, "You can agree, this phenomenon is commonplace for our country. Dammit, we know that before every visit of the higher authorities they lay fresh asphalt, and one could make a list of all that they do. Sometimes they steal, oops, I mean they paint the grass [*inogda kradut . . . fu, travu krasiat*]. All of that is outrageous, and unfortunately it's become a tradition."[42]

After the prime minister's call-in show, state-owned media moved to manage perceptions of the entire episode. The morning after Khrenov's phone call to Putin, Radio Mayak, one of the five radio stations held by the All-Russian State Television and Radio Broadcasting Company, held a call-in show to discuss the phenomenon of window dressing in contemporary Russian society.[43] The program began with laughter and a series of jokes about the doctor's last name, followed by a summary of the episode and a question to listeners about their participation in such performances. The atmosphere was of carnival in Bakhtin's sense, only the apparent aim, or at least result, of the performance seemed to be to normalize mises-en-scène.

Callers to the show spoke openly about a variety of different kinds of window dressing, at times describing their own roles, and at others enumerating various outrageous and hilarious tactics employed by others in their entourage or city: ground painted green to simulate grass; road repair paid for but undone, a staple of budgetary misdirection nearly everywhere; and a host of other diversions. A private businessman who said he had been personally involved in preparations for the visit to Ivanovo of the man to whom he referred on air as "our respected [leader]" recounted how a child had hung around the work crew, curious about what they were doing. When the child started to get in the way, irritating the crew, the foreman had joked, "Don't touch the child! He's probably an officer of the FSB."[44]

If the doctor was simply stating what everyone already knew, then what explained the reaction to his phone call—on the part of both the regional authorities, who panicked, and the rest of the country, which followed the story with great interest? Soviet norms of communication may help us understand why and how certain parties responded the way they did. In Alexei Yurchak's interpretation, in Soviet discourse pragmatic categories of meaning tended to matter to participants more than semantic ones. Yurchak writes of unanimous voting at Komsomol meetings, "To participants this was usually an act of recognition of how one must behave in a given ritualistic context in order to reproduce one's status as a social actor rather than as an act conveying 'literal' meaning."[45] In this example, as in many other instances of Soviet-era unanimous voting, the content of the proposition at hand was not what was significant. Rather, it was the fact of participating in an expression of unanimity that held meaning.

In the case of the call-in show, the young doctor had declined to follow the normal "rules of the game."[46] It was not the content of his critique that mattered so much as his decision to break an implicit social rule. The significance of the information lay in its public verbalization, not its content. The challenge to authority in the doctor's phone call and the reason for the furor it caused lay not in the situation he described, but in his decision to describe it.

In other words, calling window dressing by its name was a direct challenge to the regional administration not because the information revealed was particularly surprising to anyone, but because in so doing, the doctor challenged a means by which the state expressed its power. Participation in the ritual was what was expected; truth was beside the point. When Ivanovo hospital staff wrote anonymously that "all kinds of big cheeses from the local administration have come to the regional hospital and are deciding how to remove the stain of shame,"[47] the shame in question was not the pretense. Rather, the shame lay in the poverty of a health care system compelled to put on a show for visitors from Moscow, or in local authorities' seeming inability to control a particular employee.

The episode on Radio Mayak included a great deal of laughter—primarily laughter at descriptions of various iterations of window dressing. What was the meaning of that laughter? Soviet traditions of subversion—and post-Soviet nostalgia for such subversion—might suggest social critique and a virtual circle of intimates created in the audience through the program. However, another meaning, one consistent with the tone of other re-descriptions of Khrenov's action, also emerged.

In successfully encouraging others to share tales of window dressing on the airwaves, the program hosts managed to dilute one aspect of the doctor's phone call to Putin. Here, others also were talking openly about political secrets on the airwaves. The discussion was not part of a wave of protest that, in another national context, might have followed an event such as Khrenov's phone call. Instead, it served to render banal the seemingly extraordinary event of the evening before. How brave was the doctor, really, if others could talk about the same thing, publicly?

Second, it normalized and underlined widespread complicity in such performances as the Ivanovo hospital visit. The message seemed to be that we are all in on this together. Participation meant neither false consciousness nor an expression of a fragmented self or double consciousness. Instead, participation expressed a version of ideological fantasy, an inversion of Marxist false consciousness: "They know very well what they are doing, but still, they are doing it."[48] Khrenov emerges from the episode as an eccentric—*chudak*, an oddity for having come forward.

To the extent that Soviet tropes were present in the discussions of Khrenov's phone call, they were used to criticize the young doctor for his supposed ideological enthusiasm. When we take all of the parts of this episode together, we see that performances of and references to Soviet repertoires serve primarily to discredit persons associated with them, to normalize both administrative incompetence and participation in the political theater that conceals it, and to cast Putin in a positive light. In the end, state and media management of the event produced a complex narrative with complicated relationships to the Soviet era. In it, the Soviet Union was very much with us, but there was no direct line connecting the past and present, nor any single valence attached to the various elements of the Soviet past that make their appearance in this multilayered episode of political theater.

The Game as Such

Writing in the late 1970s of what he called "post-totalitarian" society, Czech playwright Václav Havel described the implicit dilemma faced by a greengrocer asked to place a sign with the slogan "Workers of the World Unite" in his shop window. The greengrocer, uninterested in the meaning of the slogan itself, complies in an act that signifies his understanding of his role in society. He places the sign in his window because, in his universe, this is the normal thing to do.

The ideological field in which the greengrocer lives signals everywhere to him the need to comply. Furthermore, he is aware of the predictable results of refusal to participate. In Havel's interpretation, the greengrocer, like other members of his society, has engaged in a Faustian bargain with the authorities, exchanging the loneliness and uncertainty of modern society for a reassuring blanket of ideology—consigning, in Havel's words, "reason and conscience to a higher authority."[49]

What would happen if the greengrocer should decide to withdraw from this bargain? Havel enumerates the consequences, which are both material and social: "The bill is not long in coming. He will be relieved of his post as manager of the stop and transferred to the warehouse. His pay will be reduced. His hopes for a holiday in Bulgaria will evaporate. His children's access to higher education will be threatened. His superiors will harass him and his fellow workers will wonder about him." In refusing to place the sign in his shop window, the greengrocer would face solitude and isolation, shut out from a level of material well-being offered by the system that asks of him compliance in the coproduction of ideological control over society.

For Havel, the force of this punishment awaiting the greengrocer should he decline to participate emanated not so much from his individual act of noncooperation as from the more profound rupture that noncooperation would represent for the system. Havel writes, "By breaking the rules of the game, he has disrupted the game as such. . . . He has shown everyone that it *is* possible to live within the truth, and therefore everyone who steps out of line *denies it in principle and threatens it in its entirety*."[50]

But the world of Havel's greengrocer is not the world of contemporary political theater. Today, the game cannot be disrupted in this way. Participants operate in and across multiple ideological fields that overlap and conflict with one another. In the case of the cardiologist from Ivanovo, there were multiple actors—politicians at every level, radio hosts, television producers, and ordinary citizens in the blogosphere—performing different memory plays on the same communicative stage: ironic recycling and humor; reference and recollection; evocation of sinister past experience as a means of intimidation; and reproduction of past narratives are all occurring at once in a carnival of interlinking but distinct webs of meaning.

In the presence of these multiple, overlapping registers and a widespread frank acknowledgment of performance, participants cannot as easily hide the existence of theater from themselves. In the episode described in this chapter, Russian media responded to truth-telling with laughter and derision: everyone was already in on the fact of the performance, and acknowledgment and discussion of the fact of performance were possible in a public forum. While some, like the local functionaries in Ivanovo who attempted to impugn the character of the young cardiologist, continue to behave as if this were not the case, ideology plays a different role in contemporary politics than it did in certain decades of Soviet power. In contemporary political theater, the principal purpose of performance is not to conceal some truth behind the stage curtain, but to socialize its participants to the rules of the theater.

Ideology is thus not the filament linking the Soviet past with political theater in the present. Instead, to the extent that the universes of Havel's greengrocer and the Ivanovo cardiologist share fundamental characteristics, those characteristics lie in the relationship between participation in ritual, in the case of the greengrocer, or performance, in the case of the cardiologist, and the material life of the consumer. Havel hints at this aspect of his post-totalitarian society, locating its cornerstone in the "historical encounter between dictatorship and the consumer society . . . the general willingness of consumption-oriented people to sacrifice some material certainties for the sake of their own spiritual and moral integrity."[51] Such willingness is not limited to post-totalitarian society. The dramatist suggested that post-totalitarian society serves as "a kind of warning to the West, revealing to it its own latent tendencies."[52]

In late twentieth-century Eastern Europe, the Soviet state having shifted from the violent legitimizing strategy of the 1930s to an understanding between state and society that in certain respects resembled the postwar welfare state elsewhere in Europe,[53] the price of noncompliance was in great part material. Contemporary political theater likewise rests upon a material bargain, one that extends both across time into the Soviet past and across space into other places of the global present. Returning to the scene of Putin's visit to Ivanovo, the contours of that bargain begin to come into view.

In the narrative of the young cardiologist, regional authorities in Ivanovo sought to present an image of economic progress in the health sector to the prime minister and his entourage. Having received specially allocated funds for regional development, they hoped to show—or at least believed they were expected to show—that hospital staff members were well paid, certain wings of the hospital were well equipped, and patients were cooperative and appreciative of the care they received. Additionally, as others later reported, they hoped to show that roads were freshly covered with asphalt, hospital buildings had roofs protecting patients from rain, and infrastructure in the city was well cared for.

The cardiologist's account exposed not only the artifice of regional officials and hospital employees, but also the improper use of federal funds. Implicit in his narrative was the suggestion that resources for regional development had not made their way to their intended destinations, and that this, after all, was the reason why the hospital became a site of political theater.

What was the actual material state of affairs in the health care system in Ivanovo at the time? Notwithstanding the performance that had been staged for the Moscow delegation, conditions at the regional hospital where the episode occurred were far better than in other health care facilities in the region. In investigating the call-in incident, *Komsomol'skaia pravda* reported on conditions at municipal hospital No. 1 in Ivanovo. That facility was housed in a prerevolutionary former stable, with rooms arranged shotgun style: "You open a door—and you end up in the dressing room, next—the toilet, behind it, the hall. That is, the toilet is a walk through."[54] The journalist went on to describe some of the conditions there:

> The walls are chipped and flaking. Enterprising patients paste wallpaper on them at the level of their beds, so that pieces of plaster don't fall on

their heads. Besides, they stick them with improvised means—pieces of sticking plaster. It's a picturesque scene, particularly in combination with the black mold on the ceiling—it's impossible to remove it, since the ceilings are four meters high. But the most interesting thing happens here starting at 8 o'clock in the morning. From departments that are not connected with each other by corridors—they're isolated—they bring through the sheets and mattresses for disinfection.[55]

After the phone call to Putin, local newspapers were bombarded with letters from people anxious about the quality and accessibility of health care in the region. A journalist for *Argumenty i fakty* wondered at the phenomenon: "It's true that, surprisingly, before . . . [the] speech it turns out that no one noticed the ruin. And he, the young specialist, having announced it to the whole country, is now being made to offer his apologies at length."[56]

According to the prime minister, the regional hospital in Ivanovo had received 130 million rubles from the federal budget. Such an influx of cash represented a special privilege, not only for the region, but also for the hospital itself. Most hospitals in the region were struggling with multiple challenges, including huge shortages of qualified personnel—in one hospital, only half of all shifts were staffed, and almost half of all staff worked double shifts.[57] Most often, this left patients' families to care for and feed loved ones, as well as to take turns mopping hospital floors. Further, amid gross infrastructural decay, there were limited resources for paying hospital staff—while the national minimum monthly salary had been 4,300 rubles, nurses in Ivanovo were being paid 2,660 rubles, and doctors' starting salaries were 3,560 rubles.[58]

In an interview after the incident, the doctor explained his actions by saying that people were afraid and that he had simply "voiced the mood in the city." What were people afraid of? In his view, unemployment, layoffs, economic distress.[59] He sought to call attention to two things: the low pay of health care workers, and the political behavior required by their precarious economic positions. The participation of hospital staff in the show for the Moscow delegation had been, in all likelihood, motivated by concerns about their personal economic situations.

Economic considerations motivating participation in political projects are hardly unique to political theater in Russia and Ukraine; such a calculus may be observed across economic sectors and national contexts. For example, in both Russia and the West, journalists and small media companies struggling to make ends meet may be co-opted by centralized commercial structures whose executives disseminate a point of view together with packaged content.[60]

Even as people's motivation to participate in political theater is often economic, command performances also serve a deeply political role. The phone call of the cardiologist from Ivanovo appeared to partake in a broader strategy by the Putin government at the time: to present an image of what journalists Matthews and Nemtsova called a "highly controlled version of liberalization from above that will include more freedom of expression, a friendlier face toward the West, and inviting former liberal critics to act as Kremlin advisers. He and his advisers hope that allowing a degree of free speech and creating the appearance of responsive government will keep voters happy."[61]

A journalist for *Izvestiia* observed that 2010 had seen "a new genre of links between the people and the authorities—the voice 'from Potemkin villages,'" noting further Moscow's Center for Political Technologies Alexei Makarkin's description of the government's uses for the phenomenon: a rather "vivid method of communication between the authorities and society. You know, rather than discussing this or another theme, you can take a concrete story . . . a concrete Doctor Khrenov unmasks falsifiers and those who would varnish the truth."[62]

Elements of illusion present in the televised call to the premier both concealed other aspects of contemporary political realities and suggested a complex relationship between contemporary politics and their Soviet progenitors. Here, the staged disruption of a Soviet politico-theatrical form was a vehicle for the idea that contemporary Russian politics are democratic, and that the government is responsive to citizens' concerns.

Like other pressure valves permitted in Russian media and virtual space at the time, such performances themselves together partook in a third, broader iteration of political theater. In this instance, a young doctor called to report on a performance that was Soviet in form but that expressed the economic anxieties of contemporary capitalism—all in the context of a performance of openness meant to reassure the Russian public of the responsiveness of an increasingly repressive regime.

Contemporary performances whose form may evoke historical practices of imitation or illusion attract participation because they play upon people's economic ambitions and insecurities. Today, in Russia, as in parts of Ukraine, the price to pay for stepping out of character, for removing oneself from the stage or even the theater, is not mainly political. Instead, as for Havel's greengrocer, what is mainly at stake for players in today's political theater are not political freedoms, but access to the good life in a consumer society.

 CHAPTER 3

Setting the Stage

Soviet-era repertoires had provided scripts and props for political theater in the twenty-first century, but economic and political change in the first years following the dissolution of the Soviet Union—and the shift from near universal basic welfare to the neoliberal capitalism those changes would usher in—set the stage for twenty-first-century performances.[1] This was the case across former Soviet territory, in both authoritarian and more democratic regimes.

To understand the economic context for the development of twenty-first-century political dramaturgy, this chapter returns to the 1990s, a decade before parties of power in Russia and Ukraine began to threaten people's access to infrastructure, services, and pay to elicit widespread participation in command performances. Supply chain disruptions and new border regimes resulting from the dissolution of the Soviet Union reshaped local networks of reciprocity, while privatization foreclosed access to public goods people previously had used to support themselves, leaving people more dependent on employers and local authorities than before. Changes during those years structured people's future expectations about state power, while rising economic insecurity made even marginal gains newly important for household economies.

The chapter follows a single workday in the lives of two women on either side of the Russia-Ukraine border at the end of the twentieth century to illustrate how local changes shaped the repertoire of tactics that later became available to the stagehands of political theater. The two women are Tatiana Denisovna, a middle-aged factory worker in the southwestern Russian city of Voronezh, and her sister Valentina, who has been living across the border in Ukraine, in a village in the southern reaches of Kharkiv region, since she married twenty-five years before. To protect the identities of individual interlocutors, details of the lives of the sisters have been changed in this text. In each case, the details substituted are drawn from lived experiences of other real individuals in the localities in question.

As the lives of these sisters show, even as postcommunist economic reform meant to separate political and economic relationships, people's adaptations to economic crisis reconstituted formal and informal distribution networks around economic and social institutions. In the ebb tide of Soviet power, workplace-linked services replaced universal welfare. As broken supply chains and disruption of kinship-based networks of reciprocity made even insolvent companies into lifeboats, employers gained influence over employees' behavior outside the workplace. Dispossession through enclosure made even marginal gains increasingly important to households as the loss of access to common-pool resources through privatization deprived many people of rents or usufruct to which they were already legally entitled. And authorities' later threats against services and infrastructure in the twenty-first century would be credible because of people's experience of earlier rupture.

You Haven't Seen Disorder

In 2017, a high school student recorded a contentious classroom discussion in Russia's Bryansk region. Widely circulated on social media, the recording elicited recognition among some listeners and derision among others. It told a story that resonated with both Kremlin narratives and life experiences of many Russian adults. The school discussion connected people's support for Putin with their experiences in the 1990s. Like many analyses of the global rise of so-called populist leaders, the recording explained political behavior by highlighting the role of social anxiety caused by economic loss.

The recording captured high school students voicing their dissatisfaction with United Russia. Their dissatisfaction prompted the director of their school to respond, "There was total chaos [*bespredel*] in the country.[2] I was studying at that time. It was frightening to go outside after eight o'clock in the evening. You didn't see that. You still haven't seen disorder."[3] Young people, the director implied, could not appreciate the importance of the fact that in Russia, Putin's rule had meant the reestablishment of order and security. The school director's account emphasized the role of fear—fear of chaos, of crime, of want—to account for support for Putin.

While the Bryansk school director's statements articulated personal experiences, they also resembled interpretations of the 1990s promoted by the Kremlin. To underline the accomplishments of Putin's long rule, contemporary official Russian narratives have emphasized the real privation and confusion many people experienced during that decade. The political scientist Gulnaz Sharafutdinova has argued that both contemporary Russian leaders and their media allies frequently have used the frame of the "rough 1990s" (*likhie 90-e*) to support their own legitimacy, "harnessing group emotions in the pursuit of . . . political aims."[4] Like contemporary political battles over the writing of World War II history, the first post-Soviet decade has been a key historical terrain on which Russia's political debates of the present are contested.

Economic and social changes in Russia and Ukraine during the low tide of government presence in localities in the 1990s set the stage for a resurgent state and twenty-first-century political theater. Most salient for the proliferation of command performances in the twenty-first century were not people's feelings about anarchy in the 1990s, as Russian state-led interpretations might suggest, but the specific shape of shifting expectations and material conditions that resulted from economic changes during that decade.

Peter's Soul

It would be difficult to generalize about how people who lived in the former Soviet Union felt when the bottom fell out in 1992. People experienced that period in different ways depending on their generation, lineage and connections, education, and many other factors. As is often the case in times of cataclysm and change, people were not all in it together. Kremlin narratives use the adjective *likhoi*, a word that can mean both "hard" and "intrepid," to describe the decade. At that time, most people referred to *bespredel*, the lack of restraint or rules that seemed to characterize society at the time.

But to understand how those years prepared the stage for political theater, we do not necessarily need to know how people felt or feel about that time, nor how they felt or feel about certain politicians or political parties. We can examine the details of people's lives to see how changes around them opened opportunities for the politicians who later would direct command performances.

Some scholarship, as well as some popular literature, interprets participation in political theater as authoritarian manipulation or the behavior of a backward "zombified" populace unchanged from the Soviet period with little inner life or judgment.[5] To move away from such two-dimensional caricatures toward a more complex vision of human experience and choice—even when that choice is sometimes rigidly constrained, as in the stage management of contemporary political theater—this chapter highlights salient details from individual lives.[6] Such an approach can reveal aspects of politics, and logics of political participation, that a view from above—or a view from the *theatron*, rather than the stage—does not always permit us to see. The purpose of this exercise is appreciation of the serious and rational motivations behind human behavior—even behavior that could seem, from certain perspectives, submissive or unthinking.

This exercise expressly does not involve an effort to divine the inner intentions of the protagonists of this story. Human contact and lived experience are the foundation for the observations, arguments, and interpretations presented here, but human feelings are not at its core.[7] However, we can ask: knowing what can be known about the life of a particular person, how might one expect such a person to behave in the existing circumstances?[8] Although it is not the usual role of political ethnography, such an approach is not foreign to practitioners of rational choice inquiry.[9] Here, the role of ethnographic narrative is not to evoke sympathy, but to cultivate analytic empathy, and to reap the interpretive rewards such empathy can offer.[10]

The work of two playwrights, Anton Chekhov and Bertolt Brecht, can illustrate the analytical implications of the role of sympathy, which is anchored in the subjective experience of the observer, and that of empathy, which requires knowledge of the observed. In Chekhov's 1894 short story "The Student," a widow weeps as she listens to a theological seminary student recount the apostle Peter's betrayal of Jesus in the Garden of Gethsemane. Chekhov gently reminds his reader, "If the old woman cried, it was not because he could tell a touching story, but because Peter was close to her, and with all her being she was interested in what was happening in Peter's soul."[11] The woman's tears express not sentimentality or emotionality, but immanent and profound interest.

Brecht, reflecting on Horace's *Ars Poetica* in a dialogue grappling with the sentimental in performance, writes, "Why does he say 'If you want me to weep . . .' (Si vis me flere)? Is the idea to trample on my soul until tears come and liberate me? Or is it that I should be shown episodes that soften me until I become humanely disposed?" His interlocutor responds, "What's to stop you, if you see a man suffering and are able to suffer with him?" Brecht's character replies, "Because I must know why he is suffering."[12] Considering Brecht's idea in his work on the concept of the bystander in the contemporary world, Stephen Esquith writes that "empathy is not an emotion devoid of cognitive content. In order to engage in a conversation with her [Brecht's example of a sorrowful sister], we must imagine what it is like to see the world as she sees it, feel the love she feels for her brother, and believe what she believes. We must educate our emotions, not merely succumb to an irrational identification with another, fictional or otherwise."

Writing on traditions of stagecraft in Russia to emphasize approaches insisting on detailed knowledge of others' lives as a precondition for the analytical exposition of their choices, anthropologist Alaina Lemon provides a complementary perspective. In Lemon's telling, in contrast to American method acting, which asks the actor to reach into her *own* experience to summon the emotions necessary to portray a character, Russian theatrical training in the traditions of Stanislavsky or Meyerhold demands serious, sustained, and meticulous observation of *others'* behavior and social context as a precondition for the empathy necessary for performance. That empathy, Lemon reminds us, is based on respect for the other, and not on an expectation that we are all alike.[13]

Such an exercise requires moral imagination and an effort to attend to the details of the everyday life of others. While some accounts of politics emphasize the emotions of people on the stage at times of great upheaval, this chapter's "education of emotions" refers to the reader's effort to try to understand the contours of individual lives, and to listen to what their opportunities and challenges might reveal about their relationship to politics, their material lives at a particular moment in time, and how those conditions may have shaped their expectations of politics and the state in the years to come.

This immanent interest, this reach of imagination rooted in knowledge of others' experiences, is our aim as we join the two sisters, Tatiana Denisovna and Valentina Denisovna. In this text, the sisters' lives are not hagiography, psychological portraits, or biography.[14] Their experiences provide a ground-level view of constraints that shaped people's lives in the 1990s. This view enables us to see how those constraints structured their relationships with authorities in the twenty-first century, setting the stage for the development of political theater.

The challenges these sisters faced in the 1990s are not in any way exceptional. In many ways, they represent the statistical middle. Certain details of their lives reflect particularities of the city or region in which they live. For example, the city of Voronezh experienced scheduled daily municipal water shut-offs long before the dissolution of the Soviet Union. People in nearby cities did not face this particular reality. Despite such local variations, however, regularities emerge in the sisters' relationship to their workplaces, local government officials, and their families.

We join the sisters in early 1998, a year of apparently minor significance in the context of geopolitical change.[15] The Soviet Union has dissolved, but borders are not yet fully demarcated. New versions of national currencies are untested.[16] The sisters, like so many others, continue to think of themselves as Soviet people. According to their passports, the family was Russian under Soviet rule, but their grandparents spoke Ukrainian. The extended family is spread across eleven time zones, an artifact of twentieth-century resettlements and deportations. There are cousins in the eastern Siberian city of Blagoveshchensk on the Russia-China border,[17] in the Russian region of Belgorod, in northern Kazakhstan, and in western Ukraine.

The sisters kept the jobs they worked during the last years of Soviet power, as their respective companies followed downward trajectories in increasingly import-driven economies. The two companies, formerly state-owned, have been privatized. The process left employees both largely divested of the property they together had built under socialism and more subordinate to managers than before.[18] They remain in their positions for a reason: as for many others of the sisters' age and gender, large swaths of mainly unregulated private-sector labor markets remain closed to them.[19]

By the second decade of the twenty-first century, Tatiana Denisovna and Valentina Denisovna will become bit actors in command performances. They will execute their civic duty, voting in elections secure in the knowledge of the outcome. At work, they will participate in a variety of different performances of success. Tatiana Denisovna's supervisor will send her and her coworkers out onto Soviet Square in Voronezh to express their support for the president. In the years of Kuchma's and Yanukovych's presidencies, Valentina Denisovna will ride a bus filled with other women from her village to demonstrate on Freedom Square in Kharkiv. The two will share these activities with others, university students and landless and jobless young men, who likewise cannot risk either displeasing their superiors or turning down the opportunity to earn a day's pay pretending to support politicians.

A Day in the Life of Tatiana Denisovna

With the January holidays over at last,[20] Tatiana Denisovna and her coworkers could turn from the time-intensive labor of receiving family and friends to the relatively slower but relentless cycle of normal responsibilities—factory job, housework, and care for young grandchildren.[21]

Tatiana Denisovna spent much of the following month waiting for the bus on Voroshilova Street, a main artery not far from the central districts of Voronezh. The municipal authorities faced budgetary shortfalls that year, and public transportation ran far less frequently than it had previously. That morning, she had waited for two hours at the bus stop. When the vehicle finally arrived, the embarking crowd had been so tightly packed and tensions so high that the driver had intervened. He shouted at the bundled mass to keep their tempers despite the physical discomfort and the fact that everyone was now very late for work. That winter had been especially cold, and in the christening frosts of late January the thermometers read a consistent forty degrees below freezing. Sweltering in heavy coats inside the bus, passengers looked down through frosted windows at passing cars, each occupied by only one or two people, with even greater irritation than usual.[22]

That morning, like every other, Tatiana Denisovna had risen early, while there was still water in the pipes. The municipal authorities cut the city's water supply twice a day, morning and evening, during the hours when most people were home. Before dawn, she filled from the tap a few three- and five-liter jars and, because the jars were growing increasingly difficult to find, some empty plastic soda bottles, and lined them up along the windowsill. She saved enough water for that day and, in case of what seemed like a growing possibility, a future time when the municipal authorities might decide not to turn on the water supply at all. The shut-offs had not started with the collapse of the Union. The sense of uncertainty that accompanied them, though, was new. Communal life was like that now. Garbage accumulated in the courtyard, no one replaced the lightbulb in the stairwell when it burned out, and Tatiana Denisovna could tell which of her neighbors had money by the metal doors installed at the entrance to their apartments.[23]

Morning tea was brief. Tatiana Denisovna no longer took breakfast. Lately her budget allowed her one square meal each day, usually in the company canteen. Food prices were rising steadily every month, and neither she nor her grown daughter nor her mother had received a salary or pension payment since the previous spring.[24]

Despite the fact that the factory had withheld their wages for months, Tatiana Denisovna and her coworkers continued to show up at work every day. Looking for another job was out of the question: factories around the region had closed in the last five years, and there would be few other opportunities were she to leave her position. Women her age who had worked in education or medicine had been laid off, and some with advanced degrees in engineering and other sciences now were reduced to making their living traveling abroad to buy clothes and other goods to sell at a markup at home.[25]

In addition, her apartment belonged to the company. Leaving her position would mean finding a new place to live. Without a steady income, there would be little hope of finding an apartment to rent. The job gave her a place to go and a circle of friends and acquaintances who exchanged the kind of practical information they all needed to get by: where to find the lowest price for potatoes, who could obtain discounted tickets for long-distance trains—a once staple of travel that lately had become a luxury—where one could still get in to see a doctor, and so on.[26]

For Tatiana's sister Valentina, an accountant on a struggling former state farm across the unguarded border in rural Ukraine, the situation was not much simpler. That family, too, spent most of its time and energy running to make up for unpaid wages. The new pace of life meant that, except in the dead of winter, there was little time anymore for friendship or the warm relationships they had enjoyed before the Union had dissolved. Some relationships had come to seem mercenary: everyone was after money, people no longer depended on their social relationships as much for everyday life, and many of those relationships fell into disrepair or neglect. In the wider landscape of social change and the disappearance of the organizations that used to keep order, it was hard to tell who was dependable and who was not. At work, there was no knowing which suppliers or buyers would keep their word. Now, it was every person for herself.

The former state farm to which their village was attached had been unable to compensate its workers properly ever since the livestock slaughters of the early 1990s. Then, there had been no interest in wool for several years while cheap Turkish sweaters flooded the markets. The farm leadership had taken the difficult, painful, and irrevocable decision to slaughter the herds, groups of animals that were products of generations of knowledge, careful judgment, and work.[27] Once the sheep were gone, the enterprise would not have the resources or time to reestablish them when, a few years later, demand for wool would return.

The farm did not have enough money for diesel fuel and fertilizer, either. For those as well as other things needed for large-scale agriculture, it still depended on support from the regional government. A delegation from the district office of agricultural management came around occasionally, but mainly the director was obliged to visit the district offices, especially before elections and whenever the regional office called the district leadership to demand political favors. Those visits sometimes produced promises of fuel or other materials—if the director could reliably turn out his workers at elections to express their loyal support for the hand that fed them. The visits did not, on the other hand, resolve constant problems with electricity.

The district office requested reports from the enterprise, but with the power always going on and off without warning, the computer could not be used. Without power, Valentina Denisovna could not even use the company calculator.[28]

In this context, three seasons a year, Valentina Denisovna started her day around four o'clock in the morning. She washed clothes and sheets outside in a metal tub, worked in the vegetable garden, and milked the family cow before she rode her bicycle to the former state farm office in the neighboring village. In the afternoon she would return to milk the cow, which lived in a stable on the one-story village homestead her mother-in-law shared with her sister-in-law. Then, she would lug buckets of water up the stairs to their own apartment, where she would clean before preparing the family's meals. Valentina Denisovna's mother-in-law's household followed a similar schedule, with the addition of the permanent struggle to obtain enough wood for the stove that heated the house. For that, to ensure that they received fuel to last the winter, they needed the help and support of the farm director.

It had not always been necessary to carry water. In Valentina Denisovna's village a system of pipes had been installed in the 1960s to bring water into and out of the two-story apartment building and other homes. The construction was shoddy, and the pipes were pitched improperly, leaving water to stagnate in the system. In the early 1990s the local authorities gave up trying to solve the issue and closed down the system at its source.[29] Now families in the building had to walk down the street to a well to fetch water for washing and bathing. Buckets of water were heavy, especially on the stairs, and the trips added an hour or two of work to the day.

By law, both Valentina Denisovna and her mother-in-law could privatize their housing and become homeowners. But the process was onerous and expensive. The forms, stamps, fees, and under-the-table payments were endless. Neighbors who had done it spoke of ruinous tax and utility expenses. Like many other village residents, Denisovna's family had decided it was not worth the risk. Better to keep living in their homes, stay silent, and pray that no one in the village council office would become curious or ambitious. They hoped that as long as they did not make waves and the village leadership was satisfied, they and their homes would be left alone.

The Rich Also Cry

Amid currency devaluation and hyperinflation, administrative chaos, and disruption of access to extended family caused by new border regimes and the rising costs of travel, workplaces that had been key social institutions before the Soviet collapse became even more important in subsequent years for people like Tatiana and Valentina Denisovna. Even where factories slowed production or shut down, collective farms slaughtered their herds, or funding dried up for scientific and cultural institutions, work collectives remained important social institutions and critical anchors for their employees. Though many enterprises stopped paying their employees for months at a time, workplaces remained sites of access to housing, local transportation, medical services, and informal distribution networks through which people obtained basic necessities. Later, this would make workplaces attractive sites of pressure for regional leaders seeking to deliver votes or performances of enthusiasm to national politicians.

Valentina Denisovna often found herself asking how it had come to this. She was educated, with a college degree and an office job. Yet here she was, under a cow morning and afternoon, and lugging buckets of water from one end of the street to another. This despite the fact that the family had stopped drinking milk years before. The grandchildren went without, but they were hardly alone: few families who kept a cow could afford to drink the milk themselves. Once the farm stopped paying its employees, the sale of milk at the market in the district center had become their only source of cash. Although they could produce or barter most of their necessities, the family needed that cash to buy soap, matches, and other necessities.

A few years later, they would have to sell the cow. The animal would become expensive to feed, and a cow was like an infant—someone needed to be there, without fail, to attend to her needs, to pasture and milk her twice a day. The family could not afford to sacrifice the labor of one of the adult members of the household to take care of the animal. Without a member of the older generation at home, the animal had to go.[30] Homestead production offered little shelter from the shock that buffeted large farms and factories.[31]

Despite Valentina's long hours tending her homestead, she could not afford to ignore her responsibilities at the state farm. The farm was less generous with its resources than it had been when there was still a Soviet Union. But even though the farm was now a shadow of its former self, she and the other employees depended on it more than ever before. They needed access to a dozen things the director controlled, and Valentina had seen what had happened to the small number of people on the farm who had struck out on their own.[32] They were cast out, excommunicated. The director told them the ambulance would not come for them if they were sick. Their kids lost their spots in village child-care. Some of them were evicted from their apartments.

She and her fellow villagers needed to be able to graze their cows on farm pasture, cut hay for their animals on farmland, chop wood on farm forests, and most importantly, jockey for a well-timed visit in the fall from the farm tractor to plow their homestead potato fields. The further you fell from the director's favor, the more likely you might be stuck waiting for the tractor until the spring thaw, when fields turned to mud. If, before, people could pull the director aside after a farm meeting and tell him what they really thought, now the situation was much more delicate. Surviving meant showing up and saying yessir to whatever he asked.

Now too there was no party representative to whom they could appeal for support. As a result, the director had been running roughshod over employees. Machinery—even whole tractors—kept disappearing from the equipment yard, along with other farm equipment. There were whispers that the director was selling farm property to foreign investors. In a legal sense, that property belonged to the workers. Employees were supposed to receive shares in the farm, but between the constant uncertainty about the value of money and those mysterious disappearances, it was unclear whether those shares would be worth anything at all.[33]

The situation on the farm of an accountant friend from Valentina's days as a student at the agricultural institute was no better. A few years ago, some men had arrived with briefcases. Afterward, workers had received some money in exchange for their shares. Her friend had worked for the farm for over two decades. She bought a pair of shoes with the money from her shares. The soles came off after two weeks.

Valentina Denisovna had it easier than some of her colleagues and friends. Her husband was still alive and healthy and could contribute to what she could glean from her position on the state farm. He took seasonal construction jobs in Crimea and in Poland. Her husband had tried opening a business in the village: a small kiosk selling food, cigarettes, and beer. The couple had thought the village needed more commerce: the local state store had survived the hardest years after independence, but it was hardly ever open and never had much on the shelves.

Denisovna's husband had a good sense for business. But between the certificates that always needed renewing, the incessant visits from representatives of state regulatory offices who used their positions to line their personal pockets, and the neighborhood toughs—ambitious boys connected to men who had long ago surpassed the Sicilian Cosa Nostra in organizational sophistication—who exacted payments for protection both from her husband and from his competitors, there was little way to turn a profit.[34] For those who did, the tax authorities took what remained.

The family had decided it wasn't worth the trouble. Someone else could deal with the aggravation, the pressure, and the intimations of violence. Each spring, Valentina Denisovna's husband would set off to the south or west on short-term contracts, working long hours on rickety construction sites, his pay often shorted by unscrupulous employers, praying to the Lord that his back would not fail.

Valentina's sister also depended on her workplace, but in a different way. While Valentina was out in the state farm's pasture milking, her sister watched a soap opera with her colleagues at work. Tatiana Denisovna relied on the people she worked with for food and information about food. The end of the Soviet Union had not meant the end of lines. Now she queued up for products where prices were lowest. That meant keeping track of where to go to buy basic goods. She and her coworkers traded information about flatbed trucks of vegetables that were rumored to arrive next to a certain train station at a particular hour, about where you could still buy sugar after the sugar beet processing plants had stopped operations permanently because of constant supply chain interruptions, about which market had the cheapest bulk farina. Other than information, they traded food they had been able to procure from colleagues who had relatives in the nearby countryside.[35]

For this, Tatiana Denisovna used to visit her sister regularly. The director of Valentina Denisovna's state farm had had the foresight in the 1980s to organize processing facilities on the farm's territory. In the last years of the Soviet Union, Tatiana Denisovna had been able to bring jars of tomato juice, squash, and pickles from their canning facility and farmer's cheese from Valentina's cow back to her apartment. Since the Union dissolved, train tickets had become prohibitively expensive. There were rumors that Ukraine might start to require visas. Travel cost money, and planning it seemed risky. Now the sisters only saw each other once or twice a year, and Tatiana was obligated to search for other ways to stock her pantry. Despite the fact that nowadays she rarely received a paycheck, she did not know what she would have done without her colleagues at work.

For Tatiana Denisovna, all the uncertainty and aggravation of 1998 required perseverance, but it paled in comparison to what had transpired six years earlier. That January, prices had nearly tripled in a single month and had not stopped climbing at near that rate until well into the following year. The euphoria some had felt when Boris Nikolaevich Yeltsin held a Russian flag atop that tank in Moscow passed in the blink of an eye, replaced first by apprehension and then a sensation of total insecurity, a feeling that the bottom had dropped out.

Some afternoons, Tatiana Denisovna and her colleagues would come together to participate in a national ritual. The entire country would seem to come to a halt as people gathered around televisions in government buildings, factories, hospitals, and stores to follow the travails of Maria in the Mexican soap opera *The Rich Also Cry*.[36] Maria's troubles of the heart offered viewers a temporary respite and distraction from their troubles of country and wallet.

At that time, it had seemed that the social order was collapsing. People who had stepped into the breach played by different rules, resorting to violence in new, seemingly unpredictable ways. The end of Soviet power had brought political freedoms, but it had emboldened extremists and ushered in an ideological vacuum. What were they meant to believe in now? It had also brought economic hardship and American problems that the propagandists had long described to an unbelieving public: homelessness, street violence, and insecurity.

The stress of everyday life in late winter of 1998 paled, too, in comparison with what would follow in the months to come. That summer, amid a dizzying series of changes in the government and a precipitous drop in the value of the ruble, the city would seem to grind to a halt. People in Voronezh would compare the situation to how it had been in the winter of 1991–92, not long after that night when they went to bed only to awake the next morning to discover that their country no longer existed.

In 1998, most of what people ate had been produced abroad. When the ruble plunged against Western currencies that summer, stores could not afford to pay for new inventory. Some shopkeepers resourcefully drew on the skills of shop-window artifice they had learned in Soviet days. But carefully arranged pyramids of locally produced pop and soda crackers hardly concealed the fact that little remained on the shelves. Only the candy factory in the city center would manage to continue production. The smell of chocolate wafers would waft over the hungry city, taunting the population like a Snickers commercial during the weekly television game show *Field of Miracles*.

Late that August, Tatiana Denisovna's coworker's husband would have a heart attack. Her schoolmate who worked at the clinic would recount days inundated with cases of angina and heart attacks among men who should have been too young to get sick. Tatiana Denisovna's own husband had died in a car accident in the early 1990s. Although she was only in her late forties, a number of her same-age colleagues had lost their husbands in the intervening years.[37] At the same time that failing infrastructure meant that there was more physical work to do than there were hours in the day, many families had lost one of the adults who could do it.

The same month, Tatiana Denisovna and her next-door neighbor would go to the savings bank to try to withdraw what little was left in their accounts. Six years ago, when the ruble plunged, they had lost their entire previous savings. Now, together with others harboring the same plans and fears, they would find bank doors slammed and locked in their faces.[38] They would leave quickly, feeling the temperature of the crowd rise, and return to their apartment building. Later in the evening, through the thin walls of her apartment, Tatiana Denisovna would hear the sound of someone watching the television news: while parliamentary deputies bickered among themselves, the government would appoint the second of three prime ministers in two months. Tatiana Denisovna would tune her radio to a classical music station and raise the volume as high as it would go, trying in vain to drown out pronouncements from the Duma—sounds that made her stomach turn.

Relief would arrive unexpectedly the following year. In the countryside, some farms would recover as demand for local products picked up in response to the high price of imported food. Then, in an initially bone-chilling moment on New Year's Eve 1999, Boris Nikolaevich Yeltsin would announce his resignation, and his replacement, on national television while they were all meant to be celebrating with family and close friends. Soon after, pensions would be restored and the factory would start paying her salary again.[39] For a time, the new government would seem to be doing something about all the problems.[40]

Everyone Is Dependent on the Bosses

The challenges and economic vulnerabilities Tatiana Denisovna and her sister faced in the last decade of the twentieth century tracked changes under way elsewhere in the world. Their experiences shared key features with political economies of loss in other regions of the globe: risk shift, austerity, and enclosure, as national and transnational movements transformed an unprecedented range of public goods and services into privately owned commodities with increasingly complex and opaque ownership structures.[41] In this global context of shifts in relationships between people with respect to things, people like the Denisovny experienced economic loss that politicians could use to create opportunities for securing participation and loyalty.

Although twenty-first-century performances of political theater reminded many people of Soviet-era practices, the morphology of performance—what people saw on the stage—would conceal a logic rooted in economic precarity. That precarity developed in a context in which social welfare provisions had all but entirely eroded, and in which the state unilaterally had broken the social contract underlying the final decades of the Soviet Union's existence.

As time went on, people in both rural and urban areas, people like the Denisovny, would face local leaders who would convert settled entitlements into objects of negotiation and rewards for political behavior. Amid ongoing economic stress, public servants would hold hostage people's access to public infrastructure, social services, and compensation, releasing them only in return for political favors, including participation in command performances.[42] Politicians and bureaucrats linked things people had taken for granted—salaries in enterprises dependent on the state for subsidies, certification, or tax incentives; use of public infrastructure; and access to public education and markets in consumer goods—to political support for specific candidates.

These exchanges did not benefit bit players on the stage. Usually, people see political corruption as depending on some form of a quid pro quo. Even though patron-client relationships happen between people who may not be social or economic equals, they can provide a way for the more powerful to respond to the concerns of those who have loyalty, votes, and legitimacy to offer.[43] And in other national contexts, clientelism has primarily been observed to be additive—if ultimately inefficient or maldistributive—for clients.[44] People come away from the exchange with something they did not have before. That might be a job, a loan, land, or gifts. In some forms of electoral clientelism, voters can receive concrete payments. Without this added benefit, clients might have little incentive to participate in those relationships.

For two decades, the variety of electoral clientelism present in Ukraine and Russia included both positive and negative inducements.[45] Some local state agents used positive incentives, accompanying payments with threats or offering them as a replacement for things people took for granted. In Russia, people called this "the whip and gingerbread."[46]

Mainly, though, the tools used for staging command performances were subtractive. Rather than gaining from participation, people stood to lose something if they did not comply. As local state agents threatened access to infrastructure, compensation, and services to incite people to support incumbent politicians, people understood that nonparticipation would mean loss—loss of a job, a place to live, a spot in school for their child, access to health care, or a dozen other things most people require to live a quiet and fulfilling life. Where large portions of the population received low wages and depended on public services to conduct the daily business of living, this threat of redefinition carried particular weight.

Inducements were often net negative for another reason. This had to do with the context in which electoral quids pro quo took place. At first glance, sometimes positive inducements created the appearance of benefit from participation. But if we look more closely, we see that the context affects how we should interpret the meaning of payoffs. For example, during Putin's second term as president, a Russian journalist described a typical situation:

> Voting for Candidate "Against All," like mass flight from electoral urns or conscious spoiling of ballots, was the popular response to elections without choice, because the outcome of an electoral campaign is almost always predetermined. Simple, experienced people feel this intuitively. And the more educated and enlightened part of the population will easily explain to you that well, really, life is such that with two sacks of grain, a country granny will vote how her *kolkhoz* [collective farm] chair orders her, and the latter, in his turn, for a ton of diesel fuel for seeding for a discounted loan, for a tiny subsidy will sprinkle a handful of falsified ballots in the urn. "Correct" voting is ensured by the reproduction of this order of things, when everyone all around is dependent on the bosses.[47]

In this example, a pensioner trades her vote for two sacks of grain. After this transaction, she would seem to be at least a little better off than she was before.

Once we understand the context of the exchange, however, we see that what appears to be a net benefit is nothing of the kind. First, the pensioner is not free to refuse to enter into this implicit contract. She needs the grain or its exchange value. And since the agricultural enterprise continues to govern various aspects of her life, she cannot afford to alienate the director. This ensures that she will participate in the exchange without being asked to do so.

Second, the payment she receives for her vote is not additional money in her pocket. The sacks of grain are goods already due to her by law. The director owes her the two sacks of grain as a typical payment for his lease of her land share on the territory of the former collective farm. The woman is the legal owner of the land that produces the grain. But the director's de facto control over its use and harvest allows him to extract her political cooperation in exchange for receipt of her own property. In practice, her ownership rights do not extend to use of her land.[48] This is seized by the director, who then sells her rights back to her for the price of her vote.

Amid enclosure or privatization of common-pool resources, payments in cash or kind for participation in political theater often replaced rights or entitlements of greater value that people had recently lost. When we consider these exchanges in the light of concurrent exchanges, even apparent positive incentives—vote buying or food baskets, for example—often represented not a gain but a net loss for participants, many of whom nonetheless were in no position to decline small encouragements. In political theater, people's everyday lives are filled with offers they cannot refuse.

Transactions that were losing propositions for bit actors nonetheless could yield longer-term political dividends for the local stage directors who brought people into the drama. As politicians at the national level helped themselves to the public purse, local agents ensured that people at least received a small portion in return for their support. In a context of widespread loss and insecurity, even seemingly minor payments could ensure a positive view of the patron who provided them.[49]

Everything Is Destroyed

The social and economic context in which command performances would come to proliferate in both Ukraine and Russia at the turn of the twenty-first century included tens of millions of people whose experiences resembled those of Tatiana and Valentina Denisovna—if not always in their precise, locally inflected details, then in their broad contours.

The view of this period from above is well documented. In the first years following the dissolution of the Soviet Union, with the collapse of central planning and the partial dissolution of trade ties between Soviet republics' successor states, whole areas of industry in Ukraine and Russia came to a standstill.[50] This occurred just as new national governments lifted price controls, opened their borders to imported products, privatized vast numbers of public goods,[51] and, at the behest of international lending organizations, attempted to resolve balance-of-payments problems by making dramatic cuts to state budgets rather than by raising tax revenue. Among the results of these choices were catastrophic levels of de facto unemployment, including the society-wide disappearance of salary payments for people who never formally lost their jobs.

State withdrawal from many areas of life affected people in different ways. Men suffered precipitous drops in life expectancy and a loss of social status and meaning.[52] Women, deliberately and explicitly excluded from multiple sectors in new, private labor markets,[53] constituted an educated labor force driven into other pursuits. For a time, some mothers became shuttle traders, while some daughters traded in their own bodies, at home or abroad.[54] At the same time, exclusion from labor markets did not mean a welcoming private sphere. Unable to bear the cost of providing for children in the absence of reliable public services, a whole generation of young people waited to start families. For some, a necessary wait proved too long.⁵⁵

People's experiences of governance changed dramatically within a short period. As numerous scholars noted at the time, a sense of unbounded disorder, *bespredel*, reigned in various areas of life. The temporary disappearance from view of agents of the law allowed the emergence of new, informal groups who governed territory without popular mandate.⁵⁶ For some, shared experience of state withdrawal included violence at the hands of other private citizens.⁵⁷ For others, it meant a sense that they were newly on their own and responsible for their own physical security.⁵⁸

For all, state withdrawal meant a deterioration of infrastructure and the dissolution or reshaping of institutions that formerly had structured everyday life. Liberating for some, this condition introduced new constraints for most. As supply chains broke and normal mechanisms of contract enforcement receded, wages evaporated and transportation, communication, health, and education infrastructure slowed or stopped in the absence of replenishment from the empty coffers of municipal budgets. With the temporary reduction of living to survival,⁵⁹ relationships with state representatives also changed. The belief that local leaders and state organizations had obligations of care was replaced by relationships in which people expected little responsiveness from elected authorities.⁶⁰ For the great majority, insecurity replaced dull predictability.

Across former Soviet space, people searched for metaphors to articulate the extent of the social, economic, and infrastructural destruction that followed the Soviet collapse.⁶¹ Even before state-led ideological campaigns in Russia would turn to focus on World War II, people used the aftermath of war to describe their surrounding reality. Boris Grebenshchikov's "Train on Fire" played over and over again on the airwaves, and listeners thought of its protagonist urging his regiment homeward to steward wasted land.⁶² The phrase, "Everything is destroyed, like after the war" became a refrain for the decade.⁶³

That phrase could be heard in most any context, but especially in the hinterlands, where "rusted-out factories" *were* "scattered like tombstones across the landscape"⁶⁴ and where sudden poverty and epidemics of drug dependence ruptured family ties. "Everything is destroyed, like after the war" meant both the physical destruction of the built environment and the human detritus that the period of system change had left in its wake. Together with shifts in state identity and the threats to communication within far-flung extended families that the Soviet collapse precipitated, this destruction formed part of the context for those people in Russia who listened, and understood, as

Vladimir Putin in 2005 described the dissolution of the Soviet Union as "the greatest geopolitical catastrophe of the century."

The losses of the 1990s set the stage for what would come in the next decade: politicians' use of infrastructure, services, and compensation to compel people to do their bidding. Local political entrepreneurs would leverage people's precarious access to energy, transportation, and labor compensation, linking these to cooperation in political theater. By decade's end, political parties would assume a role in local politics similar to that played by developed party machines elsewhere in the world.[65]

When it came to staging command performances, politicians' threats against existing infrastructure, services, and payments drew their credibility from the fact that the social contract had been decisively broken in recent memory.[66] Even as some threats of economic reprisal seemed immediately believable, others required confidence that local leaders would deliver on their threats, and that if a community did not behave as requested, fuel supplies would be cut off, bread deliveries would not take place, universities would close, or salaries would not be paid. The abrupt rupture of the Soviet social contract in the early 1990s became a reference point for the following years, allowing many to believe that they would lose if they did not participate—and to act accordingly.

When, a decade or more later, the Denisovny sisters would go out into city squares to demonstrate or to the urn to vote for the president, they did so under just such threats of loss: their supervisors and local leaders would threaten their jobs, the bus line, a long-promised village gas line, day care for the grandchildren, all if they did not agree to participate in command performances. The sisters would take politicians and bureaucrats at their word for the same reason their coworkers and neighbors did: because everything the bosses threatened had already happened to them, personally, once before.

 CHAPTER 4

Staging Performances

Even as the initial purpose of economic reform in Russia and Ukraine had been to extricate the state from economic life, a series of events and decisions reinforced local geographies of overlapping political authority and economic opportunity in many regions of Ukraine and Russia: the disruption and disintegration of supply chains, trade policy that threatened both domestic industry and agriculture, widespread state withdrawal from service provision, the legal or de facto transfer of responsibility for some areas of service provision to enterprises, and the privatization of common-pool resources. Those overlapping contours made it possible for local leaders in business and government to press people into theatrical service, satisfying national politicians' demands for electoral support.[1]

Signs of political theater had been afoot for a few years before command performances burst onto the national stage in both countries in 2000. In Ukraine, the early months of that year brought frenzied political activity across the country as President Leonid Kuchma pushed a constitutional referendum that would consume the population for several months. By spring, the population approved the referendum in a landslide. Its proposals, however, were not implemented. This all-Ukraine referendum marked a turning point in politics in the region, as the first instance of successful large-scale electoral dramaturgy in independent Ukraine. The plebiscite coincided with the rise to power of Vladimir Putin, whom citizens of the Russian Federation had elected president just three weeks before.

In the light of national elections in years to come, the significance of the Ukrainian referendum lay less in its immediate legal implications than in the nature of its organization and execution and in the work it did to socialize the Ukrainian public to post-Soviet political theater. In retrospect, the value of the exercise seemed pedagogical: it taught people to comply with the demands of local state agents. For at least the next decade and a half, political parties would maintain their grip on political power by staging command performances.

In both Russia and Ukraine, even though the first electoral cycles following the dissolution of the Soviet Union had been relatively competitive,[2] people throughout Ukraine understood the April referendum in 2000 to be a performance. During the months and weeks preceding the referendum, local state agents across Ukraine used a range of economic instruments to push people to participate. The presidential administration pressured institutions across Ukrainian society—universities and hospitals, national and regional press outlets, small businesses and large-scale agricultural companies—to support President Kuchma and his agenda for constitutional reform. Across the country, the consequences of refusing to comply were economic, not political.

Kuchma's referendum contained a mix of populist appeals and pro-executive measures. It proposed changes to the country's constitution that would transform the relationship between executive and legislative branches, granting broad powers to the executive and establishing an upper house of parliament. If it passed, the president would have the authority to dissolve parliament if it failed to form a stable majority within a specified period of time or to ratify the state budget. The number of parliamentary deputies would be reduced by one-third, and a new second chamber would represent the interests of the country's regions. To encourage participation, the referendum also contained a question that would eliminate immunity from prosecution for parliament members—a measure that, while popular, would not be adopted for nearly another two decades, when Volodymyr Zelensky would fulfill a promise of his presidential campaign.

A media campaign to discredit the national legislature and promote the executive branch accompanied preparation for the referendum. The national and regional press published hundreds of articles criticizing parliament members as universally corrupt. Those articles included interviews with prominent figures in the spheres of education, culture, religion, and government.[3]

The initiative asked citizens to endorse changes that the Ukrainian constitutional court had declared unconstitutional just weeks before the referendum.[4] People who took to the streets in the port city of Odesa in early April to protest the initiative claimed that the proposed changes would lead to "the reversal of democratic reforms, to the creation of a legislature in the 'pocket' of the Presidential administration, and to the final destruction of the balance of powers." They argued the referendum would place almost all power in the hands of the executive, rendering the legislative and judicial branches merely "decorative."[5]

The countrywide ballot unfolded in April, just a few months after Kuchma, buoyed by support from voters in the west of the country, had been elected to the presidency.[6] Many attributed Kuchma's rise to his having learned to speak passable Ukrainian at a time when many national politicians spoke mainly Russian. They played upon an old expression referring to travel by Christian pilgrims along rural byways, where the only way to know where to go was to ask directions. *Yazyk do Kyieva dovede*: Your tongue will lead to Kyiv. Perceptions of any flaws in Kuchma's Ukrainian would fade in subsequent years with the rise of Viktor Yanukovych, a Russophone politician whom voters took seriously but not literally and who spoke in generalities and prison jargon. Kuchma's election as chief executive in 1999 had included incidents of pressure, but the large majorities in western Ukraine who voted for him had programmatic reasons to support his candidacy against Donetsk-born Communist Party leader Petro Symonenko.

Once in office, Kuchma encouraged the development and use of regional machines to compel cooperation with the presidential administration.[7] Those machines were most effective in the eastern and southern regions of the country, where industry and large-scale agriculture were engines of local and regional economies. For observers abroad, this created an impression of people in Ukraine's east and south as having political preferences distinct from those of the rest of the country.

According to the Central Electoral Commission, 82 percent of voters—just shy of thirty million citizens—turned out for Kuchma's referendum. Of those, over 90 percent voted in favor of at least one of the proposed measures.[8] The highest rates of participation were in student dormitories and military units.[9] Turnout in the referendum was higher than it had been in the presidential elections just a few months before.[10]

While television and posters advertised the referendum as a "people's initiative," Ukrainians understood this was a euphemism. The perception of the referendum as a presidential project was so widely shared that comedians told jokes about it on national television.[11] In a televised competition of improvisational comedy advertising a "President's cup," one skit asked, "What will happen if the referendum doesn't take place?" The answer: "That can't happen, since the referendum is under the patronage of President Kuchma."[12]

"Jokes" like this made some people laugh, but they also taught the population how to behave. In her analysis of the Soviet humor magazine *Krokodil*, the anthropologist Alena Ledeneva described the pedagogy of satire amid censorship. For decades, *Krokodil* openly had acknowledged challenges of Soviet life and invited readers to laugh at those challenges. In Ledeneva's interpretation, official satirical culture not only offered a release valve, but also instructed readers in the boundaries of permissible critique.[13] Like the Ukrainian comedy skit on state television, official satire permitted the acknowledgment of an open secret—the referendum is not a "people's initiative" but a project of the president—while indicating to its audience just how far they might go. And in this case, in its criticism, the televised comedy skit served a further purpose. It reminded viewers, indirectly and through laughter, what the referendum was and what would be expected of them.

Kuchma's administration had led a countrywide campaign to collect the three million signatures required to hold the national referendum, a process that hinted at how the presidential administration intended to run the referendum itself. Municipal and state employees solicited the signatures, organizing this work during business hours. For public servants, participation in the "people's initiative" was, as one local human rights organization put it, "voluntary-obligatory"—a Soviet-era term used to describe required activities. Threats for nonparticipation in collection of signatures directly targeted people's livelihoods.

Municipal employees learned they would lose their jobs if they did not produce required quotas of signatures. State workers found their salaries withheld until they had found enough people to sign.[14] Those who worked in the private sector were not insulated from pressure. Employees of the housing and utilities authorities—people who had the power to let disruptive problems and annoyances of everyday life linger—also collected thousands of signatures.[15]

Then, in the weeks preceding the referendum, institutions whose budgets came directly or indirectly from public funds—offices of state and local government, universities, schools, hospitals, former collective farms, and others—held meetings that employees were required to attend or risk losing their jobs. At those meetings employees received instructions to deliver their own votes and those of their subordinates.[16] In many cases, supervisors physically led groups of employees en masse to precincts for early voting. Across the regions of the country, more than a third of the electorate would vote before balloting day.[17]

No One Needs This

Along Ukraine's eastern border, decades of Soviet planning had produced dense concentrations of industry and educational institutions in cities and large-scale commercial agriculture in the countryside. In the east, functionaries at every level pressured the population to participate in the referendum.[18] Local officials described a presidential administration that had mobilized the entire vertical of power: "Behind the chairman of the *kolkhoz* stands the head of the district administration, and behind him a deputy in Kyiv."[19]

Local commentators in the city of Kharkiv described managers of state enterprises across economic sectors who "forced their subordinate workers to take part in voting under threat of being fired."[20] School directors compelled teachers to threaten parents with punishment of their children at school if the parents did not participate in the referendum.[21] In several precincts, teachers delivered ballots to people's homes.[22] People described widespread campaigns of "intimidation" and "brutal pressure" at the hands of public servants and heads of public enterprises. A resident of the city of Kharkiv remarked that although such techniques had been used in the run-up to recent presidential elections, during the referendum they "touched every member, without exception, of my considerable family."[23]

University officials and prominent members of scientific and artistic establishments described experiencing pressure to endorse the project.[24] These included rectors and department heads of major universities,[25] directors of regional libraries and theaters,[26] and numerous researchers: political scientists, sociologists, psychologists, and legal scholars.[27] They, in their turn, delivered pressure and threats to university students. In the weeks leading up to the referendum, university officials gathered students in auditoriums and informed them that if they did not vote for the ballot measure, they would lose their stipends or the university would be closed.[28]

Pressure on students would not persist in all localities. The 2000 referendum was one of the last instances of national balloting before mobile phones became widely available. When they did, students were able to record and broadcast to wider publics the threats they received from university administrators, leading some of the latter eventually to abandon the practice.

In rural districts, local functionaries used a variety of techniques to produce the result desired by their superiors in Kyiv. Membership in civic organizations exposed people to pressure, especially where organizations received support from local authorities. The day before the referendum, regional representatives of women's groups held a meeting in Chuhuiv, a town of about thirty-five thousand people southeast of Kharkiv, on the highway toward Slovians'k. In that meeting, the chairman of a former collective farm and member of the district electoral commission used a commonly heard refrain to describe the referendum: "needed by no one." Then he displayed to those present a list of those who were to vote in it.[29]

On the other side of Kharkiv region, near its western border with Poltava region, the assistant director of a local NGO had impressive success recruiting new members. She bragged that a large number of local people either already had voted or had signed a paper declaring their intention to vote yes. The assistant director herself had been the first to cast a ballot.[30]

Early voting occurred throughout the city and region. Some local observers noted that officials who collected votes before the day of the referendum had done so without proper documentation and in contravention of national law. One Kharkiv resident made an official declaration to the head of the Central Electoral Commission, cataloging numerous infractions. He had watched as three strangers approached his family members at their home. One presented herself as the head of the local precinct electoral commission. The three persuaded his wife and daughters to vote on the day before the referendum. They voted on the spot, in front of the visitors, who asked for no identification and offered no envelopes for their ballots. The visitors asked them to sign for and vote on behalf of other family members. This resident expressed "incomprehension" at coordinated efforts to persuade people to vote early, "independently of whether citizens had made requests to do so or not."[31]

Workplaces were sites not only of pressure in the weeks before the referendum, but also of the voting process itself. A regional land functionary, likewise depicting the referendum as "needed by no one," described balloting in villages. The head of the former collective farm sits at his desk and calls someone in: "Ivanov, give me your ballot. Are you for the president? For (marks ballot). Now drop it in the ballot box." "Next." He imagined official figures would cite 60 percent participation but thought actual participation would amount to some 20 to 40 percent—and that people who did not show would have their ballots marked for them.[32]

In contrast to electoral contests of the previous decade, an atmosphere of fear pervaded institutions where supervisors mobilized their subordinates to participate. Always referring to others, not themselves, residents of the region would say "people are afraid" when speaking of the referendum.

Jokes using Soviet-era tropes of escape emerged and circulated among the young, educated, and relatively privileged in the city of Kharkiv: "suitcase—train—Germany," and, in reference to the hapless subway car hijacker of a Soviet saw, "next stop: Munich."[33] Local observers noted similarities with the Soviet period, underlining the fear that accompanied the referendum's implementation: "In fact, a fear of functionaries and representatives of power that had been forgotten over the last decade returned to many millions of people. Relationships between the state and citizens are returning to stereotypes of communist times, when citizens feared to express in any way a thought that differed from the official."[34]

Now, though, the fear people felt referred not to their political status but to their livelihoods. One Kharkiv resident described interactions in the hallway of her apartment building on the day of the referendum. A member of her precinct electoral commission rang at her door to ask why she was not voting. The member told her, "Because of people like you, turnout will be low and there will be unpleasantness for us at work." Meanwhile, her neighbor, a schoolteacher whose supervisor had told her to report on the number of parents who had voted, recounted, "What hysteria when it turned out that almost no one had gone [to vote]. . . . In a neighboring school they took away the students' book bags and said they'd give them back to the parents when they voted."[35]

The situation was similar in the nearby countryside. For other types of policy implementation, village council members in settlements physically close to the regional capital normally experienced greater pressure to implement policy than their colleagues in regional peripheries. Oversight of policy implementation took place mainly in settlements near regional capitals, where it was relatively easy and cheap for government officials to drop in on local council members.[36] Implementation of ordinary economic policies in the more remote countryside often went unmonitored because regional functionaries' budgets did not include fuel for transportation. But in the case of the referendum, pressure to participate suffused interactions between supervisors and subordinates throughout the territory of Kharkiv region, regardless of distance from the regional center.

Resources the government invested in the referendum accounted for this difference. Though modest in comparison to the electoral campaigns to come, state funding provided local officials enough money to extend the range of their oversight of activities in the countryside.[37] By deputizing employees of institutions from health care and education to industry and agriculture, regional officials could stretch their resources, piggybacking on existing institutions to exact pressure on people to vote.

Behind closed doors, local functionaries complained about being used in this way. Acknowledging aloud that "people are openly afraid," they expressed annoyance at the task of mobilizing the population. Some used alcohol to try to wash away the bad taste of obligatory meetings. In a settlement just beyond the Kharkiv city outskirts, local officials spoke with dread about one upcoming meeting, which would be "an even bigger drinking bout than last time."[38] Others articulated their personal feelings: "I'm not going to the referendum. The whole thing makes me nauseated."[39] During a trip to a remote rural district far away from the regional capital, a prominent former political figure in the region recounted how she had been invited to give a radio interview about her civic activities, only to be ambushed with questions about the referendum and whether she thought it necessary to vote in it. In her telling, she had answered something about "civic duty" (*grazhdanskii dolg*). Personally, however, she did not plan to go.[40]

Beyond Kharkiv, authorities used similar tactics to persuade people to participate in and vote for the referendum measures. In central Ukraine, some three hundred kilometers southwest of Kyiv, residents of the region of Vinnytsia encountered tools of pressure and persuasion in many aspects of their daily lives. Energy meter readers in every district of the region visited each house to "recommend" participation in the referendum. In Vinnytsia's municipal hospital No. 1, doctors were required to cast their ballots at work. One observer remarked that how patients voted was "right out of a detective novel." Members of the electoral commission told gravely ill patients that they understood the patients supported the referendum and that their ballots would be filled out for them so as to avoid any mistakes. On public transportation, tram and trolley operators took the microphone every two stops, announcing, "Citizens, we invite you to vote in the people's initiative referendum and to support the questions submitted for discussion."[41]

Thinking Pedagogues

Twelve hundred kilometers southwest of Kharkiv, along Ukraine's border with Poland, Slovakia, Hungary, and Romania, tactics of coercion and persuasion resembled those in the industrialized east. In the months preceding the referendum, Leonid Kuchma's administration mobilized economic and social leaders and institutions across the region of Zakarpattia, inciting their constituents to support the president.

In 1999, local economies and property rights regimes in the region had not yet changed dramatically since Soviet times. Collective farms hobbled along, not yet subject to the land reform legislation that finally would reorganize them early the following year. Hungary's Status Laws had yet to make employment opportunities abroad widely available to the large Magyar minority in the region. And it would be four years before the countries along Ukraine's western border would join the European Union, reconfiguring cross-border trade and labor flows in the region.

In Zakarpattia at that time, people's livelihoods depended on networks and resources attached to workplaces, trade unions, churches, and other organizations. Those collectivities actively and successfully encouraged their members and constituents to participate in the referendum, while political elites from regional heads to village leaders pressured the population to support the president. In Zakarpattia, such efforts were even more successful than elsewhere in the country. Some 98 percent of eligible voters in the region participated in the referendum, and between 95 and 97 percent answered yes on each of the four questions.

The regional press in Zakarpattia highlighted the presidential administration's efforts to mobilize the population. In the three and a half months leading up to the referendum, sketching a picture of total societal unanimity, the Ukrainian-language weekly *Novyny Zakarpattia* published 167 articles supporting the initiative. The newspaper reported telegrams sent from work collectives across the country in support of the referendum—from an agricultural collective near Kyiv, from workers in a bread factory near Kherson, from a district consumer union near Zhytomyr.[42] It highlighted local residents' statements, like the pensioner from the district of Svaliava who argued that "there was not a single population point without meetings at which people unanimously spoke in favor of conducting the . . . referendum."[43]

When regional leaders spoke, heads of regional committees and councils of trade unions, together with the heads of their subordinate organizations, gathered to listen. Regional leaders stressed the importance of supporting the president in order to ensure funding of social protections for their members.[44] Political parties of various stripes lined up behind the president, and social, political, and economic institutions in every sector participated in the campaign. The entire apparatus of administrative power stood together in support of the referendum: functionaries from regional and district officials,[45] village heads,[46] directors of youth social services,[47] and head doctors of district hospitals[48] publicly articulated their support. In January, the heads of nine political parties came out in favor of the referendum.[49]

In this relatively land-poor, mountainous region, numerous pro-referendum messages connected the effort to a contemporaneous presidential decree on the reorganization of the agricultural sector.[50] Those messages reminded residents that if they wished to receive plots of land from collective farms, and if they wished to avoid "complete collapse" of agricultural production,[51] they should support the president.

Anticipating possible objections to an effort of such scale and intensity, the regional press published comments addressing many people's main concern about the referendum: namely, the expense of the campaign. One citizen of Chop argued in a letter to the editor that echoed many similar interventions in the press: "Some say that the situation in Ukraine is so tense. There's not enough money. And now quite a bit is going for the referendum. Let it. At least we'll know for what concretely our taxes went."[52]

The administration's efforts extended beyond the state and public sector to include religious organizations and civic associations. Heads of churches, who were important in providing and maintaining basic social protection in the first years after the dissolution of the Soviet Union, actively promoted the president's agenda. Religious leaders made recurrent public appeals for unity and support of Kuchma.[53] Christian churches of all denominations joined in the effort. Leaders of Roman and Greek Catholic communities, Lutherans, Evangelicals, Baptists, and Seventh-day Adventists signed public letters in support of the referendum.[54] Civic associations with a variety of missions, from a district organization for parents of disabled children to a cooperative of victims of Soviet political repression,[55] called for continuing the "unanimity" residents of the region had expressed in the presidential elections—to give the president extraordinary powers over the parliament.

Few groups were as active in promoting the president's referendum as elementary and high school teachers and university administrators. The presidential administration mobilized educators at every level to participate in the referendum and to enjoin their clients—parents and university students—to do the same. In Zakarpattia and throughout the country, teachers in elementary, middle, and high schools gathered to discuss the necessity of the referendum.[56]

When, a decade and a half later, Ukrainian showman-turned-president Volodymyr Zelensky's television character Vasily Goloborodko would suddenly rise from humble history teacher to the presidency, his character did so because of a viral video of an expletive-laden political rant of Goloborodko reacting to his supervisor, who had insisted Goloborodko's students leave the classroom to set up the school for election day. That episode touched a nerve; the story it told reminded Ukrainian television audiences of years of mobilization of the educational system for political aims.

Teachers participated in initiative groups organizing for the referendum, and the regional press frequently quoted teachers endorsing it.[57] Sending clear signals to those served by public education, newspaper articles identified teachers and school directors by their name, their position, and the name and location of the school where they taught.[58] In Khust district, when a math teacher in a village orphanage provided a detailed set of recommendations to the regional paper specifying that parliamentary deputies should answer for their actions, the headline took on a mildly threatening tone. Changing the meaning of the math teacher's words with the help of an ellipsis not required by the column width, the copy editor penned a headline, "Everyone . . . will be held personally responsible."[59]

The head of Zakarpattia's Department of Education publicly signaled Kuchma's expectations to teachers, telling readers of *Novyny Zakarpattia* that "thinking pedagogues" supported the president's initiative.[60] In this multilingual region, teachers of Ukrainian language and literature received special attention.[61] In the town of Berehove, the director of a Ukrainian-language preparatory high school and head of a council of school directors likewise promoted the referendum, enjoining employees and the public to protect the "joyful, smiling faces of our children" by voting in it.[62] A school director in the city of Mukachevo who also served on his district council assured readers that through his "daily interactions with teachers, medical practitioners, parents of schoolchildren and villagers" he had become "convinced that an absolute majority" supported the president.[63]

By March, the list of public supporters of the referendum in the education sector expanded to include sixteen heads of educational institutions accredited in the region.[64] Meanwhile, school directors led initiative groups that prepared Ukrainian society for the referendum.[65] Nearly every university student in Zakarpattia receiving a tuition stipend found the name of her rector or director on that list.

One of the people on that list was a man named Slyvka, rector of a major regional university in Uzhhorod, a medieval and Baroque city of pedestrian paths lined with linden and cherry trees, flush against the border with Slovakia. Though Slyvka supported Kuchma's referendum, in subsequent years he would draw a line when it came to compelling his students to participate in regime directives. By 2004, the campaign of Viktor Yanukovych had placed such intense pressure on university hierarchies that Slyvka's refusal to force students to participate in pro-regime demonstrations had become a much remarked-upon exception to the rule.[66]

By May of that year, Slyvka was dead. Official reports attributed his demise to suicide, but local narratives cried murder, connecting the rector's death to his rejection of demands to mobilize his students for political purposes. The national weekly *Dzerkalo Tyzhnia* described the death as "a question without answers."⁶⁷ People personally close to the rector described a horrible end, with multiple stab wounds to the spine.⁶⁸

Local journalists reported that "all of Zakarpattia buzzed like a disturbed beehive: 'They killed the rector, and the police and prosecutors are protecting the murderers!'"⁶⁹ During Slyvka's funeral, usually bustling cafés in the vibrant downtown pedestrian zone of Uzhhorod were silent and empty. The city was elsewhere that day.⁷⁰ Locally, people argued that the university was a prize the regional governor coveted because of its economic significance and the possibilities it offered "to have political influence on students and teachers."⁷¹

Following Slyvka's death, the governor appointed his own brother to replace the rector. The local press interpreted the move as an effort to align university hierarchies with the Social Democratic Party of Ukraine for electoral purposes. "If [the rector] . . . still somehow held back the ardor of the SD-niks trying to turn the university into the propaganda wing of its party, now . . . [the university] with its collective of more than 3,000 people has passed into the power of the SDPU(o) completely."⁷²

They Can Simply Be Commanded

Across the country, pressure to participate moved down the power vertical from the national to the local level. The method of delivery varied according to individuals' places in administrative hierarchies.⁷³ In most workplaces, supervisors delivered requirements and threats verbally. Rank-and-file employees received these threats at special obligatory group meetings or in person.⁷⁴ Middle managers received instructions over the telephone,⁷⁵ while other employees received them in individual meetings behind closed doors.⁷⁶

In early 2000, supervisors delivered threats both explicitly and through that discursive system of hints, nods, and winks known in Ukraine and Russia as "understandings."⁷⁷ In Ukraine, the use of understandings under Kuchma and Yanukovych had become a widely enough recognized social fact that by 2004, the sung and chanted mantra of the Orange demonstrations—"No to falsification! No to machination! No to understandings! No to lies!"—referenced them directly.

Such implicit instructions served not only to communicate threats, but also to indicate the boundaries of political community. As in late Soviet politics, people who both understood the literal implications of such messages and accepted their performative meaning formed a sort of fraternity. Even as many experienced political pressure as socially isolating, this shared implicit understanding strengthened social bonds for others who participated—and for some, provided a possible flashpoint for resistance.

At the highest levels, responsibility for securing participation in political theater was explicit and transmitted in written form.[78] A highly placed Russian functionary and head of regional electoral headquarters of United Russia in the region of Sverdlovsk described how ministerial-level tasks for elections were allocated: the Ministry of Health received instructions to provide lists of proxies in each of the institutions in its sphere to oversee electoral activities, while the Ministry of Social Welfare was to provide information about individual pensioners to United Russia.[79]

Further down the administrative ladder at the regional and local level, state employees, including those working in the social sphere, came to understand that their job description included the obligation to stage elections, and that working as a public servant meant working for the incumbent. When the deputy director of education in Kherson region of Ukraine visited schools in the town of Nova Kakhovka to campaign for Viktor Yanukovych in 2004, "his main argument was that since schools belong to the state, teachers are required to vote for the representatives of state power."[80] In 2011, employees of Gazprom in the city of Tomsk experienced a standard iteration of implicit threats when they were blackmailed with potential layoffs, with bosses "sort of suggesting that they vote for United Russia."[81]

Pressure articulated through administrative hierarchies extended not only to public servants and public-sector workers, but also to their kin and client networks. A journalist in Russia's northwest wrote in 2011 that "people on the state payroll and workers in state and municipal enterprises need not be motivated to voting, they can simply be commanded. In Voronezh region teachers, doctors, librarians were proposed to enroll in the ranks of United Russia supporters and, naturally, vote for the party. Besides, people on the state payroll must agitate their relatives for the party; doctors—their patients; teachers—the parents."[82] Some agitation within networks could be subtle, but this was not always the case. At a 2004 meeting of village heads and state-owned businesses in the Ukrainian city of Bila Tserkva in Kyiv region, the head of state administration told those present that anyone who did not help to ensure victory for Yanukovych "would never set foot in Bila Tserkva after [election day] October 31."[83]

Party enrollment and voting were mainly private, individual acts which ultimately were knowable through election results. But command performances could also be highly visible affairs. In 2013, writing in the central Ukrainian city of Dnipropetrovsk as authorities organized demonstrations against the Revolution of Dignity, historian Anna Abakunova described an unremarkable event that corralled public-sector workers in a public space. To organize a rally in support of then-president Yanukovych,

> all civil servants were herded in. . . . All the teachers were ordered to let the children skip the sixth and seventh classes of the day. The teachers themselves had to sign some papers that they would appear at a rally in Hloba Park. In answer to the question what would happen if one did not sign, management responded that one had better sign. Thus everyone appeared at the appointed hour at the designated location. There were several thousand people, that is all the government employees. Even teachers from nearby cities were brought in in an organized fashion—from Nikopol, Dniprodzerzhyns'k, and so on.[84]

The audience for such coordinated public demonstrations of the state's capacity to elicit performance would include all those who witnessed the spectacle of thousands of schoolteachers rallying in favor of a widely despised national political leader.

Tactics used in Ukraine at the turn of the millennium brought the state into every area of life, and they followed a pattern that would be used repeatedly and with striking uniformity over the following decade and a half in both Ukraine and Russia. In Ukraine, local authorities tied access to wages, infrastructure, and necessary services to electoral outcomes, threatening services from residential gas line construction in Poltava and Vinnytsia regions[85] to cattle vaccinations in Sumy region.[86] After the massive street demonstrations of the Orange Revolution of 2004, such techniques disappeared temporarily from national-level politics under the presidential administration of Viktor Yushchenko. But coercive practices—and elections as mass theater—rapidly resurfaced just a few years later in many regions of the country. In Russia, the use of these mechanisms would intensify during some periods, then recede to some extent, then appear again, seeming to peak in 2011. Following widespread demonstrations between 2011 and 2013, the Russian state entered a new phase of control with additional tools. Not only economic sanctions but also political persecution could result from noncompliance.[87]

Techniques to entice people's participation in command performances relied on durable, underlying structural conditions. Because of this, political elites could choose to activate them, or not, at any point in time. With attention to maintenance of local networks and capacity, parties and incumbents could keep alive the possibility of future manipulation through periods of electoral loss, reawakening those techniques when they returned to power. In Ukraine in 2006, international observers rejoiced over the apparent victory of "Western" forces and the disappearance of electoral coercion at the national level. But in the regions, the machines that compelled participation had simply moved their operations to a lower level of government, continuing to manipulate municipal and local rural elections and providing services that the traditional state no longer could or would provide.[88]

What to Do If They Force You to Vote for United Russia

During the following decade, the tools used to motivate participation in Ukraine's 2000 referendum developed into an ever-evolving constellation of episodically mobilized techniques. These included a mixed repertoire of punishment, outright vote buying, paid participation in the election "carousels" that bused voters from one polling station to another, payment for participation in street demonstrations, and subtractive tactics that threatened people's wages, benefits, and access to services and infrastructure.[89]

In each case, tactics involved a quid pro quo in which individuals or groups furnished political support in exchange for access to scarce resources. Some looked like everyday clientelism. In February 2002, the Ukrainian city of Kherson reportedly received ten new municipal trolley buses in return for promised support for the incumbent electoral bloc.[90] In Russia's western Urals, the mayor of the city of Izhevsk required local veterans' organizations to turn out votes for United Russia in order to receive funding.[91] People in both countries, especially people with access to welfare state benefits—elders, veterans of labor and war, and others—would receive food packages in exchange for a promise to participate in elections. Combinations of tactics meant that street demonstrations and national elections evolved into complex phenomena, with some participation coerced, some paid, some given out of political conviction, and some a mixture of these.

Political theater flourished in areas with dense concentrations of people and industry.[92] Supervisors threatened collective punishment in a round robin form, what Russians refer to as *krugovaia poruka*, or joint responsibility.[93] Threats of collective punishment were especially credible in places where the boundaries of electoral precincts overlapped with social institutions. These included students registered in university dormitories, factory workers voting in company towns, and people living on some large-scale agricultural enterprises. Recalcitrant villages sometimes saw all-important bread deliveries halted,[94] and resistant civic associations could find themselves evicted from offices they rented.[95]

Over time, collective threats gave way to surveillance of individuals. As mobile telephones became more widely available, employers commonly required employees to save photos of their completed ballot on their phones.[96] Even people who could not afford their own mobile phones could confront this requirement. In a post titled, "Did your boss ask you to take a picture of your ballot with a check in the needed box?" a journalist from the Russian Urals city of Yekaterinburg made explicit a typical situation: "Let's say a village teacher or factory worker doesn't want to lose his job. They gave him a special telephone so that he could photograph a 'correct' ballot and report to his boss."[97]

Employers who used telephones to check compliance provoked creative responses. By 2011, texts and videos posted on the ru.net—the Russian-language internet—with titles like "What to do if they force you to vote for United Russia" instructed voters on how to use black threads, thin pieces of wire, or squares of transparent film to create photos of ballots with a check in the "right" place before indicating their actual preference in ink.[98] In Ukraine, since numerous parties engaged in vote buying, this offered a potentially lucrative opportunity to those willing to avail themselves of it. Web publications with titles such as "The elections are coming: how to earn money on vote buying while maintaining your integrity (instructions)" taught people how to receive money from multiple parties by sending different overseers falsified evidence of "correct" balloting.[99]

Over time and especially, in some estimations, in poorer regions[100] or in places where middle managers themselves exerted only pro forma pressure on employees,[101] enforcement became a problem. In response, election organizers adapted their tactics, using more explicit methods of vote buying and bolder tools of falsification, such as sacks of ballots filled out in advance and deposited at particular polling stations.[102]

Tactics that depended on collective enforcement had the best chance of success in places like eastern and southern Ukraine, with their numerous large universities, hospitals, industrial enterprises, and agricultural enterprises, or in Russian company towns. In such contexts, a variety of different spheres of life overlapped. In a company town or on a large farm, multiple aspects of people's lives were bound up in one another,[103] allowing local elites credibly to invoke the possibility of both individual and collective punishment in the event of noncompliance. Later, just such contexts would be host in Russia to attempts to secure participation in higher-stakes activities—namely, to recruit contract soldiers for the war in Ukraine.[104]

In all these places, paymasters and political representatives either were the very same individuals, or they were members of the same administrative hierarchy. Often, majorities of electoral commissions drew on a single work collective, permitting leaders of enterprises and state offices to pressure those overseeing balloting processes and counting votes.[105] Years after the dissolution of the Soviet Union, in much of post-Soviet space, spheres of economic and political activity still overlapped, allowing politicians to tug at strings that touched multiple sites of survival and social reproduction.

The Birthday of Bourgeois

Across Ukraine and the Russian Federation, the tactics politicians used to secure participation in command performances shared certain commonalities. In the first decade of the twenty-first century, politicians and their agents leveraged three categories of goods to encourage participation in political theater: financial compensation for work; access to necessary infrastructure; and access to services.[106] Supervisors across a wide variety of types of institutions and companies pressured their subordinates to comply: vote for a particular candidate or participate in a certain demonstration or risk losing your job or, in the case of university students, your stipend or place at university. In many cases, employers would claim that their enterprise risked bankruptcy and closure if employees did not comply.[107]

Financial tactics threatened the livelihoods of a variety of categories of citizens. Public-sector employees, including teachers and hospital workers,[108] employees of state-owned enterprises, and employees of enterprises receiving subsidies or tax benefits from the state all received threats of salary loss or, in some cases, loss of their jobs because of closure of enterprises or turnover in state administration if the right candidate did not win. Pensioners faced threats of cuts, delays, or redefinition in pension payments. University students faced threats either of withheld stipends, closure of their universities, or the withdrawal of plans to grant their university national status. Farmworkers and worker-shareholders in large-scale or state-held agricultural enterprises encountered withholding of wages or in-kind payments—both of which in turn affected private-sector smallholder agriculture. And public institutions as well as small business owners received intensified attention from regulatory agencies.[109]

Politicians acting to ensure particular election outcomes targeted access to critical infrastructure: electricity provision, heating fuel, and municipal water supplies. In an instance that would be repeated in villages across Ukraine and Russia, people living in rural areas of Vinnytsia region of Ukraine learned gas line construction would halt if they did not vote according to the announced preferences of the presidential administration.[110] In the countryside, employers curtailed access to pasture for livestock; to irrigation and fertilizer infrastructure, or tractors and combines; to storage facilities for grain; and a host of other resources and infrastructure that employees who were also homesteaders needed but only large farms could provide. In some villages, politicians threatened to suspend or stop twice-weekly or weekly deliveries of bread. In both cities and the countryside, people whose access to housing was linked to employment faced threats of losing their apartments.

Rural transportation infrastructure was a common target of politicians weaponizing state budgets to compel participation in political theater. In 2004, voters in Novi Sanzhary district of the Poltava region of Ukraine found that not only bread deliveries, but also bus service stopped for three days after residents ignored farm directors' demands they sign a statement indicating their intention to vote for a particular candidate.[111] In Russia in 2011, the vice premier of the republican government of Udmurtia told residents of the city of Glazov, which had voted for the Communist Party, that because of their choice the city would receive fewer resources for repairing roads. In his comments, the vice premier referred to the example of the city of Sarapul, which had voted "correctly" and would receive three times more than Glazov.[112] The vice premier's frank statement not only commented on an ongoing situation, but also served as warning for communities that might cast their ballots for opposition parties or candidates in the future.

Such tactics gained effectiveness amid the decaying infrastructure characteristic of post-Soviet space outside major metropolises. In a reversal of what the political scientist Paul Martin Sacks, writing of Irish political machines, called "imaginary patronage," in which politicians take credit for goods that publics would have received in any case,[113] people in Ukraine and Russia sometimes interpreted infrastructure failures as electoral threats or punishment. This allowed politicians to piggyback on infrastructural deterioration to attempt to control electoral and other political behavior.

Just such an incident occurred following elections in Ukraine in 1999. For weeks, rolling blackouts darkened the city of Kharkiv. The blackouts lasted several hours, their timing unannounced. Local televised news reports at the time told of people trapped in elevators in apartment buildings, unaware the electricity supply would be cut at that moment, and of other inconveniences that frayed the nerves of the population. Some interpreted the outages as retribution for municipal districts' electoral choices in the recent presidential election, like the local farmers who were in the city to exchange information about diesel prices. They complained that they had missed episodes of a popular television miniseries, *The Birthday of Bourgeois*, as a result of the outages, noting that a part of the city center housing the security services never lacked power.[114] Whether the blackouts actually had been politically motivated was beside the point. Amid other, similar threats, people interpreted them as if they had been, and announced their intention to behave accordingly at the polls the next time.

Electoral tactics also included limiting access to social services such as medical care and education, which employers or health care providers could refuse to offer. In many locations, some hospital patients would receive surgery only once they cast a ballot for the right candidate. Individual village residents who did not support incumbent politicians could lose access to ambulance services. And schools targeted parents through their children, who could receive grades that reflected their parents' voting behavior. Noncompliant parents stood to lose access to public preschool places altogether.

Taken together, these tactics posed a potential threat to almost all aspects of people's daily material existence: their livelihoods, their children's future, their home life. Political elites transformed entitlements, redefining them as perks people would receive as a reward for loyalty and participation in political spectacle.[115] The system that grew up around and through political theater recast rights as privileges people could gain through loyalty to political incumbents.[116] This was a fundamental shift in the social contract, a new politicization of the responsibilities of the state toward citizens and citizens toward the state.

These tactics both redefined and reflected a redefinition of the relationship between public or publicly funded institutions and politicians. The politics of spectacle politicized not only government bureaucracies, but also a much broader swath of public institutions and private enterprises benefiting from state subsidies or preferential tax regimes. For the purposes of political theater, schoolteachers and other public-sector workers were subordinate to the politicians who ensured their employment. As such, they were expected to comply with demands to enter the stage.

While parties of power mobilized public institutions for electoral spectacle, the use of coercive tactics was not confined to institutions receiving public money. Private enterprises also were vulnerable and would be targeted by tax inspectorates and politicized local regulatory agencies. Virtually any private enterprise with a physical footprint could be pressured, as seemingly simple but necessary things like certificates of compliance with fire codes or other safety regulations became objects of political manipulation.

Pressure tactics were economical for incumbents because they drew on existing hierarchies that ordinarily served other purposes.[117] In universities, deans and professors asked students to perform political tasks. Some of these were an extension of everyday life: faculty might often make mundane extracurricular demands of students on the order of moving tables in a conference room. With command performances, attendance at political meetings and rallies became part of this ordinary repertoire of participation and help.

In twenty-first-century Ukraine and Russia, politicians and their agents filled spaces from which state and party seemed to have nearly completely withdrawn just a few years before. The ebb of state power in the post-Soviet decade gave way in the new century to its flow back into the cracks of everyday life, widening small fissures into much deeper divides. Access to pensions, wages, education, health care, housing, transportation infrastructure, and other items became conditional on support for parties of power and participation in command performances. Over time, the demands of parties of power expanded into ever-widening spheres, affecting not only traditional sites of politics but private or publicly regulated ones as well—hospital beds, second-grade classrooms, public transportation. Everywhere people might encounter public servants, middle managers, and educational and care professionals, there was an opportunity for incumbent politicians to compel participation in political theater. A decade on, the contours of this pressure would change as local economies adapted to new rounds of enclosure and privatization. But the stage management of political theater would continue to bring the state into people's living rooms, affecting some people much more than others and creating a new sense of division and polarization.

# Chapter 5

Improvisation

In years to come, bosses and paymasters in large cities and company towns would continue enforcing their demands to support political incumbents. They did so with threats of collective punishment and by exerting pressure through the administrative hierarchies of social and economic institutions. This approach worked best where industry and large-scale agriculture continued to dominate regional economies. In Ukraine, among these were the coal-mining country and centers of heavy industry of the Donbas and the vast fields of sunflowers and sugar beets in the east, where companies retained their former scale and organizational structure. But elsewhere, outside industrial centers, policy makers and local elites continued to disassemble economic institutions that dated from the Soviet era, privatizing land and other resources that had been attached to those institutions. In Ukraine's western regions, new and more stringent border regimes accompanying the accession of neighboring countries to the European Union produced changes in the structure of local economies.[1] The resulting shifts in the local economies of many small towns and villages changed the mechanisms through which local leaders called people to participate in political theater.

Unlike the meeting halls of factories and large farms where state and party agents delivered barely veiled threats to assembled groups of workers, in small towns and villages, state and party agents now turned to private and individual persuasion and coercion. What began at the turn of the millennium as a near total system of control based on collective responsibility evolved into a decentralized set of practices that involved some portions of the population but not others, individualizing risk and further reshaping boundaries between state and society. In other localities, the ways elites responded to economic changes in the twenty-first century transformed both the reach and the nature of the state and its relationship to people living on its territory, ultimately creating far-reaching consequences for the unity of the polity.

One of the places where twenty-first-century changes in economic relations shifted patterns of people's participation in political theater was Zakarpattia, a region in western Ukraine at the edge of the Pannonian basin. There, the threat of collective punishment that had hung over people's heads a decade earlier became a political economy of individualized coercion. Villages in the southwestern corner of Zakarpattia had been part of Hungary for centuries and were incorporated into the Ukrainian SSR in the first years after World War II. More than twice as far from Kyiv as from Budapest, that part of Zakarpattia is demographically distinct from its neighbors and both ethnically and linguistically diverse. In the early 2000s, about 12 percent of the population in the region identified as Magyar and spoke Hungarian at home and in a broad variety of community cultural institutions, including schools, churches, and clubs.[2] Like the twenty-first-century financial ties with Moscow that fed economic development in certain communities along Ukraine's eastern border, deep cultural, administrative, and financial connections to an external homeland helped sustain Zakarpattia's Magyar communities through years of neglect by Kyiv.[3]

Majority Magyar villages in Zakarpattia were Party of Regions territory while Viktor Yanukovych was president. The party had built a powerful organization in the region under Yanukovych, and local Magyars supported him for a variety of reasons. After the Orange demonstrations on Kyiv's Maidan in 2004, the Party of Regions enjoyed programmatic support from the Hungarian-speaking population. Despite initial cooperation between the government and a regional ethnic association, the Kárpátaljai Magyar Kulturális Szövetség (KMKSZ), many Magyars grew alienated from the government of President Viktor Yushchenko. Although a native son of Zakarpattia, Viktor Baloha, headed Yushchenko's presidential administration, Yushchenko's government had adopted increasingly aggressive policies that seemed to the local population to define national identity and the boundaries of the demos in ethnic and linguistic terms—terms that excluded Magyars and other minority populations—rather than in the civic terms specified in the Ukrainian constitution.[4]

In those years, stories circulated in the region of layoffs for Hungarian-speaking teachers in elementary schools, among many other instances of reported discrimination.[5] At the same time, national media increasingly focused on historical controversies surrounding the genocide of Ukrainians during Stalin's terror famine of the 1930s—the Holodomor—discussions of which saturated airwaves throughout the country. The mid-twentieth century had brought numerous horrors for the residents of Zakarpattia, but those horrors had not included Stalin's starvation campaigns. Unable to relate to a centerpiece in the national narrative under President Yushchenko and aggrieved by the unrecognized suffering of their own families during the war, some Magyars pulled away from identification with the Ukrainian state.[6]

This alienation grew amid economic and social stress. Despite Yushchenko's emphasis on Ukrainian linguistic identity, Ukrainianization policies in Ukraine's southwest, in Crimea, and in other predominantly Russian-speaking regions of the country remained unfunded mandates. In the southwest, the budgets of local libraries strained under efforts to acquire Ukrainian-language materials, and many rural parents had difficulty obtaining quality instruction in the Ukrainian language for their children. Adults educated in the Soviet period never had occasion to learn the language in a classroom. As a result, they were unable to access certain labor markets.[7] Much of the rural Magyar population continued to engage mainly in homestead production, sending their children abroad to work in Hungary.

This situation, together with land privatization and the rise of new border security regimes, gave rise in the second decade of the twenty-first century to new tools of cooperation between citizens and party or state agents. Some of those tools looked like payoffs, as agents distributed cash with suggestions to vote for particular candidates. Amid enclosure movements and spiraling economic insecurity, many voters understood those payments as paltry gestures at compensation for benefits or rents they were due. But with household budgets strained, those payments represented offers most people could not refuse.

When party agents approached them with payoffs or pressure, people had no competing sources of authority to which to turn. While representatives of Yulia Tymoshenko's Fatherland party also distributed cash payments, targeting mainly Ukrainian-speaking villagers who were more likely to vote for the bloc,[8] until 2014 the Party of Regions exercised an indirect and superficially barely discernible influence on most areas of life. But as André Simonyi has shown in his political ethnography of a pair of villages in the region, three key sets of figures governed access to basic necessities: the village mayor, a large landholder, and local religious institutions.[9] All three were directly or indirectly associated with Yanukovych's Party of Regions and drew influence from this connection.

State and party agents faced their own challenges. Under pressure from their supervisors to deliver votes, yet often without additional resources at their disposal to do so, local agents in the countryside improvised approaches to securing broad participation in electoral performances. The threats they delivered were particular, calibrated to individual households' needs and fears. Party agents visiting rural households drew on a diverse tool-kit, delivering threats to some people, and money, firewood, or groceries to others.[10] Contact was selective: local agents understood local conditions, and they knew their neighbors. They knew who would cooperate, and they knew who was not worth the bother or expense.

State and party agents delivered pressure and payment door to door in the enclosed courtyards of village homes. Barking dogs often would announce the arrival of the party representative, usually a village official, who drove or walked down village streets where homes were just a few meters apart. Agents would call out to residents, waiting outside the outer gates of village homesteads before entering courtyards. Once inside, they conversed with members of the household. On some pensioners' homesteads, which on most days would see a continuous flow of neighbors throughout the day to drop off provisions, collect funds for the cemetery, or trade a favor for a jar of homemade wine or moonshine, the arrival of an agent was visitors' cue to quit the premises.

This was the moment at which cash would change hands. In the 2010 Ukrainian presidential elections, which at the time even the prime minister of Canada had described as free and fair, most people described having received 200 UAH to vote for Yanukovych, with an additional 200 UAH for a party-list vote. By 2014, partly in response to political instability and currency devaluation, the price had risen to 500 UAH in some places, even as it remained at 200 UAH in others.[11] By 2019, it had risen to 1,000 UAH—a sum that amid war and debt-driven currency devaluation represented no significant increase in value for voters.

Payments typically amounted to a bit less than a week's pension or minimum salary, enough to make an important difference in the monthly budget of a single pensioner. Across Ukraine, people received the same amount for their votes. The amounts people reported receiving in villages and those quoted in national newspapers were the same. For a family budget, one such payment could mean the cost of transportation for a month, the cost of food for one person for two weeks, or two weeks of water and electricity.

When party agents arrived at the gate, the conversation that would follow depended on tacit, shared understandings of the meaning of the payment. Those understandings echoed the system of hints, nods, and winks about which people had sung and chanted during Ukraine's 2004 Orange Revolution: "No to falsification! No to machination! No to understandings! No to lies!" In many cases, there was nothing to sign nor even any need for explicit identification of the candidate for whom the person would vote: "It's more like, 'there's an election coming up, we need to get out the vote for Yanukovych.'"[12]

Mechanisms of coercion and persuasion did not change appreciably even when the party in power did.[13] After the events of early spring 2014, while the country nervously awaited presidential elections in the wake of the Russian Federation's actions in Crimea and the start of the war in the Donbas, president-to-be Petro Poroshenko's organization used some of the same techniques to secure voter support.

This ritual exchange, familiar to Ukrainians across the country, would continue during Poroshenko's presidency. In late March 2019, on the eve of Ukraine's presidential elections, Studio Kvartal-95, the comedy troupe of Volodymyr Zelensky, enacted a caricature on national television, provoking laughter from the studio audience. In their skit, then-president Petro Poroshenko visits the home of Andriy Parubiy, chairman of the Ukrainian parliament. Upon arrival, Poroshenko hands flowers to Parubiy's wife and one thousand UAH to Parubiy, saying, "You understand for whom to vote in the next elections."[14] The punch line follows when Poroshenko offers the same sum to Parubiy's wife in exchange for her vote—minus the value of the flowers he had just given her. The joke made explicit the relationship between net payoffs and entitlements in political theater: what is given in one area will be taken away in another. Like Kvartal's satirical portrayal of Poroshenko and Parubiy, exchanges often took place in the context of an ongoing relationship, where a failure to live up to the bargain could provoke future problems.

In small towns and villages where collective pressure was not possible, local agents, anxious to be certain that their efforts in the weeks and months prior to elections would produce the desired results at the ballot box, tried to ensure compliance through other means. Party agents would require that people bring their cell phones into the voting booth, taking and sending a photo of their paper ballot to prove they had voted according to the arrangement. Over time, this practice, like all other tools of pressure and coercion, would give rise to improvisations intended to circumvent it.[15]

Village pensioners in Ukraine's southwest who did not possess cell phones thought that the small size of their communities allowed local electoral officials to know who voted and how. Others believed this not to be the case and explained their compliance in a different register. For them, cooperation existed in a moral economy whose underlying logic was rooted in a social contract. People framed compliance as a matter of ethics: "It's up to people's conscience what they do at the ballot box." Few viewed accepting payment for votes as a moral good: "People know that it's not correct, but they think, 'If they're giving it out, why shouldn't I take it?'" In this local moral universe such an exchange, once begun, required completion: "No one knows how others vote. People receive the money, and then it's up to their conscience how they vote." In the words of another villager, "Ukrainians have *religion*: 'I took the money, so I'm obligated before God to do what I said I would, to vote for [a particular candidate]."[16]

Godforsaken Country

When Ukraine's western neighbors joined the EU in 2004, the organization expanded security along the border with Ukraine. This and concurrent land privatization led to the partition and loss of rural space in communities along the border. As a result, many in rural southwest Ukraine abandoned agrarian livelihoods.[17] The reconfiguration of household economies pushed local leaders who also confronted economic risk in their personal lives to expand their own spheres of activity. This expansion exposed other community members to new pressures to comply with demands to participate in command performances.

For a decade and a half following the dissolution of the Soviet Union, rural communities in the southwest had lived on the fumes of the former system. Many people eked out modest livelihoods based on small-scale agricultural production and remittance labor, relying on services still provided by what was left of collective farms and other legacy institutions. They could not easily travel west themselves, but they sold produce, meat, and dairy products to local markets and consumers from countries just beyond the border. Describing the area as "forgotten by God," villagers would echo the lyrics of the Russian pop star Andrei Gubin's song "Boy Drifter" ("Mal'chik brodiaga"), heard daily in villages on radio waves throughout the late 1990s and beyond.[18]

At the turn of the millennium, when politicians had mobilized institutions for participation in Ukraine's nationwide referendum, most collective farms in the southwest still operated. In this land-poor area, as in some other regions west of the Dnieper, chairmen of former collective farms did not act in 2000 to preserve their enterprises and material assets in the face of centralized pressure to reorganize and distribute land and assets to worker-shareholders.[19] In the southwest, local authorities exercised less active oversight in the day-to-day business of commercial agriculture than in Ukraine's east. The result was just what farm directors in the east had sought to avoid: land fragmentation.

Over the next decade, many people found they no longer could afford to farm small, scattered plots often far from roads and irrigation. They leased their land to local bosses who reconstituted large-scale production, hiring for cheap day labor a much smaller proportion of the rural population than had worked on the collectives. In one pair of villages in the southwest, the collective farm at the heart of rural life for a half century was divided into two private enterprises, one of which soon ballooned to include an expanse of territory larger than the original collective. Almost everyone who had resided in adjoining villages during the Soviet period now leased land to that farm. Those who still farmed themselves kept small homesteads built on the garden plots people had cultivated under Soviet rule.

With dwindling of opportunities in commercial agriculture, young people quit the village. In the historically Magyar settlements that lined areas of Ukraine's borders with Slovakia, Hungary, and Romania, families took advantage of the recently instituted Hungarian status laws, which provided benefits to ethnic Hungarians in countries that had been part of the post–World War I Trianon settlement.[20] Grown children went abroad to be educated and to work in Hungary.[21] Their movement formed new connections and affiliations that a decade later would bring prime minister Viktor Orbán's party into this corner of Ukraine. Hungarian state-funded cultural organizations operating in the region nourished social institutions that distributed funds to the rural population in Ukraine. Members of Ukrainian local government, meanwhile, had deepened their wealth and their ties to figures in the regional and national government, extending the reach of the state into the hinterland.

When countries on Ukraine's western border became part of an expanded European Union in 2004, villages in the southwest underwent a profound transformation in the organization of economic life, as communities oriented themselves away from homestead agriculture and toward petty commerce, encouraging the development of transportation infrastructure that would link border crossings to towns and cities in the interior.[22]

With EU expansion toward the east, Brussels had demanded increased security along the border with Ukraine, so the security cordon widened along its length to accommodate the new measures. Residents of agrarian communities now could expect several days in jail if they were found too close to the demarcated border.²³ Many found it difficult to communicate with the soldiers who stopped people in the fields. The young men deployed to the border were Russian speakers from eastern Ukraine who spoke neither Ukrainian nor Hungarian. To protect soldiers from pressure to bend the rules for their relatives, the logic went, local men did not serve in the border zone.

Jail also was made more likely by the fact that the new soldiers were unfamiliar with the faces and habits of villagers. No one in his right or sober mind would take something as important as a passport with him to do agricultural work, but it was dangerous to be caught without papers. Reinforced border security meant immediate loss of access to pasture for animals, hunting grounds and streams for fishing, and haying in common fields. This hardship was accompanied by other losses. In some settlements, household garden plots and privately owned fields were seized through eminent domain.

The expanded border zone affected even those who worked in nearby cities: municipal budgets at that time reduced spending on rural transportation routes, and some bus routes now ran two or three times a day rather than every two hours. In heavy snow, sometimes the bus did not come at all. To get to town, people had to walk to the bus stop in a neighboring village. In winter, border guards would misinterpret the sight of people trudging north toward the city, thinking they were attempting to cross the border. They would lock people up for three days until the mayor arrived to vouch for them. The risk of imprisonment was a constant companion, the mayor's help their only possible recourse.²⁴

New exposure to European Union regulations governing dairy products and meat affected agrarian livelihoods in the borderland. Before EU accession, rural households would sell milk, farmer's cheese, sour cream, and meat to people from across the border who would come to buy high-quality, lower-priced food from villages in Ukraine. When Slovakia joined the EU, this changed. Now, certification was needed, and cross-border food sales were unprofitable. With the exception of the odd relative who might visit from a neighboring village across the border and take home a jackrabbit after placing a bill in the palm of the right customs agent, people's chances to sell meat and milk disappeared.

People in the borderlands also complained of smaller, everyday frictions. Along the EU border, hardened security changed rural soundscapes, breaking nocturnal peace and depriving village residents of sleep. Most village households kept a dog or two. The dogs' job was to alert their masters of visitors and keep the foxes away. With EU expansion, soldiers guarding the border on the Ukrainian side began to change shifts in the middle of the night. Personnel carriers would pass through villages in the wee hours. The vehicles would set off a chorus of village dogs who would continue to bark long after the trucks had passed. This helped drive some villagers who still had a choice to abandon homestead production, or at least their chickens, in favor of an hourly wage.

Over time, livelihoods came to depend less on people's own labor and more on global supply chains. In the borderlands, pressures on commercial and household agriculture pushed some rural households further away from farming and toward trade. In one border village, entrepreneurs from a nearby city opened kiosks in village homes they rented for a small fee. There, they sold consumer goods produced mainly in China to EU shoppers from Slovakia seeking bargains amid pressure on their own economies at home.

Local commerce was intense closest to the border. In one village with a pedestrian crossing, visitors from Slovakia visiting roadside kiosks would rarely walk farther than a bend in the road a few hundred yards from the border crossing. Just beyond the bend, it was possible to forget that the border, or the border crossing, was even there. There, even as border kiosks flourished just a few dozen steps away, the owner of a single privately owned store struggled and eventually closed the business.

Trade would prove an unstable source of revenue for all. Fluctuations in currency markets reverberated quickly, creating sudden shifts in demand and closing businesses. The entrepreneurs could move their business to a different setting, but the rural households who had sold their livestock and rented out their property for the stores could be left with no income and spoiled farmland.

All along the border between this part of Ukraine and Slovakia, Hungary, and Romania, border commerce brought temporary rent and a daily wage to village communities. Checkpoints would open, reorienting local economic activity and transforming fields into built environment, and then unexpectedly close, leaving rural communities in the lurch. Some who had constructed houses in the expectation of access to border commerce left their homes empty as other villages became crossing spots.[25]

Some saw business decline as border crossings opened in other villages with better roads. As commerce evaporated, people felt the change in their daily lives, and people talked about the EU border the way they had talked about economic crisis following the dissolution of the Soviet Union: "Before we ate salami, now [we eat] bread and butter."[26]

From their perspective, the causes of that decline were not great upheavals but small shifts: a new border crossing down the road; a change in the quantity of gasoline people were allowed to hold in their car's tank when crossing back into the EU, where fuel was more expensive; suddenly fewer customers for ice cream at a roadside kiosk. On the Ukrainian side, the profound insecurity of people's material lives in the twenty-first century meant that minor, ordinary changes in regulations that must have seemed minuscule from the vantage point of Brussels could redirect the household budgets and economic strategies of entire villages. Such small changes would make big differences in how people would be pulled into participation in command performances.

People Are Afraid

In this corner of Ukraine, people knew about vote buying and intimidation but rarely openly discussed either. Some knew how exchanges worked in their own communities but had little notion of manipulation outside their village councils.[27] If they lived in ignorance of the pressures to which their extended family members in nearby villages or their countrymen beyond the region were subjected, it was, they said, because they were afraid to ask.

When villagers repeated the refrain, "people are afraid," they referred to the shadow of possible economic consequences should they fail to cooperate in electoral mobilization.[28] They worried about how politics might affect already fragile family budgets, not physical retribution or state-sponsored violence. Economic insecurity, not political repression, suffused discussions. People spoke of their fear of losing income or status, falling through the cracks, failing their children.

Amid this insecurity, obedience and loyalty to local leaders were the currencies that could buy rural dwellers access to pasture, firewood, and other necessities. Arrangements with elected village representatives made survival possible in rural settlements whose land or population had been abandoned by commercial agriculture.[29] The dependence on local elites translated into easy compliance with the periodic campaigns of parties of power to elicit their participation.

Electoral manipulation usually appears in the political science literature as episodic, confined to the ballot box or the weeks prior to elections. But the evolution of relationships between political and economic institutions at the local level meant not only that people encountered possible threats or implicit pressure in virtually every area of their lives, but also that knowledge of past and future threats and pressure influenced their lives between electoral cycles and performances. As local leaders used existing social, political, and economic hierarchies to incite people to participate in political theater, people closely monitored their behavior with state agents in every interaction, keeping the future in mind.

How people behaved at key moments for incumbents could influence their lives and livelihoods the rest of the time. In the countryside, an individual's refusal to cooperate or a misstep could result in longer-term consequences for her and her family. The fear that accompanied state agents' tactics suffused the everyday, pulsing at low frequency, rarely alarming, but an ever-present tension. Even though performances of political theater were episodic, the tools of stagecraft could provoke anxiety even in the off-season.

The decline of local agriculture and the arrival of global trade left people more vulnerable than before to changes in the world beyond their villages. Those vulnerabilities shaped local concerns. If in the first years after Ukrainian independence people feared an early freeze, a wet spring, or an arid summer, now the departure of children for remittance labor, or unexpected shifts in borders, infrastructure, and markets buffeted household economies.

The specific wellsprings of those fears changed over time as the economic landscape shifted. People worried about building repairs, water lines, access to gas lines to cook with and heat their homes, and places to socialize and worship.[30] With European Union expansion in May 2004, people on the Ukrainian side expressed fears about changing prices and the foreigners who camped in their fields to cross the border at night—including the Chinese migrants who they feared "carried infection."[31]

Though they underproduced, collective farms had provided steady work, fodder for people's animals, plowing of household garden plots, and refrigeration both for the milk of household cows and human bodies awaiting burial. With farm reorganization, large-scale agriculture increasingly relied on a small number of day laborers rather than farm members. With newly grown children gone to work abroad or in the city, the older generations left behind worried about their own illness or, for those who still tended livestock, a sick cow dying in pasture and no way to bring her home. The political ethnographer André Simonyi writes of fears in the region that extended beyond the material into anxieties about human dignity, telling of a widow who worried about dying alone inside her home: with no one to put shoes on her body, others would see her bare feet.[32]

Even in settlements close to urban centers, people were left largely to their own devices, depending on themselves and their closely knit networks of kin and neighbors for survival. In this part of Zakarpattia, a tightly controlled international border guarded by Ukrainian troops was just a few kilometers away. But no internal security forces or police officers patrolled or were otherwise visible in villages of the area. Residents ensured their own physical security and managed their own conflicts.[33] When in the middle of the night physical confrontations broke out in front of the village tavern or when people discovered theft from the fields, villagers along the border settled disputes without reference to external authority.

The relative absence of traditional police functions of the state within communities did not mean that border settlements lived free from state control. Even as members of borderland communities continued to regulate internal conflict without the direct help of the state, changes in security at the state's edge had fundamentally reshaped economic activity within the borderlands. Those changes unfolded in ways that directly impacted communities and their members' capacity to maintain political autonomy in the face of local politicians' demands.

Villagers' access to essential services required they remain in the good graces of local religious as well as political leaders. Local ministers and priests did little to mask their political convictions in Sunday sermons. Sometimes, they preached a nativist politics reminiscent of ideas promulgated by Hungarian political parties on the right: the village "will be better when there are more children, Magyar people."[34] Local religious leaders of the Lutheran and Greek Catholic churches were imbricated in local Magyar cultural associations with ties to party politics in Hungary, while the Greek Catholic church received resources from Hungarian organizations working closely with the Party of Regions. Cooperation with the Party of Regions included both programmatic and financial support from Viktor Orbán's party, Fidesz.[35]

A positive relationship with those local religious leaders helped secure access to essential services. Local churches not only were connected to transnational networks through which resources flowed, but also purveyed a variety of social services supplementing a moribund state social safety net and extending from cradle to grave.[36] The demise of the collective farm meant that for the end of life—a constant preoccupation for aging rural populations—there were no local funerary services. The collective farm had once provided refrigeration for the corpses of the deceased in one village, but the new farm director no longer extended this service. Now, to be put in the ground without delay, villagers depended on access to burial services provided by the Lutheran church. Failing to pay an annual fee to the church, they said, could result in the minister's refusal to bury you.[37]

Economic insecurity exposed not only individual homesteads, but also individual education and social services to political intervention. Schools faced aging infrastructure and inadequate resources for both staff and pupils. In a large rural elementary school coping with typical budget constraints, the toilets were in an unheated cement outbuilding: six small holes in the ground and no running water. Schoolteachers gave a week at the end of summer—a time during which many were busy putting up fruits and vegetables for the winter—to paint and repair classrooms in preparation for the school year. A village library was the sole remaining place to borrow books after the library in a neighboring, larger settlement was repurposed. It had electricity to light its dim halls for only a few hours each day.[38]

To solve such problems, schools and preschools required ongoing active support from local elected officials. Like their counterparts in areas where industry and large-scale agriculture dominated the economy, local politicians used schools as conduits to obtain electoral support. Officials' interventions had become so reliable and acute that by the beginning of the school year in 2017, parents in the region formally begged local leaders not to ruin the September 1 holiday by distributing alphabet books with politicians' photos to first graders on their first day of school. Instead, they urged, politicians could wait at least until school was in session on the second day.[39]

The Road Is Leveled before Him

Economic insecurity not only exposed people to pressure from local authorities, but also reshaped the structure of local authority. As in areas with concentrated populations, where paymasters served in multiple roles that gave them control over the populations they served, personnel overlap was common in rural communities dependent on smallholder agriculture and border commerce. Overlap between administrative spheres allowed party operatives to compel villagers to participate in command performances.

Local elites' own insecurity contributed to that overlap. Many had responded to budgetary pressure in their own households by taking up paying positions across different fields of political and economic activity. Village priests sought funding from international humanitarian and religious organizations. Professionals in education, finding their government salaries insufficient for a decent life, turned to political work. Elected rural leaders and their staff sought supplemental sources of income. For rural representatives, work for political parties was a reliable source of access to additional resources.

Village authorities oversaw public functions from land enclosure to the distribution of pensions and welfare benefits, and people depended on their goodwill for myriad and complex informal and semiformal economic arrangements. Around election time, parties of power that were tightly imbricated within executive administrative structures deputized those agents to incite their constituencies' participation in command performances.

For those who worked, prayed, and lived in their jurisdictions, local elites' expanded role often meant new possibilities for the staging of electoral dramaturgy. And as local balances of power shifted among elites, pressure came from different corners of village life.

In the first years following collective farm reorganization in 2000, one local farm director had paid people in wheat in exchange for the use of their fields. Like many directors, he delivered the grain once a year in early fall, when commodity prices were low.[40] Each year, he paid out less, avoiding taxation by signing eleven-month contracts and shorting land share owners part of their compensation.[41] The farm specialized in grain and oilseeds. By 2011, the director paid people in potatoes that had been grown in nitrogen-poor soil—the kind of potatoes that fall apart in a pot of boiling water. For households that cultivated their potatoes in fields behind their homes, this was a useless and low-quality form of compensation, and they felt free to let the director know as much.[42] Anger and near physical confrontation played out in village courtyards on delivery day.

Those low rents on land shares caused the farm director to lose influence in the community. But even as his political power faded, other local leaders' discretion increased. The loss of income from their land shares contributed to people's insecurity, feeding anxieties about the loss of common pasture and alienation of other community land resources. The village mayor controlled the fate of those resources, and the waning of the farm director's influence allowed the mayor to accumulate political and material power as he solicited cooperation in national elections.

The village mayor was the godfather of a child of a major regional political figure. Because of that, villagers said, "the road is leveled before him."[43] Widely reviled by residents of the village, he was tolerated because the alternatives were outsiders, Russians who had moved to the area in recent years and now expressed interest in standing for public office. The mayor repeatedly prevailed in local elections, which in some years maintained a semblance of competition even when elections for national executives did not.

Among his functions, the village mayor oversaw use and ownership of homesteads and pasture. He carefully tended villagers' perpetual fears of an incipient threat of land alienation. Such anxieties seemed justified by a long trajectory starting in the 1990s of gradual erosion of the commons, the margins of which somehow always seemed to end up part of the mayor's family's wealth.

Around 2004, just before the opening of a pedestrian crossing to Slovakia at one end of the village, people who lived in homes next to the border told of both concrete threats and diffuse anxieties that the mayor would assist those who would take the land for commercial concerns.[44] They had already lost to the mayor's homestead part of the commons next to the bus stop. The resulting narrowing of the space meant tractors could no longer pass through to reach hayfields. Villagers' fears soon materialized, as pensioners whose homesteads abutted barbed wire became commercial establishments offering provisions and bicycles to shoppers from Slovakia.[45]

Then, a few years later, around 2007, villagers again described threats that the mayor would privatize a triangle of land that included the path villagers used to bring their cows to pasture.[46] Without access to the path, the shepherd whom villagers collectively chipped in to hire would have to follow a winding road behind the village, adding more than two kilometers to the animals' walk and making midday milking impossible. As a result, people could keep the animals only at a loss.[47]

In the following years, even as economic stress caused most households to give up their cows, the mayor would expand his land and livestock holdings. When a local couple separated, the husband having taken to drink, the mayor purchased their well-placed house "for a loaf of bread."[48] By 2010, his homestead was said to include at least one hundred hectares of wheat and scores of pigs. Requiring a facility to store the grain, the mayor looked for a site on which to have a granary built. He found it nearby, on the territory of several Roma homes that had been destroyed in floods the previous year. The mayor, the story went, then captured government flood payments for rebuilding the homes to subsidize his new construction—to which someone then set fire.[49]

Even people's ability to remain in their homes came to depend on the mayor's whim. In some cases, these were houses occupied by the same families for generations, acquired with the earnings of family members who had journeyed to America on five-year contracts after the collapse of the Austro-Hungarian Empire to roll tobacco in the cigar factories of Florida's Gulf Coast or to smelt steel in the hills of Pennsylvania. Others were houses people had built with their own hands after the bombardments of World War II. A few houses used to belong to Jewish families. Others in the area had petitioned to acquire those buildings—as well as personal items remaining in them—from local authorities after their neighbors were deported to Auschwitz.[50] In these villages, most families had not privatized their houses after Ukrainian independence. The process was expensive and risky. Calling attention to their case by filing for ownership papers could prompt threats of expropriation, so many chose to stay quiet in hopes of avoiding the mayor's gaze.[51]

So when, just before elections, the mayor's secretary rolled up to their front gates bearing cash on behalf of the Party of Regions, most villagers chose to accept the money. Some, like the widowed mothers of daughters whose adult children now contributed their labor and earnings to their husbands' households, had an immediate need. Others accepted the money because to do otherwise could risk irritating a public official who might, at any moment, decide to pursue their homestead land—their livelihood and last bulwark against economic crisis, the one thing over which "people would kill one another."[52] For them, vote buying was not an additive benefit so much as a poisoned gift, an offer they could not refuse.

We'll Take Your Son

Like many other party agents, local officials would use cash in some cases and pressure in others. Outside company towns and centers of industry, mechanisms of coercion and persuasion were contingent, variable across space, and depended on local adaptations and improvisations. As agents worked with few additional resources to deliver their supervisors' requirements for votes, they often needed to improvise. That improvisation required sensitivity to the nature of people's motivations and anxieties and knowledge of where and how to use limited resources effectively. As they mobilized people for electoral theater, local agents focused on the specific shape of people's fears. They knew who was vulnerable and how.

In the early 2000s, electoral dramaturgy had relied on tightly coordinated and centralized choreographies that depended on the concentrations of industry and population that were an inheritance of Soviet central planning.[53] Later, as party agents in the provinces parried demands from the center using resources and leverage already available to them, creatively withholding or redefining goods and services to maximize participation, that dramaturgy changed form. Imagined as music rather than theater, command performances at the turn of the millennium had been symphonic orchestras. A decade later, they became collections of jazz combos all playing the same changes.

Tactics varied from village to village, as local agents calibrated their actions to specific locations as well as their own particular varieties of influence. Because of the private nature of the interactions between party representatives and individual villagers, few people could be certain what specific threats or incentives their immediate neighbors faced. Villagers rarely knew how tactics worked in neighboring villages, and the resulting fragmentation of knowledge about practices fed a rumor mill. At the time of the May 2014 special presidential elections in Ukraine, some would complain that in neighboring villages "they gave out money, but we received nothing."[54]

CHAPTER 5

For some local agents, electoral mobilization was an unfunded mandate. While some party agents received cash to distribute to would-be voters, others received few additional tools or resources to pressure or entice people to participate. Required to deliver demonstrators in the streets and votes to incumbents or risk losing their own jobs, benefits, or access to services, these stage managers and stagehands of political theater improvised, using the infrastructure and services to which their jobs gave them access. Local state agents used their discretion to reallocate or withhold existing resources, creatively providing incentives for people to participate.

One mayor's secretary, a voluble and enthusiastic Hungarian-speaking woman married to a Russian man, could rarely be found in the mayor's office, which abutted the village tavern and was usually kept locked. Her frequent absences were due in part to the fact that like other village women with official positions, she kept a homestead requiring hours of backbreaking labor. Despite her higher education, every day she found herself under a cow. Sometimes, she was absent from her position in the mayor's office because in order to make ends meet she had taken another part-time job on the government payroll.

Her other official position was with the local draft board. As part of the military commission, she had access to lists of young men eligible for obligatory army service. For years, people in this area as in many other parts of the country regularly had bought their sons out of army service, six months at a time. Locally, the price was widely known. For several years it hovered at about one hundred dollars.[55] Once the war started in the east, as young men from neighboring villages were mobilized, the price rose to ten to twelve times that amount.[56]

The Donbas front, though far away, felt close in other ways. The local price of avoiding conscription reflected a widespread though not unanimously held belief that the populations of border villages in the southwest had been targeted for mobilization. Echoing an accusation that later would be publicly levied by Fidesz party representatives in Hungary[57] and Russian foreign minister Sergei Lavrov,[58] a local Lutheran minister complained that young men from neighboring villages, almost all Magyars and very few Ukrainians, were being sent to the front: "This is not right." In response to being targeted in this way, he argued, they were "paying a lot of money not to be sent."[59]

Even before the mobilization of local residents for war, people living in the shadow of the border knew at close range the conditions in which young army recruits lived and worked. Villagers regularly interacted with the troops who reinforced, at the European Union's behest, the thickly surveilled border fence. Soldiers were billeted in local villages, digging potatoes from local gardens because their own army could not feed them. When war came, villagers lamented that those taken for military service on the front "have no uniforms, they left in sneakers."[60]

Young men of draft or service age in good health were important sources of labor for village homesteads. For farming families supporting already fragile household economies, even the temporary loss of a son could place great economic stress on the family and a broader circle of dependents. During the Soviet period, some had been able to make informal agreements to have their sons posted close by. Now that was no longer possible: "Officers today are not like that."[61] As with housing or pasture, the mayor's secretary's discretion in sending, or not sending, names and files up the bureaucratic chain was a resource that local families could not afford to lose.

Villagers reported that during electoral campaigns, the mayor's secretary made effective use of this power as she carried out her other administrative duties for the mayor and her party. During the 2010 election, villagers reported an uncharacteristically high level of participation in the electoral process: about 70 percent of the village had participated in voting. They credited the mayor's secretary. In a political economy of loss, villagers described a menace of what would become, in the following years, the possibility of ultimate loss: "People were threatened: 'If you don't vote [for Yanukovych], we'll take your son into the army.'"[62]

Baby Yanukovych

As economic relationships fragmented and became decentralized, pockets of concentrated political power remained where local figures controlled both labor pools and production factors. Like their counterparts in industrialized areas, these local actors commanded considerable influence and maintained the ability to mobilize voters. This was most often the case for supervisors of public-sector workers—like the school director in a mountain village popular with skiing tourists who would require his teachers to show him their completed ballots—but it also included the directors of private enterprises.[63]

Along Ukraine's border with Slovakia, the director of a large-scale agricultural operation was the area's largest landowner. A former automobile parts warehouse worker, he directed the enterprise to which most of the people in the village leased their land.[64] He was rumored to have served time in prison in the Soviet period and was believed to maintain a close connection to Viktor Baloha, the regional political and business figure with a national profile.[65]

Regardless of the director's actual relationship with Baloha, belief in it was enough to shape behavior locally.

The farm director had seen his political influence with the local population wane with his declining lease payments to villagers for his company's use of their fields. He needed to find other ways to turn out votes: no longer would a word of support for the president from the farm director lead the community to fall neatly in line behind him, as had been the case for his predecessor a decade before.

Even as the director lost influence over the nominal owners of former *kolkhoz* land, one part of the rural population remained vulnerable to pressure from his office. In some villages, unregistered Romani settlements that had been present for generations abutted officially registered streets. Romani people, separated from access to field and pasture after land privatization, worked in a monopsonic labor market—that is, one controlled by a sole buyer. Their only option for selling their labor was the former collective farm.

Romani people in this region had long been sedentary, living in homes at the ends of some villages' streets. Then, when Soviet cadres arrived in the region to collectivize agriculture in the late 1940s and early 1950s, Roma were made members of the collectives. While Romani communities faced many of the same economic constraints as their ethnically Ukrainian and Magyar neighbors, their fortunes changed a half century later, when shares in the reorganized collective farms finally were distributed to their members. They would not share in the wealth: Romani people in the region describe having been excluded from land distribution. As a result, Romani families generally did not have access to property that could generate surplus value.[66]

In the first decades of the twenty-first century, Romani settlements had expanded from the ends of villages into unused fields. Newly built homes unconnected to village infrastructure lacked independent access to water, electricity, or gas. Without registered homesteads or access to water, Romani communities' household-level agricultural production was necessarily limited. Romani settlements sometimes occupied parcels of land less favorable for production. In one village, the street along which Roma families had constructed homes stretched into fields that regularly flooded in spring, leaving household gardens on that side of the village with a growing season one month shorter than those on the other side.[67]

By the second decade of the new millennium, Romani people could find regular jobs only through a small number of employers. Romani men in most settlements south of Uzhhorod were employed as day laborers. In those villages, the farm director sent his signature blue vans to collect and deliver men from the Roma settlements twice a day to work in fields he leased from the ethnically Ukrainian and Hungarian villagers who had received *kolkhoz* land. The vans were such a regular fixture that people in the area told time by their passage.⁶⁸

For the equivalent of a few dollars a day, Romani men performed some of the same seasonal labor that itinerant residents of mountain communities to the north customarily performed in the fields of southwest Russia and eastern Ukraine.⁶⁹ Their ethnic Ukrainian and Magyar neighbors, mirroring tropes about colonized populations elsewhere in the world, described local Romani people as constitutionally fitter than themselves for punishing midsummer agricultural labor in unshaded heat. Despite spending their entire lives in the area, Romani men often were undocumented.⁷⁰ This, combined with the contingent character of this labor and the absence of other job opportunities, placed Romani men at the mercy of their bosses' requests.

In this region, Romani families' dependence on the good graces of powerful local figures also extended to their own community leaders. Adjoining but in many ways separate from Magyar and Ukrainian village communities, Roma communities were governed by representatives who presided over multiple aspects of economic and social life. Like their ethnically Ukrainian and Hungarian neighbors, Romani people turned to community leaders for access to key economic resources.

The leader and district-level deputy of a Romani community of one thousand people commanded an economic structure typical of settlements in the region. Charged with managing numerous challenges, he worked to create housing for new families, negotiate relationships with the police, and obtain access to infrastructure. Members of a neighboring community regularly appealed to him for help, as in an incident when other villagers had blocked access to the only water pump, telling Romani residents instead to fetch water from the river. And women in his community who earned their living selling clothes door to door to Ukrainian and Magyar households depended on him for weekly transportation to a city several hours to the east, where they purchased their inventory.⁷¹

This leader was widely appreciated by his constituents, and his name and political affiliations were widely known. He made plain his expectations for constituents. On the eve of the 2010 presidential elections in Ukraine, his sister birthed a child. The family named him Yanukovych, after the soon-to-be-elected president.⁷² The local and national press reported that following the elections, the family moved into a new house, drove a new red Ukrainian-produced car, and hung a Party of Regions flag in front of the home.⁷³

Enticements to participate in electoral manipulation accompanied such signals. Roma men often figured in local journalists' accounts of voting carousels, and their leaders were described as participating in sometimes organized violent intimidation of electoral officials.[74] In such accounts, Romani men followed a process recognizable throughout Ukraine and Russia: they would disembark from buses or vans near voting precincts throughout the region,[75] receive a shot of liquor or up to 200 UAH for a completed ballot, and collect an empty ballot for deposit at the next precinct.[76] In 2012, the Committee of Voters of Ukraine reported that at one local polling station, groups of Roma men were led in to vote ten at a time and then paid just a few dozen meters away.[77]

When used widely, techniques that relied on payment could be expensive. These were mainly useful at the margins, especially in closely contested parliamentary and local elections, rather than presidential races.[78] Where regional party agents and leaders could entice directors of companies like the former collective farm to deliver employees like Zakarpattia's Roma to the voting booth en masse and cheaply, they did so. In many other cases, party agents creatively relied on resources already available to them as they parried pressure from the center.

She Doesn't Even Try

Despite the uniformity of techniques state agents used to pressure people into participation, the incentives that drove people to comply with their demands were neither distributed evenly across territory nor relative to distance from capital cities.[79] Across both countries, people's experiences of interaction with state agents varied from street to street and from household to household. Some administrative regions and districts were home to many more institutions that could compel participation in theater than others. But even within these areas, even next-door neighbors frequently did not share similar experiences of coercion or persuasion. Whether and to what extent people would be drawn into participation in electoral performances came to depend on how their households were embedded in local economies, and on the specificities of local state agents' improvisations.

Party representatives calibrated their threats to individual fears but were selective in targeting voters. Some in Russia and Ukraine who held jobs that did not expose them to coercion and who lived in places where paymasters have no role in government of political parties were able to live lives relatively free of pressure from state agents. The result was a motley combination of calls to support specific incumbents and people who participated regardless of economic incentives. In this system, some experienced political participation as command performance, and others felt they were presented with choices that aligned with their interests or beliefs.

Erzsébet Kovács was one rural constituent in Ukraine's southwest who escaped harassment by party agents. Neighbors remarked that the local party representative "doesn't even try. She knows who will take it and who won't."[80] Grandmother Erzsi lived with her husband in a long house, built before the world wars, in one of the small villages that dot the flatlands a few kilometers inland from Ukraine's border with Slovakia. The house stood up well against time, though unlike most other homes in the village, few renovations had been done for several decades. In 2009, Grandmother Erzsi and her husband, both in their late eighties, worked the cornfields behind their home, caring for hens in their courtyard. They enjoyed each other's company and lived simply, subsisting mainly on bread and small amounts of pork fat they fried over a fire in their courtyard. Their adult children were successful in their careers, following the paths of previous village generations who had grown up in the close-knit agrarian society and then struck out on their own. One daughter left to work in the European Union, and another had a good job and apartment in the nearby city of Uzhhorod. Although financial resources were available to them, as far as anyone around them could tell, Grandmother Erzsi and her husband spent none on themselves.

When, in late fall or early winter of 2009, agents of the Party of Regions conducted visits to homes in this village and neighboring settlements, they acted as they had in previous years and skipped Grandmother Erzsi's house. Local party operatives understood what Grandmother Erzsi's neighbors likewise knew. The older couple could not be bought, and there was no point in spending money on their votes. The result of this exception was that Grandmother Erzsi and her husband had no direct experience of pressure from political parties. At the end of the first decade of the twenty-first century, their world did not include state coercion or persuasion.

Grandmother Erzsi and her husband may have been exceptions. Among families stretched to a near breaking point by prices for heating fuel, transportation, food, and the education of the younger generation, few saw themselves as having the luxury of refusing the payments offered by local officials. But their experience highlights a critical aspect of the exercise of state and party power in this period. Unlike some authoritarian regimes, where members of particular ethnic groups or other solidarities might receive exceptional treatment, party agents in this rural hinterland tailored coercive measures at the level of individual households and according to the particularities of specific families.

CHAPTER 5

Neighbors with otherwise similar-seeming lives thus could inhabit radically different worlds when it came to their experience with state and party agents. Some lived under threat of life and livelihood, while others were left alone. In a single rural settlement or city apartment block, some people perceived themselves as living in freedom even as their neighbors lived with pressure to perform in political theater.

For those exposed to pressure to perform, political authority extended into nearly aspect of their lives. Politicians and state agents redefined fulfillment of basic human needs—warmth, light, ideas, health—as delivery of privileges for which the state had an obligation only toward those who supported particular politicians or parties, not toward the population as a whole. Over time, differences in people's experience of state pressure based on their material circumstances would become a deeper divide, as people living in one and the same place developed radically different understandings of what it meant to participate in politics.

# Chapter 6

Meanings of Participation

Over time, the meaning and salience of political participation changed for people who were drawn into performances. The lengthy time horizons and social imbrication of the complex political and moral economies behind political theater produce their own universes of meaning and interpretive frames. Where politicians direct political theater, parallel interpretations of political participation can take hold within populations on the same territory. This chapter narrates an episode in Kyiv on the eve of the violence that would roil the Ukrainian capital over the following months. The episode illuminates the epistemological space between people mobilized for and socialized by political theater and drawn into its social contract, and those who held on to a vision of political participation as expression of choice, however limited the menu of options might be.

Sandwiches for the Opposition

Residents of the Ukrainian capital awoke to disturbing news on the morning of December 11, 2013: the previous night, the government of President Viktor Yanukovych had ordered hundreds of special forces of the Ministry of the Interior onto a frigid Independence Square, where some ten thousand protesters had been gathering peacefully since late November. That night, members of the special forces had cleared the space of tents and barricades and engaged protesters in a nearby intersection in an hours-long physical standoff.[1]

Parts of Ukrainian society responded immediately. In the wake of the troops' arrival and ahead of a concert on the square by the popular Ukrainian rock group Okean Elzy, taxi drivers converged on the city center, delivering a new wave of protesters whose numbers would swell in the following forty-eight hours to near two hundred thousand.[2]

The next morning, accompanied by the United States ambassador to Ukraine, Geoffrey Pyatt, and a small security entourage, American assistant secretary of state Victoria Nuland visited the square. Approaching members of the special forces and individual demonstrators, and trailed by journalists who captured the event, Nuland held open before her a white plastic shopping bag. In it, both bread rolls and tea biscuits were visible to the cameras.[3]

Russian and Ukrainian media, as well as news outlets in the United States, covered and commented on the event. Widely circulated photos and videos showed the American assistant secretary of state urging soldiers and demonstrators to help themselves to food from the plastic bag. A soldier smiles in silence as he hesitates and then accepts a bread roll. Acknowledging the food, demonstrators say "thank you" and "God bless you."[4] Nuland described her visit as ordinary manners: "I didn't think I could go down empty-handed, given what everybody had been through."[5]

In contrast to Nuland's apparent equanimity, Russian media outlets erupted in a furor. Their outrage focused on the tea biscuits visible in the plastic bag. Headlines foregrounded the food: "Nuland and Pyatt distribute tea biscuits on Maidan to activists and *siloviki*," "The State Department distributes tea biscuits on Maidan," and "Deputy U.S. Secretary of State distributes tea biscuits and rolls to people on Maidan."[6]

Nuland quickly moved to respond. In a meeting a few days later at the American Enterprise Institute in Washington, DC, she amended versions circulating in Russian media: "First of all, to correct some *disinformaciya*, they were sandwiches, not cookies."[7] She reminded the public that she had distributed food not only to protesters, but also to members of the special forces. Nuland's international interlocutors appeared bored with her attention to such a seemingly trivial detail. In an interview with CNN's Christiane Amanpour several months after the incident, Nuland again reminded viewers she had brought "sandwiches" to both Maidan protesters and Berkut forces. Amanpour responded, "Let's get—we'll move past the sandwiches."[8]

MEANINGS OF PARTICIPATION 115

But the tea biscuit controversy lived on in Russian media. Two years after the incident, a Russian news service revisited the question of whether Nuland had distributed tea biscuits or sandwiches. RIA Novosti announced to readers, "Ukrainian Ministry of Foreign Affairs: Nuland Distributed to Maidan Participants Namely Tea Biscuits." The service quoted Oleksii Makeiev, director of the political department of Ukraine's Ministry of Foreign Affairs, in an interview on Latvian radio. In the interview, Makeiev made an ambiguous statement about Nuland's gesture: "Many of those who ate those tea biscuits did not go out onto Maidan for that."[9] More than seven years after the initial event, TVC Moscow reported in May 2021 that "the having-distributed-biscuits-on-Maidan Nuland is heading to Ukraine."[10]

Why did Russian and Ukrainian news sources care so much about the tea biscuits? And why would an American deputy secretary of state take time, even half in jest, to issue a correction about having distributed sandwiches rather than cookies? For Ukrainians and Russians watching news footage of the deputy secretary of state on Independence Square, the plastic bag Nuland carried was a familiar sight. It resembled the white plastic sacks of food used by political campaigns in both countries. In a common variation on the exchanges underlying the stagecraft of political theater, political parties distributed food to their constituencies in return for support. Charitable organizations officially unaffiliated with candidates or parties acted on their behalf, using this type of sack and setting up tents as "free social assistance points" for distribution.[11]

During electoral campaigns in Ukraine, acceptance of those plastic sacks usually acknowledged a quid pro quo. Sometimes the arrangement was implicit. At other times, teachers and other municipal employees who had been enlisted to distribute the bags to potential voters would ask voters to sign an agreement on receipt of the bag. That agreement would indicate an intention to vote for a specific party or candidate.

The contents of those assistance packages mattered to observers interpreting Nuland's gestures. They help explain the intensity of the reactions she elicited. The bags political parties distributed typically included buckwheat, cooking oil, sugar, tea, and condensed milk.[12] Nearly invariably, they include tea biscuits. They never contain sandwiches.

For those who saw sandwiches in the bag held by the American deputy secretary of state, Nuland's gesture represented solidarity with people who had taken to the streets to protest a corrupt and repressive government. Distributing food, Nuland inhabited a role—and invoked a trope—immediately recognizable in the context. Over the course of the previous weeks, groups of Ukrainian women had formed kitchen brigades to sustain the thousands of protesters, men and women, camped on Independence Square.[13]

In this interpretation, Victoria Nuland's distribution of sandwiches had been a simple and human gesture, a breaking of bread with both those who had suffered for their beliefs and those who had been ordered to destroy the physical infrastructure of a peaceful protest. In the days after her visit to Maidan, Nuland repeatedly sought to reassure those who would listen that she had distributed food not only to protesters, but also to soldiers. For those who saw no meaningful distinction between sandwiches and tea biscuits, the distribution of food to both groups conveyed neutrality: her act was a peacemaker's gesture.

For those who saw tea biscuits in Nuland's bag, her distribution of food meant something else entirely. Read through the lens of the stagecraft of political theater, Nuland's offer, and demonstrators' acceptance of the contents of the plastic bag, looked like evidence of a political relationship. In this interpretation, demonstrators and members of the special forces who took biscuits from an American deputy secretary of state acknowledged a relationship of patronage. Acceptance of food indicated loyalty toward a foreign state. It seemed to confirm that recipients were agents of a foreign power, the United States.

Nuland's insistence that she had distributed food not only to protesters but also to members of the special forces did little to shift the perspective of those used to seeing or participating in paid or incited protest. For them, Nuland's apparently even-handed interaction with members of Ukrainian society who found themselves on different sides of the barricades looked like a broad claim of control. By turning to both sides, Nuland symbolically acknowledged a relationship not only with the opposition but also with the Ukrainian state itself. As Amanpour put it, "the Russian foreign minister . . . blames the United States, saying that you have to control your clients, as they call it—the Kyiv government."[14]

The tea biscuits were not the only reason some saw Nuland's visit as proof that the United States was meddling in Ukrainian politics. Coverage of the tea biscuit controversy repeated Russian journalists' tropes about previous episodes of mass protest in Ukraine. During the Orange Revolution of 2004, amid other so-called color revolutions that swept across former Soviet space during the prior decade,[15] Russian-language media had portrayed protesters as drugged shills for the United States Department of State.

At that time, Russian and Ukrainian media reported Viktor Yanukovych's wife's false claim that protesters on Independence Square had received "American" *valenki*, or traditional felted wool boots, and oranges injected with narcotics.¹⁶ Some received her claim with trepidation. Others laughed. For twenty-first-century middle-class Ukrainian urbanites, *valenki* were among the least American objects imaginable. Felted boots symbolized the very opposite of a modern and wealthy citizenry. In cities at that time, only the poor, the old, and the very young wore them. But in the countryside, on very cold days, plenty of people still pulled them on as boot liners. For practical-minded Yanukovych supporters, the idea that demonstrators spending frigid days and nights on Kyiv's central square might receive boot liners from America plausibly sounded like a foreign power was providing relevant material assistance to a protest movement seeking to overturn the result of their votes.

In 2013, questions about the sponsorship of mass protest resonated not only with media coverage of previous protests, but also with the experience of many people in both countries who had not participated in anti-regime demonstrations. For over a decade, political parties across the spectrum had pressured and paid people to assemble in crowds supporting their candidates. Ukrainian oligarchs footed the bill, and politicians hired people using online databases and social networking sites. Networked brokers would offer applicants day jobs as demonstrators at competitive rates.¹⁷ These practices mirrored developments in Russia, where United Russia had moved away from the use of state-sponsored groups like *Nashi* and toward the use of crowds for hire—*Landsknecht*—even though the use of such crowds would not always prefigure electoral success. By the time Ukrainians gathered on Independence Square in the final months of 2013, much of the country had had direct experience of political participation as either command performance or paid activity.

For many Ukrainians, the absence of pressure and payment was precisely what had distinguished the protests of late 2013 and early 2014 from demonstrations since the Orange Revolution. From their perspective, participants had gathered on Independence Square because they believed in a cause, not because they had been paid. For these participants and their allies, the mass protests they would come to describe as the Revolution of Dignity represented redemption of a politics that had grown cynical. But for some others, the widespread existence of paid protest and command performances had made Russian media's accusations of foreign intervention in Ukrainian civil society perfectly believable.

The dispute over the content of Nuland's plastic bag on Independence Square was thus neither an argument about food nor even about partisanship. Instead, it was a disagreement about hermeneutics. Dominant interpretations of Victoria Nuland's gesture—apolitical solidarity with human beings caught in a difficult confrontation, or affirmation of a patron-client relationship involving a foreign power and Ukrainian citizens—expressed two distinct and contradictory understandings of the meaning of political participation. Like the pro-Yeltsin graffiti that appeared in Voronezh in 1996, these two versions of participation seemed nearly indistinguishable in form, yet they conveyed entirely different understandings of reality.

This similarity of form gave participants and observers room to attribute different meanings to the same event. As a result, two distinct epistemic worlds flowed from a single, seemingly trivial difference in perception regarding a single object. People attached whole—and wholly divergent—universes of meaning to an imagined sandwich roll or tea biscuit.

Falsification Is Too Simple an Explanation

On the eve of the 2012 parliamentary elections in Russia, the sociologist Grigorii Yudin summarized these divergent meanings, describing those elections not as a contest between parties or candidates, but as a competition between two understandings of the same event. When people showed up at precincts to vote, he argued, some would think of their participation as choice, *vybory*. Others, meanwhile, would imagine their act as balloting, *golosovanie*. Elections meant "conscious political choice," while balloting referred to an "administrative event for the demonstration and consolidation of loyalty to the authorities."[18]

Writing of Senegal in the late 1990s, the political scientist Frederic Schaffer had asked what democracy might mean to people in countries that had recently put in place a system of competitive elections. Schaffer argued that his Wolof and francophone interlocutors used the word *demokaraasi* mainly to refer to how their communities assured their security, not to how they selected leaders.[19] People assign a range of meanings to the concept *demokratiia*, and only some have to do with electoral choice.[20] In Russia and Ukraine, the practice of political theater encouraged the development of two distinct sets of meanings around political participation.

Where political theater is prevalent and most people see the purpose of elections as an opportunity to express fealty, it may be meaningless to speak to those participants of a rigged or falsified process. From their point of view, elections that are about loyalty rather than choice are no less real for being so. Many of the people who saw tea biscuits in Victoria Nuland's bag would have viewed accusations against their candidate of electoral manipulation or falsification not as descriptions of fact, but as markers of someone else's political identity—proof of the accuser's membership in an alien political camp.

In Russian electoral politics, politicians had constrained elements of competition that would be necessary for the victory of a liberal democratic model. At the same time, they preserved a semblance of democratic form that never ushered choice from the stage entirely. This effectively accommodated and encouraged the reproduction of both systems of meaning on the same territory, making possible the simultaneous presence of divergent registers.[21]

This duality was not limited to elections. The cultural anthropologist Natalia Rudakova has documented two registers in Soviet journalism. She argued that both truth-seeking and propagandistic models were present.[22] After the Soviet Union came apart, market pressures on newspapers led to the gradual abandonment of one of these registers—the truth-seeking one—leaving a profession exposed to pressure from parties of power.

In both Russian and Ukrainian elections, one of these registers has been more dominant than the other at different times. In Russia, some sociologists described the vacillation between frames as indications of a political struggle between society and state, the outcome of which was a victory for parties of power and a system of meaning emphasizing duty, fealty, and obligation. The sociologist Vladimir Rimskii noted in 2011 that "naturally, citizens wanted the political class to reflect their interests, but the political class wanted to use resources of those same politics to solve their problems. . . . Sometime between 1999 and 2000 the political class won."[23]

In Ukraine, the number of plays present on the stage at any given time has varied. The country has held more and less competitive elections, and leaders have leaned toward or away from democratic practice. At times, both registers have circulated simultaneously. There have been exceptions, as in Kuchma's 2000 referendum, when only balloting was present, and Ukraine's 2019 presidential elections, which offered a recognizable choice. In the latter case, Russians were watching closely. A Voronezh journalist observed that the Ukrainian elections "really became elections in the strictest sense of the word." She went on to describe the elections' arc as dramatic theater, "starting with the very fact of the nomination of the young showman as candidate for the highest office and ending with a sharp political battle with a triumphal result for him."[24]

Analyzing politics in Russia and Ukraine through the lens of these two distinct registers, we can observe the emergence and reproduction of two systems of meaning surrounding political participation. This approach permits us to examine both command performances and democratic institutions without reifying one set of experiences and interpretations as more real or genuine than the other. Analyzing meaning-making, we can break through one of the central analytic impasses in the literature on political subjectivity in authoritarianism: the question of dissimulation.

The intellectual genealogy of *Homo sovieticus* and his close relatives—the unconscious actors that densely populate the literature on authoritarian and totalitarian regimes—highlights a subject position that explains complicity in performance as deception or self-deception.[25] Such accounts range from Marx's notion of false consciousness to Lisa Wedeen's account of Syrian politics under Hafez al-Assad, where people made to participate in a shared charade are aware that both they and others act "as if" they supported their president.[26] More recent iterations may be found in the analytical apposition used in Ukraine following the Revolution of Dignity, which contrasted submissive people with Soviet mentalities and "tolerant" liberals.[27] Scholarship on Russia likewise sometimes examines support for Vladimir Putin using the logic of dissimulation, asking whether his popularity as measured in public opinion surveys is genuine or false, if respondents are "lying to pollsters."[28]

This dyad—democratic politics and its memetic, compromised twin—flows from models of human subjectivity that dominated the study of the Soviet Union in the West and now silently underpin the study of politics in its successor states. These models posit only two types of animals in the zoo, two varieties of human being. These two species, the collaborator and the dissenter, inhabit commentary about Russian and Ukrainian politics and political discourse in many other national contexts. On the one hand, there is the successfully colonized mind—in its less formal versions, the zombie and the uneducated dupe—the purportedly unthinking collaborator cooperating with the projects of authoritarian leaders, exercising no independent agency. At the other end of the spectrum is the resisting liberal subject, valiantly bucking the chains of oppression and resisting the projects of dominating states. Such subjects, fists clenched and raised in outward expressions of dissent, inhabit the literatures on revolution and social movements. In their quieter manifestations they engage in what appear to be everyday acts of resistance, as in the seminal works of political scientist James C. Scott on this subject.[29] These are the low-level functionaries who slow work to a sloth's pace, the waiter who spits in the soup.

In an influential critique, the anthropologist Alexei Yurchak argued that this binary does not represent the only type of possible postsocialist subjectivity or discursive reproduction.[30] The dyad of the post-Enlightenment liberal subject with its corollary, the resisting subaltern, and the seemingly dominated, quiescent, totalitarian subject is not the only lens through which to regard political performance. Inquiry into the supposed inner dispositions of political actors is not the only way to analyze participation in political theater, and a presumption of clear separation between state and society is not the only possible point of departure.

Yurchak, in his critique of interpretations that read command performances of support for leaders as expressions of dissimulation, pointed to the late Soviet shift toward performative, as opposed to constative, or literal meaning. In this shift, different elements of ritual action came to assume greater or lesser importance. Of elections, Yurchak wrote, "In such a context, it may be less important for whom one votes than that one votes." He went on to elaborate that the literal meaning of the ballot—the choice of a candidate—is secondary to its performative meaning, which may result in the provision of other goods: "A successful execution of the ritual of voting will enable other important practices and events to happen, such as the reproduction of the institution itself and of one's position as its member . . . with all the possibilities that follow from that position."[31]

Yet despite Yurchak's late Soviet shift toward performative meanings, literal meanings of political participation, including the idea that elections were or should be about choice, also circulated within the population.[32] That idea was part of the reservoir of meanings from which people drew to make sense of changing politics after the dissolution of the Soviet Union. In the late Soviet period, participation in elections that involved neither contention nor surprise had been a constituent feature of citizenship. Today, for those who think of elections as obligation, the point is not to choose leaders but to be part of a political community in which people express membership through the liturgy of leader selection.

In political theater, this is a material bargain. While the form of such elections resembles practices Yurchak described, their content and driving force include a social contract in which economic insecurity drives people onto the stage. Taken together, the theatrical form and economic content of political theater have repercussions not only for how people understand their own politics, but also how they interpret the political actions and intentions of compatriots with whom they may disagree.

During the first two decades of the twenty-first century in Russia and Ukraine, a portion of the population lived within a democratic model, however constrained. Some had sufficient economic means and autonomy to live beyond the reach of the stage managers of command performances. Others maintained a principled belief in elections as choice. For this portion of the population, elections remained a mechanism for expressing individual agency and for choosing leaders.

At the same time, other members of the polity continued to experience elections as balloting. For those who saw elections in this way, participation in democracy came to mean declaring loyalty to *patria* and leader and fealty to local elites at the ballot.[33] This register made possible the finding of political scientists Irina Soboleva and Regina Smyth that Putin supporters see themselves as out to "defend democracy."[34] In the American context, it also may explain how, against all other logic, certain trespassers on the US Capitol on January 6, 2021, could have seen themselves as defending the Constitution.

The nature of electoral support for parties of power and the problem of societal consensus around practices like electoral manipulation come into view when we distinguish between registers of choice and loyalty. Where some people see elections or other demonstrations as an occasion for showing that they belong to a community of supporters rather than as an articulation of choice, the very idea of electoral manipulation or falsification—which comes down to misrepresentation of choice—loses meaning. Debates about the popularity of politicians can become *faux questions*. Of elections in Russia, the sociologists Lev Gudkov and Georgii Saratov wrote,

> Those are not elections but a ritual of demonstration of loyalty to the regime, a ceremony of an "acclamation" of power. It is namely because of this that with such a crude identification of every anomaly with "falsification" (ballot stuffing and forgery, carousels, and so forth), the very essence of social conformism and mass behavior in conditions of an authoritarian regime is lost. Falsification is too simple an explanation, convenient for political declarations but absolutely inappropriate for the tasks of scientific or analytical work and the study of the mass nature of totalitarian and authoritarian regimes.[35]

To better understand the societal effects of electoral manipulation, we need to account for the emic meanings of political action, to distinguish between things people might do, like pressuring employees to vote or otherwise manipulating elections to deliver votes, and the concepts we use to analyze what they do.

A solution can be an analytical framework that allows us a broader view of human motivation: to acknowledge that some participants in elections see themselves as mere players on a stage, while others think of themselves as actively participating, whether in an act of democratic choice or an act of loyalty and obligation. Such an approach neither denies the possibility of dissimulation, nor invests all explanatory value in the role and importance of performance.

Every Vote Can Become the Decisive One

Soviet people had used registers of both obligation and choice to talk about elections and other forms of political participation. Soviet elections mainly had been occasions for shared festivity and opportunities for upward mobility, not mechanisms for aggregating preferences. With the dissolution of the Soviet Union, the register of obligation receded, and for a time, choice emerged as the way most people understood the act of dropping a ballot in an urn.

In 1973, on the occasion of a Union-wide election, the Soviet magazine *Ogonek* had described a typical scene. Flowers, flags, and posters adorned city and village streets filled with people. The magazine announced that "on all soviet land—from Brest to Crimea, from Novaia Zemlia to Kushka whirled a spirit of great festivity, soviet people hurried to fulfill their civic duty, to give their voice to their electors to local Councils of workers' deputies."[36] The social meaning of Soviet elections derived not only from their demonstrations of loyalty, but also from their conviviality. Participants recall the surrounding festivities shared with intimates, but also with an imagined community of citizens across the Soviet Union.[37] Often, late Soviet elections were occasions for celebration: for dressing up and enjoying a holiday atmosphere with children and friends, listening to music, and eating foods not always available during the rest of the year.[38]

Economic opportunity and social pressure accompanied that conviviality. Writing in the late 1970s, the sociologists Victor Zaslavsky and Robert J. Brym argued that Soviet elections contributed to regime continuity by offering economic incentives to organizers and by socializing the population to comply with party demands. Contrary to claims in the literature at the time, Zaslavsky and Brym thought there was insufficient evidence to conclude that frequent elections legitimated the Soviet regime in the eyes of the population.[39] Instead, they argued, elections reproduced the power of the regime because participants in electoral agitation were offered a path to upward mobility—even as the general population understood the "fictitious nature" of official ideology but participated nonetheless.[40] Social pressure helped mobilize voters, as local agitators charged with assuring the participation of individuals communicated to them a message of complicity: "Please don't get me into trouble, you may have to do this someday."[41]

As early as 1927, a Western commentator had noted the disciplining role of Soviet elections, observing that "what is elsewhere a riot of discord is here a device for registering unanimity."[42] At the same time, glimpses of a rights-based vision of political participation appear in the documentary record even decades into Soviet rule. The historian Alsu Tagirova, writing of a 1967 report produced by the Alma Ata regional committee for the Central Committee of the Communist Party of Kazakhstan, describes voters' penciled notations on ballots in that republic. Amid many patriotic messages, a few inscriptions came to the attention of the authorities. These complained that elections offered no choice, asking "When are you going to stop playing at democracy?" or "Elections are when there is something to choose from." A few notations admonished others not to privilege performative over literal meanings of voting: "Think about it and do not raise your hand mechanically in favor."[43]

After the dissolution of the Soviet Union, even as the press sometimes continued to invoke registers of civic duty, national elections rapidly took on a different purpose and meaning, acting as devices for registering choice rather than unanimity.[44] In both Russia and independent Ukraine, press coverage included intense and rigorous debate of both party platforms and the social and economic problems of the day. In national newspapers published in Moscow and Kyiv, where social and political change had been most immediate and discernible, this was to be expected. But it was also true in less expected places.

In the provinces, many papers had been unable to publish, or publish as often, in the lean years following the dissolution of the Union. Despite the evaporation of ideological control, economic factors made conditions difficult for much of the regional press: supply chain disruptions, budgetary pressures on the papers and their dedicated staff members, and suddenly constrained means of both institutional and private subscribers.

Despite these challenges, the newspaper *Kommuna* in the southwestern Russian city of Voronezh continued to offer daily, in-depth coverage of regional politics. Published in the heart of Russia's conservative so-called rust belt, *Kommuna* approached elections as matters of consequence for the selection of leaders at the regional and national level.

Political participation as loyalty and political participation as choice coexisted in the pages of *Kommuna*. Sometimes the newspaper mixed registers, as in the journalist who noted, "The number of those voting significantly exceeded the number of those fulfilling their civic duty two years ago."[45] But for most of that decade, choice was the dominant register in electoral politics as *Kommuna*'s editorial board saw it. Its writers described elections as a way for citizens to influence the direction of politics.

In the pages of *Kommuna*, voters in Voronezh openly worried about whom to choose to represent them in the country's legislature. Readers encountered spirited deliberations in print just five years after tanks had rolled through Moscow in the attempted coup of August 1991, when Soviet television viewers learned something was amiss by turning on their televisions to find nothing but the ballet *Swan Lake*, and a mere two years after Boris Yeltsin presided over the shelling of the Russian parliament building. An associate professor at Voronezh State University warned readers that "it's possible that this is our last chance to influence the fate of the country.... Will we be able to use that chance correctly? We simply have no right to make mistakes. Unfortunately, there are reasons to be alarmed."[46]

In 1995, a sense of urgency and concern suffused coverage in *Kommuna*. Part of that urgency stemmed from a proposal by the regional governor earlier that year to suspend elections until stability had been achieved. The paper ran numerous open letters in support of the opposition candidate.[47] Headlines reminded readers, "Every vote can become the decisive one."[48] Journalists urged voters to mobilize and made explicit how they understood their own participation: "I'll go, but not because I'm being convinced from every side to fulfill my civic duty.... Possibly, this is my last chance to believe that my voice can still decide something, can influence something."[49] Responding to growing despondence among the population about the responsiveness of elected officials to their concerns, a professor of sociology made the case for the importance of elections despite the difficulties of forging genuine parliamentarism.[50]

Amid intensive coverage of candidates and wide-ranging discussion of the significance of elections, letters to the editor focused on support for opposition candidates, with many readers expressing unwillingness to resign themselves to supporting politicians who were "carving up the pie" for themselves.[51] Those letters expressed not only understandings of elections as choice, but also a wide variety of both programmatic and material reasons for supporting candidates, as in the case of the deputy who had assisted a single mother of two young children unable to pay for a gas line to her village home.[52]

Fatigue with unbridled executive power, corruption among legislators, and the predations of amoral businessmen dominated coverage of people's concerns. These themes also figured prominently in *Kommuna*'s political cartoons. One featured a mug-shot poster titled "Wanted by the police." Holding a banner lettered "Congressional candidates" to paste onto the poster, an onlooker notes, "We'll just change the title."[53] Another spoke directly to the widely perceived crisis, criticizing the politics of loyalty to the president. It pictured a seesaw balanced on a bound volume of the Constitution of the Russian Federation. Boris Yeltsin was seated on the ground on one end, the judicial and legislative branches aloft on the other. Its caption read, "Our President is unbalanced [*neuravnoveshennyi*]."⁵⁴

Civic Obligation

Most scholarship about elections in autocracies focuses on what elections do for political leaders, rather than what participants think elections mean. Studies have shown how authoritarian elections can generate legitimacy⁵⁵ while leaving regimes vulnerable to evolving opposition tactics.⁵⁶ They have revealed how authoritarian elections serve as external and internal signaling mechanisms,⁵⁷ as in recent cases of regional leaders who commit electoral fraud in order to demonstrate their loyalty.⁵⁸ And they have shown how elections demonstrate leaders' firm grip on power to constituencies or act as pressure valves.⁵⁹ But the challenges of research in authoritarian contexts make it difficult to study what elections mean for actors on the stage.⁶⁰

For clues, we can look at how political concepts are understood and practiced in different contexts, and how the meanings that attach to them can change over time.⁶¹ Oleg Kharkhordin has shown that political concepts like state, nation, friendship, virtue, and republic have taken on a wide variety of different meanings from one century to the next in Russia.⁶² But such shifts also can occur more rapidly. In twenty-first-century Russia and Ukraine, as command performances became regular parts of political life, the meanings that attached to electoral participation also shifted, moving from the predominantly rights-based frame of the 1990s to a frame that emphasized fealty and obligation.

In the space of a few years, the vigorous debates about politicians' responsibilities toward people that had graced the pages of *Kommuna* gave way to language emphasizing people's responsibility toward politicians. In the new millennium, "civic duty" (*grazhdanskii dolg*) quickly emerged as the dominant way to describe political participation in Russia. In 2006, a Russian voter who described having been compelled to vote (*zastavliaiut*) framed her participation in this way: "I am a sovereign's [*gosudarev*] person and therefore am obligated to give back my civic duty."⁶³ Seven years into Vladimir Putin's rule, a survey in Russia reported that three times as many respondents explained their participation in elections in terms of civic duty as those who voted to express their opinion or affect the outcome.⁶⁴ In recent years, tenth and eleventh graders in Russian schools participated in lessons titled, "Elections are my civic duty."⁶⁵

In Ukraine, the frame of civic duty was intermittently present and could mean something slightly different. At the time of Kuchma's 2000 referendum in Ukraine, discussion of civic duty had resembled Soviet discourse surrounding fulfillment of production quotas. Journalists made pronouncements such as "by April 16th, almost 50 percent of voters had fulfilled their civic duty ahead of time."[66] But in other years, command performances mixed with democratic forms of participation in equal measure. In areas dominated by the Party of Regions, which more than other parties relied on political theater to achieve its political aims, the meaning of civic duty often resembled its meaning in Russia. Elsewhere in Ukraine, and across the country since the Party of Region's dispersal in 2014, the meaning of civic duty or obligation could refer to the responsibility of making a choice—a recognized feature of citizenship in established liberal democracies[67]—rather than obedience in a process with a known outcome.

In the following years, registers of duty and obligation in Ukraine invoked responsibility for the country and its future. In 2019, stars of television, film, and music posted images of themselves voting or going to vote, while commentators observed that "celebrities did not stay on the sidelines during the elections and fulfilled their civic obligation."[68] The metropolitan of the Kirovohrads'ka diocese of the Ukrainian Orthodox Church observed, "Why should we, as Orthodox people, as residents of this country, give away the right to decide the fate of our country, our church, to someone else for us? . . . Taking part in elections is a holy and sacred right."[69]

They Have Stopped Believing Their Promises

Disaffection with traditional forms of democratic political participation was a key precondition for development of political theater and the spread of the register of obligation. By the early 2000s, many people in Russia felt they had few opportunities to participate in political processes that meaningfully addressed their concerns. Disillusioned with the choices offered in electoral politics, many people withdrew from participation. Their exit created a vacuum, and political technologists leaped into the breach, creating staged productions that looked like the institutions from which people had withdrawn.

Notwithstanding the Kremlin's tightening grip on the press, Russian regional media chronicled this process of withdrawal and replacement. By the 2000s, Voronezh's *Kommuna*, whose pages had documented the raging policy debates of the 1990s, had established itself as a voice cooperating with the party of power. The newspaper sometimes openly criticized deputies of United Russia. Still, the Putin administration accredited *Kommuna* journalists for meetings with the president.[70] Throughout the first decade of the new century, the paper carefully reported on social and economic conditions in the region.

In and around Voronezh, many of the concerns people expressed in the early 2000s were kitchen-table issues: the cost of utilities, the availability of social services, access to heating fuel.[71] Responding to people's urgent daily needs, politicians offered material help in exchange for promises of support. In rural areas, local leaders sensitive to people's challenges talked about gasification. Before 2000, only 18 percent of the region's rural population had access to natural gas in their homes. That meant hours of labor preparing firewood or purchasing coal, stoking furnaces, and dealing with soot and dust. At that time, hot running water remained a dream for the vast majority of people in rural areas.[72]

Beyond dissatisfaction with daily living conditions, the fate of things people had built during the Soviet period most rankled the population. In rural areas, the fact that elected representatives had themselves appropriated what the population had built, or were failing to constrain others who did, disappointed many. Struggling economically, people felt disillusioned about prospects for responsive government. A member of the Voronezh regional veterans' council echoed a common refrain: "People who gave their life-long intellectual resource to the state find themselves in fact below the poverty line. We can't agree that the fruits of our labor—factories and plants, energy outputs and ore deposits, the oil and gas trades and all the rest—should suddenly find themselves in the hands of those who had and have no relationship to them. And now they're taking land from the peasant for next to nothing."[73] A sense of betrayal about enclosure and privatization was in part a product of the conditions in which people had spent their efforts. Postwar reconstruction had been difficult, with some people working knee-deep in the ashes of cataclysmic destruction. That some of the beneficiaries of privatization or enclosure now populated the halls of government while the population continued to struggle turned many people off to politics. At that time, Russians in the provinces distanced themselves from political participation because they felt the exercise was meaningless, that their representatives had forgotten about them.[74] Citing a refrain recognizable to people in consolidated democracies, a local journalist wrote of local people's feelings toward politicians, "They have stopped believing their promises."[75]

Even so, people were disappointed in concrete policy outcomes, not in democracy itself. The chairman of the regional legislature argued, "People want to believe in government [*vlast'*], they want to have an awareness that this government was chosen by them independently."[76]

Early in the new millennium, elections as choice came to hold little appeal—the government seemed unresponsive, and there were no meaningful choices. Yet the idea of elections as duty or obligation had not yet taken hold as the dominant way of understanding the meaning of political participation. *Kommuna* reported on a national poll of rural and urban households in which only 23 percent of respondents said voting was a responsibility or obligation of each citizen.[77] Over and over, reporters noted that among the population, the question was not for which candidate to vote, but whether to go to the polls at all.[78] As reforms in Moscow placed more and more power in the hands of the executive, the legislative branch seemed not only corrupt but also impotent. People's interest drifted away from parliamentary elections.[79]

In Voronezh region, with the proliferation of both pressure to support incumbents and dirty electoral tricks, people became even more annoyed with and distant from politics. The chairman of the Voronezh regional legislature publicly observed that voters reacted badly to active support by local government for particular candidates and that this turned them off to elections in general.[80] In the first decade under Putin, so-called black PR had proliferated in the region, discrediting not only individual candidates but also elections themselves.

Some aspiring legislators turned conventional clientelism on its head, advertising false promises of food or even attacking a candidate by giving out overly extravagant bags of food in the candidate's name, suggesting corruption.[81] Tricksters tried to sow confusion, discrediting social welfare programs and casting blame on candidates for vote buying even when none was happening.[82] The regional press saw the problem clearly and worried openly about the effects of electoral manipulation on democracy. A journalist for *Kommuna* argued, "The use of dirty tricks threatens to turn elections into a farce.... Such methods are a direct violation of the law, the discrediting of the very idea of democratic elections.... While it is not yet too late, it is necessary to return the running of electoral campaigns to a lawful, constructive course."[83]

Meanwhile, local organizations struggled to involve a disengaged population. Young people were challenged to compete in knowledge of the constitution, electoral law, and events "connected with human rights." Elections were framed as duty and responsibility to the country, not as an obligation to a leader. In 2007, a winning short poem in one Voronezh school competition read, "For the first time I vote / The first time, like the first grade / I take responsibility / for Russia now."[84]

Biscuit Politics

Political systems that rely on performances of democratic institutions present a problem of nomenclature. Command performances not only shape electoral and other political outcomes, but also transform in significant ways how people understand political participation. It is not enough to speak only of the political economies of exchange that underlie performances or of the arrangement of players on the stage, because political theater does work in the world: politics are different after the show is over.

What kind of political order does the practice of political theater produce? Writing in 1989 of the historicity and patronal politics of the postcolonial African state, the French sociologist Jean-François Bayart referred to *la politique du ventre*—the politics of the stomach. Analyzing how indigenous political elites accumulated and leveraged power through control of material goods, Bayart proposed the concept to revise Western analytical models of African statehood and the normative baggage they conveyed. Like Bayart's *politique du ventre*, the dominant interpretations that emerged from the controversy surrounding Victoria Nuland's distribution of food in Kyiv's Independence Square suggest different ways to think about contemporary political orders.

For people in Russia and Ukraine, the two objects at the center of the dispute over the meaning of Deputy Secretary of State Nuland's action—sandwiches and biscuits—each signified a recognizable civilizational order. Each object mapped onto semiotic fields and broader systems of value that emerged in part from the twenty-first-century staging of command performances. For local observers, Nuland's sandwiches symbolized a political order emphasizing choice and legitimacy, the rights the state secures for citizens, access to a welfare state, elections that are for choosing, and a clear conceptual separation between public and private spheres. The biscuits, on the other hand, suggested not rights but fealty, citizen obligations toward the state, and strict legality or dictatorship of the law (*diktatura zakona*).

In biscuit politics, the responsibilities of the state toward its citizens are politicized: rights are goods linked to political loyalty, and the state's obligation is toward those who support particular politicians or parties. Biscuit politics express a relationship of responsibility between state and society in which the modern welfare state gives way to selective expressions of *caritas*. Leaders communicate a personal interest in people's well-being while encouraging members to care for one another and themselves. Think of Putin on New Year's Eve, addressing the nation in 2019: "Our spiritual generosity . . . is needed during the holidays and every day, when we support those who need help, who are alone or sick."[85] The language is of care, rather than rights.

Unlike grassroots mobilizations, command demonstrations are not sites of critique but representations of states' or political parties' interests. In biscuit politics, a demonstration is by definition a tool of the state, a show of support by and for the party of power. It is not a tool of the domestic opposition. For people who think within this frame, it follows that if a demonstration does not represent the interests of the state or the incumbent party, the demonstration must necessarily represent the interests of a foreign power. From this perspective, assembly is guided and paid for by particular interests, and organized voluntaristic opposition is impossible. Protest, therefore, must be mise-en-scène by forces allied either with the incumbent political party or with foreign entities.

In biscuit politics, demonstrations represent the interests of the group that provides material support for the event. This contrasts with sandwich politics, where people see mass protest as the expression—sometimes spontaneous, usually sincere—of individual citizens' political will. Through their participation, people signal cooperation and affiliation. From this perspective, people who assemble in the name of anti-regime political ends engage not in representation but in a rejection of community. For many of those who participate in political theater, disruptive street protest to question the legitimacy of an electoral outcome signals a turn away from political community. In Ukraine, this idea was at the root of some popular criticism in some circles both of Euromaidan and, a decade earlier, the Orange demonstrations.

Despite this shift in interpretive frames, regimes that rely on political theater remain situated squarely within modern traditions of statehood. Even as people's local experiences may be different from those in countries where fiscal obligation is one of the main obligations to the state, places where command performances proliferate are "normal countries,"[86] and participation in political theater is one of the ways people fulfill their obligations.[87] For many who participate, coercion or pressure to participate does not make such requirements seem extraordinary. After all, even in wealthy polities with robust representative institutions, fiscal and other obligations to the state may be received as coercive measures—in the United States, some do not want their taxes to pay for wars, while others may resist the use of taxpayer dollars for reproductive health services. In this sense, in contemporary Russia and Ukraine, regardless of levels of political repression at any given moment, pressure to participate in command performances might best be understood not within frameworks of authoritarian social mobilization, but rather as an activity typical of contemporary statehood in a capitalist order.

People in Russia and Ukraine who see themselves as participating in biscuit politics often do not experience a feeling of a lack of agency, and they may reject accounts that describe them in these terms. Instead, they see their participation as partaking in a logic of exchange in which they have an assigned role, a social meaning. Distinct in key ways from categories of analysis ordinarily used to examine politics in this region—liberalism and conservatism, resistance and collaboration, individualism and collectivism—sandwich and biscuit politics bundle values in a way that resonates with emic understandings of the meanings people in the region attach to political participation.

It may be tempting to imagine that biscuit and sandwich politics are simply different names for conservative and liberal politics or collectivist and individual philosophies. But biscuit politics emerge from a pattern of practices that cohere around economies of material exchange. It might be possible to imagine continuity between these two systems of value—biscuit and sandwich politics—and the dual consciousness present in the literature on Soviet-era practices of dissimulation. Such an argument might hold that Soviet antinomies of independent thought and state or party loyalty, held simultaneously within individuals' minds,[88] reproduced themselves in the population after the dissolution of the Soviet empire. According to this logic, today's supporters of parties of power would likewise be engaged in a complex dance of self-deception. But even as Soviet statism required consistent loyalty to national organizations and ideals, biscuit politics instead depend on periodic demonstrations of local fealty. Biscuit politics express an underlying set of local economic relationships. They do not indicate, or do not indicate reliably, acceptance of an ideology.

Politicians in Russia and Ukraine might like observers to think otherwise. Since 2013, biscuit politics in both Russia and Ukraine have been accompanied by intensive state-led ideological work focusing on national identity.[89] In biscuit politics, economies of exchange are individualized and particular. Today, the staging of political theater no longer depends on bargains between collectives and their bosses (*krugovaia poruka*) but instead turns on exchanges between individuals and local elites. After enclosure and privatization, the systems that brought people onto the stage of political theater increasingly depended on societal atomization and individual fealty rather than collective feelings of belonging and responsibility. In this way, like a tarp loosely tied across a tent fixed by stakes in the ground, national and collectivist ideologies promoted by the Russian state rest awkwardly and insecurely, yet very visibly, atop a politics that depends on individual transactions. Although biscuit politics instantiate values, they are based on a set of transactions. Change the transactions, and the values may change as well. The tarp can blow away.

The register of obligation, emphasizing loyalty, sociality, and community over choice, is not new but was present in the late Soviet period. The legal historian Aurore Chaigneau, writing on the normative power of property law in Soviet Russia,[90] described an understanding of property as principally an obligation, rather than a right—*devoir de* rather than *droit à*—a vision consistent with the primacy of obligations over rights in contemporary statism in both Russia and Ukraine. But the social and economic context in which obligation resurfaced in the twenty-first century generated new meanings and frictions. The practice of political theater transformed the loyalty to fatherland or party required of Soviet subjects into fealty to local officials. Over time, while state-led discourses of national belonging overlaid these relationships,[91] political economies of accountability remained local.

Both biscuit and sandwich politics and their central registers—fealty or obligation versus choice—are defined in large part by the existence of the other register. We can understand these two approaches to politics not as signifier and signified, not democracy and its imitation, but as two distinct forms of representation, each possessing an internally coherent logic, each integral in itself, and each in a continual process of redefinition in opposition to the other.

If we turn the lens to look through its other end, the view of politics can be nearly the same. Each side sees the other as participating in theater rather than in so-called genuine or authentic political action. For some participants in biscuit politics, the fact that many people regularly have been offered money for demonstrating or voting lends credibility to accusations that any protest or mobilization has been paid for. Seen from the vantage point of those who participate in political theater and support parties of power, the actors in this drama execute similar acts, but the roles are reversed. For them, it is the opposition demonstrators who enact an inauthentic politics as unwitting shills in the service of outside forces.

From this perspective, participation in political theater is neither a sign of what Russians and Ukrainians call "zombification," nor an indication of an alignment of interests between dramaturge and bit players. If liberal models of democracy frame political participation as the representation of interests, biscuit politics move away from a representational mode and toward a transactional one. For politicians operating within the framework of biscuit politics, mobilization for political theater is a tool to be, or stay, elected. For all the participants, participation in political theater is a means to maintain privileges they formerly understood as rights.

In contemporary Russian and Ukrainian politics, the shift toward civic obligation as the main way in which people understand elections also meant a change in temporality, a shift toward the importance of the here and now. The stage management of political theater was a move away from the future orientation of communism to present exchange. This temporal shift mirrored the post-Soviet transformation of informal economies from complex transactions based on *blat* with long time horizons, to more quid pro quo transactions with short time horizons, such as bribery, vote buying, and other forms of exchange.[92]

Curiously, twenty-first-century politicians appealed to the ideals of citizen obligation and responsibility amid the disappearance of the idea of obligation from other areas of life. Scholars and economic actors have noted the relative *absence* of the concept of obligation in postcommunist market relations, in which contract enforcement and rule of law, among others, are not central values.[93] It may be that in this breach, state discourses valuing responsibility and obligation held a certain appeal.

All of this is not only a story about how political economy changes the meanings of political participation. It is also a story about how form matters. Today, the theatrical form chosen for state-led performances plays an important role in tracing new boundaries around the imagined polity. In Aristotelian theater, the form typical of state-led performance, the dramaturge draws spectators into the plot, involving their emotions in the action and leading them to catharsis. By design, this theatrical form creates feelings of community. It may account for some of the political success of Ukrainian president Volodymyr Zelensky, who draws on Aristotelian dramatic forms in both his comedy troupe's patriotic musical performances and for presidential ceremony. Bertolt Brecht described the Aristotelian theater as a form that "wears down [the spectator's] capacity for action."

The dramaturgy of protest tends to follow the conventions of what Brecht described as epic theater, encouraging spectators to face the problems of society and to seek to change them. Epic theatrical forms provoke the audience, "arousing his capacity for action"[94] without necessarily prompting the creation of durable solidarities. The tactics of political opposition in Russia ask people to reflect upon and confront flaws in the system, often by highlighting the absurdity of the regime's demands. By design, they solicit thought, rather than sympathy.

In contrast, by engaging participants in a common experience, command performances in the tradition of dramatic theater create complicity and bonds among participants—even if those bonds turn out to be bonds of political opposition. Writing during the season of protest in Russia in 2011–12, the political scientist Nikolai Petrov noted that such gatherings "turn perfectly loyal voters against their candidate."[95] In Russia and Ukraine, twenty-first-century command performances began as mises-en-scène of democratic institutions, but they end by marking and hardening conceptual boundaries of the demos within national communities. They permit the formation of a "we, the people" as a subset of the polity, identifiable by the presence of bodies on the stage. Gabowitsch writes, "If the liberal grammar risks degrading people's most valued connections by forcing them to act individually, the grammar of attachment potentially collapses into populism, when rules substitute abstract, easily manipulable entities, 'false synonyms' for specific, local common places."[96] In biscuit politics, participation in political theater—whether electoral contests, street demonstrations, or other performances of democratic politics—can be a mechanism for signaling loyalty and a form of conviviality. It also may provide the foundation for the evolution of political forms that may, eventually, more resemble pale versions of fascism than performances of democracy.

 CHAPTER 7

States of Ambiguity

On May 9, 2015, the seventieth anniversary of the end of World War II in Europe, half a million people bearing photographs and Russian flags processed along a central boulevard in Moscow. The photographs they carried were portraits of relatives—fathers and mothers, grandfathers and grandmothers, cousins, brothers, sisters, aunts, and uncles—who had perished as Soviet soldiers in World War II, the Great Patriotic War. Some participants bore standards displaying not photos, but the name of a fallen soldier. The Moscow procession offered a synonym[1] for an initiative that grassroots organizers originally had christened "Immortal Regiment."[2] That initiative had lately attracted the attention, interest, and—like other instances of civic mobilization—participation of the authorities.[3]

The trajectory of Immortal Regiment, a movement to remember the war dead, from its roots as a Siberian local social action to its eventual partial co-option by state agents across the Russian Federation, would come to reflect the paradoxes and ambiguities of social mobilization in an era of political theater. Immortal Regiment, its official imitators, and the controversy that swirled around it in the spring of 2015 crystallized key debates about the nature of political action in both Russia and Ukraine. Those debates turned around the authenticity of political expression and the boundary between state and society. The movement and its Kremlin imitators also highlighted an important advantage of political theater for incumbent political leaders.

Soviet leaders meant for performances to create unicity in meaning and form. Contemporary political theater gives rise to multiple interpretations, creating ambiguity and inspiring doubt.[4]

This chapter narrates the development of Immortal Regiment and its state-led mirror image, interrogating the debates that arose about the movement. It then shows how in Russia and Ukraine, broadly enmeshed relationships between civic associations and state institutions are both a consequence of market pressures and a reason why distinguishing between any state-led and grassroots participation—between political theater and traditional forms of democratic participation—is not a straightforward matter. The chapter concludes with a discussion of the ambiguity and uncertainty that results from performances of political theater, arguing that irony and multiplicity are no longer solely instruments of disenchantment, but also tools of state power.

One Country—One Regiment

In 2015, Immortal Regiment processions occurred in a broader context of attention not only to war memorialization involving Russian state institutions, commercial entities, and societal organizations, but also to death generally—what the Slavicist Maksim Hanukai has described as Russia's "spectral" practices.[5] Two years before, following a sixteen-year campaign by veteran combatant officers to establish a resting place for the country's war dead, a Federal Military Memorial Cemetery had opened just outside Moscow. The sociologist Mischa Gabowitsch recounted how the memorial territory, modeled on Arlington National Cemetery, meant to commemorate the sacrifices of Russia's military but instead had come to be used for the interment only of high-ranking officers who, moreover, had not perished in recent conflicts.[6] Their sites occupied only a tiny fraction of the vast territory of the cemetery. At its opening, the vast expanse mainly lay empty, awaiting the arrival of war dead.

By any measure, Immortal Regiment had enjoyed phenomenal success in the three years since its official inception in the Siberian city of Tomsk.[7] By May 2015, a full 13 percent of those polled by the Russian polling agency VTsIOM said they had personally participated in the initiative, 93 percent said they knew about it, and 96 percent expressed approval of Immortal Regiment.[8] There were good reasons for this. Its originators described Immortal Regiment as a civic initiative, not a movement,[9] and their stated purpose was affective: the "preservation in each family of the personal memory of the generation of the Great Patriotic War."[10]

The organizers' concept was "one country—one regiment."[11] Whether the country in question was the Soviet Union or Russia remained open to interpretation. The initiative would consolidate not only bonds of national identity within the Russian Federation, but also ties among those who shared a common Soviet past. For the organizers, the initiative was apolitical and noncommercial, uniting people "independent of faith, ethnicity, political and other views."[12] They meant for Immortal Regiment to be a genuinely grassroots effort, not a project of the state or any political party or particular interest.

Immortal Regiment found broad and deep resonance among a population long exposed to official commemorations and cinematic representations of the war, but which had had few opportunities for collective expression of personal or family history.[13] The founder of Immortal Regiment poignantly highlighted how people remembered the war and its heavy price—in school, in children's courtyard games, in the stories of family members, and from "the neighbor in the staircase who had drunk everything but his Order of the Red Banner."[14]

Under Soviet rule, some state-led commemorations had focused on individual contributions and loss. The permanent exhibition in Kyiv's National Museum of the History of Ukraine in the Second World War long drew visitors' attention to the lives and sacrifices of persons, rather than only nations and armies.[15] Immortal Regiment processions gave people something different: the chance to participate actively and to declare publicly, "This is my family's story, and it is part of a larger national story."

The anthropologist Serguei Oushakine has written of Russian nationalists' search for "inalienable cultural symbols" like the Great Patriotic War in his analysis of the connections between postcommunist trauma and social memory.[16] Immortal Regiment made a broad social appeal, linking personal and family tragedy and a larger national narrative. Although family stories previously had been absent from most commemoration, representations in popular culture had been part of the fabric of everyday life in Russia for decades. Those cultural references served as touchstones for Immortal Regiment, offering a repertoire of shared, deeply felt meanings.

The logo of Immortal Regiment, a white crane rising out of a red star, was legible to all its participants. The crane evoked the lyrics of a ballad universally known across the country and widely sung and listened to in commemoration of the war dead. The lyrics of "Zhuravli" were lines penned by the Dagestani poet and translator of Russian classical verse Rasul Gamzatov following a trip to Hiroshima. The poem, translated into Russian and published in 1968, described spirits of soldiers, transformed as white cranes, rising from battlefields. The creators of both the poem and the insignia of Immortal Regiment meant to fashion apolitical expressions of loving memory. People who joined the movement in its early years, and many who later participated, describe feeling precisely such unicity and spiritual connection with fallen kin.[17]

Organizers of Immortal Regiment Moscow seemed to have other goals in mind. On Victory Day in 2015, Russian state television broadcast Immortal Regiment Moscow's participation in that day's celebrations. On screen, Immortal Regiment columns marched under the narration of the cineaste Nikita Mikhalkov and the bombastic media personality and political commentator Vladimir Solov'ev. Their talking points captured in visual imagery the unfathomable shared experience of Soviet people and their heirs. Twenty-seven million Soviet people had fallen in the war; if a minute of silence were to be dedicated to each of them, "the country would fall silent for more than fifty years." If the war dead were to march by the grandstand, day and night, the parade would last nineteen days.[18]

That year, participation in Immortal Regiment extended across the territory of the Russian Federation, with parades in cities across its eleven time zones. On the shores of the Baltic Sea, the lyrics of "Katyusha" rang out in Kaliningrad. Participants raised their voices in unaccompanied song about the love of a faithful girl for her warrior-protector, evoking at the same time the eponymous World War II field artillery. They chanted repeatedly, "Thank you."[19]

More than nine thousand kilometers to the east in a small city overlooking Russia's border with China, forty-five hundred people, many of them children, marched down the streets of Blagoveshchensk. That procession unfolded in the context of extensive local official celebrations, with schoolchildren handing out thousands of St. George's ribbons. A "Victory Trolley" playing films and songs about the war plied the city street. That evening, Russian and Chinese authorities coordinated a fireworks display on both banks of the Amur-Heilongjiang River.[20]

On Russia's southwestern border, in the city of Voronezh, where the front had lingered, and where a single battle in the summer of 1942 had claimed the lives of nearly three hundred thousand Soviet soldiers, eight thousand people participated in the parade. There, many held portraits in their hands rather than on standards.[21] To the north, near Russia's border with Finland, participants paraded down streets in Karelia as part of official celebrations.[22] Parallel to these in-person demonstrations, a movement of virtual commemoration took place as former Soviet citizens across the world posted names and photographs on the initiative website.

In 2015, Immortal Regiment columns also marched beyond the boundaries of sovereign Russian territory. Processions took place across Central Asia, in the Baltic states—now members of the European Union—and in Ukraine. Participants marched in Berlin, New York, Washington, Ottawa, and Toronto. They processed in Tel Aviv, Oslo, Seoul, and other cities. Across the Northern Hemisphere, standard-bearing participants displayed photographs of Soviet soldiers and St. George's ribbons, waved Soviet flags, and sang "Katyusha." Internationally, as across Russia, in each city the announced purpose of the processions was the same: expression of personal, even private memory of loved ones and appreciation and respect for their sacrifice.

Symbols used by Immortal Regiment were, at that particular moment in time, hardly politically neutral. In 2015, the backdrop to the Victory Day parade was the war in Ukraine's Donbas, which brought with it not only frequent projections in Russian media about so-called fascists in power in Kyiv, but also the half-secret repatriation of Russian soldiers' remains.[23]

The St. George's ribbon, a decoration that conjured both Imperial Russian and Soviet World War II–era associations, accompanied participants from Khabarovsk to Toronto.[24] During the previous year's celebration, it had adorned the uniform of every participant in the military parade across Red Square. For some, the ribbon's subsequent ubiquity as a fashion accessory may have emptied it of meaning. For many others, the ribbon expressed allegiance to a particular vision of politics and to the party with which Vladimir Putin was associated, United Russia.[25] A Moscow-based blog argued that "the powers speak completely openly: a renewed cult of Victory should become a 'civic religion,' 'a crystallization point' of the Russian political nation, and 'St. George's ribbons' a sign of belonging to the 'Putin majority.'"[26] For anthropologist Oushakine, the ribbons both connected people and were empty signifiers acting as substitute for memory that people invested with various meanings.[27]

In Ukraine, the St. George's ribbon had taken on a very specific meaning.[28] There, pro-Russian proxy locals and Russian special forces alike had adopted the St. George's ribbon as symbol of their cause. Its colors were so unmistakably linked to the Russian annexation of Crimea, the conflict in the Donbas, and the provocateurs who traveled to eastern Ukrainian cities in spring 2014 that some in Ukraine had come to refer to people wearing those colors as "*Kolorady*"—Colorado potato beetles, the black-and-orange-backed scourge of Russian and Ukrainian summers that arrive in droves in spring. In the context of the war, the ribbon provoked verbally violent responses that seemed to reference the repertoire of techniques even children knew for eliminating the garden pests: "Burn them, crush their tanks."[29] When in early summer of

2014, scores of people died in the Black Sea port of Odesa in a deliberately set fire in the labor unions' building, some Russian reports, as well as a widely circulated internet meme, suggested that as smoke consumed offices and asphyxiated those inside, certain members of the crowd outside had shouted "burn, Colorado, burn."[30]

A Nauseatingly Distasteful Spectacle

While May 2015 brought a previously unimaginable breadth to participation in the Immortal Regiment movement, it also brought, amid a complex symbolic landscape, accusations of fakery, recrimination, and state capture. Despite its explicitly civic mission, Immortal Regiment could not escape the authorities' warm embrace. Vladimir Putin, the head of state, marched in the first rows of the Immortal Regiment procession during Victory Day celebrations in Moscow. No special fanfare accompanied him, but his participation was featured on state television.

Some immediately discounted the significance of Putin among those leading the procession. If the head of state wanted to participate as a citizen, where else would he march but in the first row?[31] When interviewed for television afterward, the president spoke of his happiness at having his soldier father with him that day on Red Square, if only in a photograph.[32] He added that "the value of this initiative is that it was born not in offices, not in administrative structures, but in the hearts of our people. It shows that respect with which we regard the generation that defended the country."[33] On state television, a commentator noted the absence of symbols of political parties in the procession: "This is truly a people's movement [*narodnoe dvizhenie*]."[34]

In the provinces, indications soon emerged that some participation in the initiative that year had been vigorously organized by local figures eager to please the Kremlin—and that some standard bearers were partaking in commemoration of a broadly social, rather than a personal or family memory.[35] Some stories came to light in the friction created when organizers in some localities kept people from participating in the processions. After an incident in a small administrative center of Voronezh region in which organizers prevented some local residents from joining the parade, a reporter commented,

> And a young mom is right to ask me: for whom was this holiday conceived, for whom was such a wonderful tradition born? For bureaucrats? For "window dressing" and governors' video reports—they say,

look what BEAUTIFUL and organized columns we had! Everything is spic and span for the television image: the people exultantly remember their heroes! Yes, the organizers from Buturlinovka really put in maximum effort, you have to give them that. Probably the schoolchildren and the production workers in the columns felt a spiritual lift. But what about all the others?[36]

Suggestions that some processions had been composed not mainly of local residents but rather of others who had come to participate in a performance also appeared indirectly and, it would seem, inadvertently in the narratives of participants. Suspicions of state complicity extended beyond hints of local bureaucratic enthusiasm or observations about the participation of politicians in the processions. On May 8, in a village of the Russian Far East near the city of Khabarovsk, a band of schoolchildren and adults, including young girls costumed in Red Army uniforms, had paraded through village streets carrying flowers and photographs. A local organizer reported that the parade received a warm reception from the local population. She observed that "after the passage of the columns one of the village residents came up to me and said she had seen her father on one of the signs and asked to be photographed with it."[37] Indeed, shortly after the televised Victory Day procession, a series of photos concerning Immortal Regiment appeared in virtual space; the photos appeared to suggest some participants had carried not photos of their relatives, but standards bearing the image of soldiers unrelated to them. An image of a pile of standards seemingly tossed aground in a corner after the procession caught some observers' imagination and ignited a verbal firestorm in Russian social media. Reports—quickly denounced as themselves "fake"[38]—that people on the state payroll had been bused in and paid 300 rubles for participation in a "paid fake gathering" (*oplachennaia massovka*) added fuel to the fire.[39]

Some expressed skepticism that it could be possible to orchestrate such an event. From their point of view, it was savagery to imagine that people's tragic family histories could be targets for such manipulation. One commenter offered as proof that the processions were genuine the observation that "they were with children, which is very important, because at the fake mass Crimean demonstration there was not a single child: people don't bring children to work."[40]

The sheer enormity of the affront dominated responses to suspicions and accusations of fakery or hints that the initiative might not, in fact, be a grassroots movement. Official sources and ordinary people alike expressed outrage at the accusation that participants had not been sincere in their acts, while those persuaded that some of the Victory Day processions had been orchestrated by administrative structures expressed revulsion at the idea that their personal memories of dead parents and grandparents had been violated.

Those who saw in the processions a Kremlin project had expressed disgust not at the movement itself but at the idea of the craven use of painful family memories—a fact that seemed to pass unnoticed by those who offered criticism in trolling attacks. In a blog entry for radio station Ekho Moskvy, the journalist Evgenii Kiselev wrote, "On May 9 I celebrated my Victory Day—not that nauseatingly distasteful and thoroughly false spectacle that our rulers arranged, that sucked people's memory about the war like a leech."[41] On air, the journalist and opposition figure Ksenia Larina declared of the use of photographs that had been "held like shovels" by people who had no relationship to them, "It's worse than profanity. It's a stinking cliché. Imitation. It's using people."[42] Some outrage emanated from the fact that for some, the popular character of Immortal Regiment had provided a contrast or a counterpoint,[43] rather than a complement, to official politics and celebrations, to the "new tanks, rocket launchers, hundred and fifty airplanes over the Kremlin."[44]

To many, the idea of Immortal Regiment as a contrast to official commemoration seemed intuitive. It mirrored a binary that long had characterized popular understandings of Victory Day commemorations: there were official public celebrations organized by Moscow—or there were not, as had been also been the case[45]—and there were initiatives and commemorations organized at the local level. At times, members of an older generation whose life experience included the war and postwar years publicly bemoaned the former. Vladislav Gubskii, a seventy-year-old professor of journalism at Tomsk State University,[46] wrote, "From year to year the important, the natural meaning of this holiday departs together with the inevitable, gradual departure from life of those people [veterans of the war]. It is turning into some kind of masquerade in which young people portray soldiers of a far-off war; the holiday is becoming an excessively organized, pompous, formal event [*meropriiatie*] that politicians, 'official figures,' and the current opposition use for their own aims."[47] But despite this contrast between, as Gabowitsch has written, "the powers and the people, private and public discursive regimes, owners and renters of the ideological 'apartment,'" state-society linkages for Soviet-era Victory Day commemorations were more complex than the binary would suggest.[48]

This was the case for Immortal Regiment. Organizers of the initiative later revealed that they indeed had encountered attempts at state capture.

They responded by publicizing examples of offenses against the nonpolitical character of the movement. As Gabowitsch also has noted, on the initiative's website, a tongue-in-cheek section entitled "Hauptwache," or military jail, enumerated a limited number of infractions of their charter rules: "It's obvious that if the Charter is broken, if people, especially schoolchildren, are put in the regiment on the ninth of May by order or a 'please kindly,' if bureaucrat or politician 'generals' appear in the Regiment, if the Regiment becomes a background for political advertisement, party logotypes and movements—the Regiment will cease to be a people's initiative."[49] Seeking to preserve the social character of the initiative and following reports that in the regions people were being offered salaried work to participate, organizers wrote to President Putin with a filial appeal "as grandchildren and great-grandchildren of soldiers to the son of a soldier"[50] for protection from absorption into state structures.[51] The president responded in Russian media, issuing a warning of his own that cautioned against the "bureaucratization" of Immortal Regiment.[52]

Blue Maidan

People across Russia and the world had embraced the mission of Immortal Regiment. But despite the movement's exclusively affective goals nearly universally shared among the population, questions about whether processions had been a performance gained traction in public discourse to the point of compelling a response from the authorities.

Doubts about the authenticity of Immortal Regiment were not unique to the initiative. After the dissolution of the Soviet Union, associational life in both Russia and Ukraine had taken on a variety of forms, even as some people shunned organized associations.[53] Some grassroots movements pursued, and achieved, concrete goals.[54] Other nongovernmental organizations existed only on paper, while some putatively independent associations were in fact deeply embedded in state networks. Meanwhile, as the new millennium advanced, observers saw social organizations that were direct descendants of Soviet-era associations as "decorative institutions" existing solely to collect the dues of their members.[55]

As the years wore on, people across former Soviet space developed repertoires of communication and interaction that transcended conventional organizational forms and generated new forms of community.[56] The sociologist Tatiana Barchunova has described the evolution of Total Dictations, another Siberian civic initiative later subject to Kremlin attempts at appropriation, which brings people together across Russia and the globe to sit and handwrite dictated texts in Russian.⁵⁷ Movements included communities across ideological spectra, spreading horizontally across space while existing in a relationship Gabowitsch describes as "parasitical on, or a response to, a repertoire deployed by the state."⁵⁸

Still other social mobilizations bore a formal resemblance to traditional civic activism but included practices typical of political theater. Gatherings orchestrated by the authorities had long been a feature of political mobilization in post-Soviet space, and pro-regime demonstration had become an increasingly common feature of the political landscape of the previous decade.⁵⁹ As political scientists Scott Radnitz has shown in Kyrgyzstan and Graeme Robertson has analyzed in Russia, apparent grassroots protests sometimes were elite-led protests coordinated by state actors with members of the public as paid extras.⁶⁰ The presence of associations as performance, together with the muddled relationship between state and society expressed in those movements, influenced public perceptions of civic engagement and the environment in which genuine efforts at civic engagement developed.

The frequency of gatherings said by some to be elite-led projects had accelerated as the Putin government responded to the threat of "color revolutions" that roiled post-Soviet space in the first few years of the new millennium.⁶¹ In Russia, large groups of people who took to the streets in all temperatures to show their support for the president grew to be such a frequent occurrence that, a decade into the new millennium, they had a name. Detractors baptized pro-regime demonstrations "Putings," an amalgam of Putin and *miting*, or demonstration, and used the term to distinguish social movements orchestrated from above from grassroots mobilization.⁶²

Across the border in Ukraine, pro-regime movements traced a similar trajectory across city squares in the first decade of the new millennium. Whereas in Russia, a single party stood behind most official demonstrations, in Ukraine, various political parties organized public manifestations. As a result, questions enveloped perceptions of even the most fervently consummated protests.⁶³ Even Ukraine's "Revolution of Dignity," which had led to the flight of President Viktor Yanukovych and which many participants understood to be a pure distillation of philosophical commitment to positive European values, provoked suspicion in the provinces. On Maidan, protesters had burned automobile tires. For most people in Ukraine in 2014, a tire was an expensive commodity. Far from the capital, people wondered who must stand behind the demonstrations, for there was "so much money in those piles of tires."⁶⁴

Incumbent politicians most often used the techniques in question, but opposition parties also adopted them. For years, reports abounded in Ukraine of both Party of Regions and Fatherland party supporters paid to demonstrate in the capital city.⁶⁵ Certain higher-level actors, meanwhile, understood that they would be rewarded later with political posts or factory ownership for their participation in the oppositions' street orchestrations.⁶⁶ By autumn 2013, such techniques had been refined and used to such an extent that political parties at first offered rent-a-crowd participants in the city of Dnipropetrovsk time-and-a-half if they were "subjected to beatings,"⁶⁷ and opposition recruiters were said to visit southwestern borderland villages to offer short-term jobs to young people willing to travel to Kyiv to protest on Maidan.⁶⁸

A common perspective on the nature of pro-regime demonstrations had earlier crystallized in a photo essay titled "Holubyi Maidan," or Blue Maidan, published on the website of the newspaper *Ukrains'ka Pravda* during the 2007 crisis that followed then-president Viktor Yushchenko's decree dissolving the Ukrainian parliament.⁶⁹ The title was a reference to the Party of Regions supporters who, to protest that decree, had taken to the streets of Kyiv. Maidan had been a central gathering point for the massive Orange demonstrations that had taken place just two years before and for the nationalist protests of previous years. Seven years later, it would become the site of the mass violence that would shake Kyiv and, ultimately, the international state system. In the photo essay, among the photographs of people waving blue flags and banners was a picture taken by the photographer as he pointed the camera at the ground. The image was of cobblestones. If one looked closely, the husks of sunflower seeds were visible in the cracks among the stones.⁷⁰

This photo conveyed a simple story: Party of Regions protesters had consumed the sunflower seeds and then spat the husks onto the hallowed ground of Maidan. Such an image attributed a Soviet identity and cultural background of those who had come to protest the decree—and suggested that "Blue" visitors to Kyiv from the east had treated the city like a Soviet train station. The message of the photo corresponded to a widespread belief among some members of the Orange constituency that the Party of Regions protesters were participating in an "artificial" political action, that the demonstrators had come to Maidan because they had been paid for their time, and not because they believed in a cause. It encapsulated a trope about two Ukraines—one liberal, democratic, Western-leaning, and one clinging to Soviet-era mentalities and practices yet ready to receive financial compensation for participation—that continued for years to saturate discourse about the country outside Ukraine and in some circles within it.⁷¹

According to this interpretation, superficial similarities between mass mobilizations in 2004 and 2013–14 and the far smaller gatherings of 2007 belied a fundamental difference between the two: the first were expressions of voluntary civic participation,[72] while the other was ostensibly motivated by economic interest, rather than principled political conviction.[73] As one observer noted at the time, "[Pro-regime] protests taken in the West as signs of grassroots political passion are often more a matter of dollars and cents." In Ukraine in 2007, this meant that individual participants were paid about 130 UAH (twenty-six dollars) to attend demonstrations in Kyiv for a day.[74] The idea of compensation was one of the elements that had outraged some observers about the possibility that some people had been paid or compelled to participate in Immortal Regiment. Accepting money in return for expression of respect for the dead was vulgar, even unimaginable.

Apart from presuming to adjudicate the epistemologically slippery question of personal intent, such interpretations ignored the real, as opposed to rumored, organizational role of both domestic and foreign entities in mass protest.[75] Even the Orange mobilizations in Ukraine, where national politicians had stood at the epicenter, had been the result both of an outpouring of voluntary public support and of tight orchestration in which protest entrepreneurs with experience in mobilization during the Soviet period had played a central role.[76] Chief among the architects of the mass demonstrations had been Taras Stets'kiv and Volodymyr Filenko, themselves members of the national legislature.[77] Stets'kiv, Filenko, and others had set and met quotas for public mobilization, created scripts and staging for protest events, coordinated action with youth organizations, and planned and executed marches, rallies, and other mass demonstrations. Their stage management of the rallies gave those events the "appearance of popular celebrations."[78] The atmosphere of freedom that many who participated in the Orange demonstrations described had been possible only because of context of careful, deliberate operational planning by individuals who inhabited both civic and state roles.

Immortal Regiment was hardly the first civil society initiative or social movement in the region to have encountered questions about the nature of people's participation or involvement with political parties in power. The notion that some people might have been pressured or paid to participate in Immortal Regiment processions seemed credible to some, and raised anxieties for others, in part because of the proliferation of dramaturgy in the political life of both countries in the twenty-first century. Suspicions about state capture of Immortal Regiment arose in part from obvious signs of appropriation, but also from people's understanding of the way civil society worked in Russia at that time. In a regional context where decades of public gatherings across the political spectrum had involved state actors and, lately, remuneration, it was not difficult for some observers to believe that some participants in Immortal Regiment might have been organized, pressured, or paid for. This uncertain belief would be the beginning, not the end, of ambiguities that would serve the interests of parties of power.

Or Risk Living Badly

For many onlookers, the possibility that Immortal Regiment had been captured by Kremlin interests did not greatly distinguish it from many other civic associations. Associations long had experienced state influence not only through direct political interference, but also through funding mechanisms. Direct remuneration for participation in demonstrations was not politicians' only path of influence on groups of everyday citizens. Wherever people tried to work together to solve society's problems, the same economic pressures that drove some to participate in electoral political theater also brought the state back into civic life. People cooperated not because they necessarily shared the programmatic or ideological perspectives of incumbent political parties or politicians, but because they were exposed to pressures of survival in market economies, and sometimes local politicians were there to help. This had implications for how people understood and evaluated state involvement in civic organizations.

State influence on associational life was not an all-or-nothing proposition. Genuinely grassroots organizations that brought people together to tackle real-world problems could nonetheless encounter pressure from local bureaucrats or politicians. Anxieties about state co-optation were part of broader structural features of associational life in the region; underlying those anxieties was a political economy that nudged societal actors toward cooperation with state agents for want of other options.

Amid the political, economic, and social chaos left in the wake of the dissolution of the Union, some people had sought to create civic organizations in order to improve their standard of living. Civic associations often sought funding not only to support operational activities but also to secure a stable salary.[79] Some organizations were created solely for the purpose of obtaining financial support. Postsocialist civic organizations entered the vernacular in the form of such aphorisms as "One actor is a monologue. Two is a dialogue. Three is an NGO."[80] Here, neo-Tocquevillian traditions reigned, but with a market twist: association was valuable because it generated social capital, and the meaning of social capital was primarily linked to the access it provided to material goods.[81]

Postsocialist labor markets changed economic opportunity structures for some, both driving people to organize and imposing time and financial constraints on their abilities to do so.⁸² People struggling with the increased labor burden of multiple jobs and, in some cases, the demands of growing their own food had an incentive to join organizations that might offer access to economic goods, as trade unions and other organizations had done during the Soviet period.⁸³ At the same time, amid the collapse of public-sector employment and newly discriminatory labor markets, women, scientific workers, and many others lost access to regular income streams. Interest-based NGOs often were left with a narrow dues base and could not pay for programmatic activities.⁸⁴

Meanwhile, stringent and seemingly arbitrary regulatory and tax regimes compelled many civic associations to keep their operational costs low, avoiding major projects. Some commentators attributed the situation to rules that starved civic associations of resources:

> The status of a "nonprofit organization" in Ukraine means the absence of even a minimal item of income: holding charitable fairs, selling your own goods, and so on—even in the case when the received funds go toward prescribed activity. In this way, NGOs turn out to be radically unviable and weak, as far as they completely depend on the availability of a benefactor and his moods. With this policy the state drives NGOs into survival mode, which ensures it relative calm: no one is particularly fooled—everyone's au courant [*usi pry dili*].⁸⁵

In some cases, the state fostered its own legitimacy by according some minimal support to civil society—all the while creating obstacles that prevented third-sector institutions from generating credible challenges to state power.

In subsequent years, the Kremlin would co-opt and support movements and organizations that otherwise might pose a threat to the regime.⁸⁶ Adept and well-connected civic organizations, so long as they did not address themes that could be seen as challenging powerful interests, could turn this strategy to their own benefit. As the director of one such organization in Russia put it, "I don't fight with the state. I take advantage of power."⁸⁷

Members of civic organizations in both countries lived in the awareness that, at some point, they might need to turn to the state for funding. This awareness shaped the choices they made about the character of the work they undertook and the links they forged with other civic associations. Even organizations relying primarily on private or foreign support acted with a possible future relationship with state structures in mind. For Ukrainian associations, "even those who call themselves 'social organizations' are certain that it's simpler to make an arrangement with the authorities than to engage the genuine support of the public."⁸⁸

The funding opportunities available to civic organizations thus encouraged persistent close links with state institutions.[89] In some cases, this meant that state representatives who controlled civic organizations' purse strings could mobilize those organizations for political theater.[90] At a chapter meeting of a women's organization in a small Ukrainian settlement between Kharkiv and Poltava in 2000, one convener reminded the group that the head of district state administration had enjoined female enterprise directors to become part of the national organization, remarking that otherwise they risked "living badly."[91]

Reliance on state funding bound the fortunes of civic associations to those of specific political elites and political parties. At the same time, the fiscal condition of many civic associations remained unstable because of periodic political campaigns against NGOs. Some politicians and bureaucrats thought of civil society as destructive opposition.[92] The government "attack on 'grant eaters'" (*hrantoidy*) under Kuchma, like Russian legislation at about the same time, targeted Ukrainian civic organizations that received funds from abroad.[93] Civic associations faced a choice: either foster a closer relationship with politicians and bureaucrats, potentially submitting to ideological control, or risk dissolution for lack of resources.

In Ukraine, this was true at the local level across the political spectrum. After the 2004 Orange demonstrations, at a moment in Ukrainian politics when many had expected the flourishing of associational life and for political institutions to be more open to civic participation and input, civic organizations in eastern Ukraine providing genuine services to marginalized groups became the target of harassment by state officials. The officials in question were newly appointed to government jobs in recognition of their political service, not their expertise. Career public servants complained "they're not specialists [*ne fakhivtsi*]" but were awarded positions "because they stood on the Maidan and are being compensated for their revolutionary work."[94] As one new district-level official put it, "the president, in thanks, appointed me to this position."[95]

Harassment of civic associations likewise took place under different political administrations and took a number of forms. After the Orange demonstrations in the city of Kharkiv, this included repossession of computer and other equipment obtained from state agencies through a competitive grant process, demands for recertification and relicensing of long-established organizations, and even unannounced "checks" (*proverki*) at a shelter for women seeking to free themselves from domestic violence (such shelters are, of necessity, at undisclosed locations and do not ordinarily receive visitors).

A newly installed local politician had instigated those checks, believing that the shelter in question was unnecessary because, in his view, domestic violence was a "family issue" rather than a matter for societal or government concern. The leader of one service provision organization was concerned: "The situation for women has gotten worse. We have to start again from zero."[96]

Over time, as harassment of civic associations in both countries continued and, in Russia, intensified, organizations lost resources or were absorbed into state institutions.[97] In some people's eyes, the resulting blurring of boundaries between state and societal actors hollowed out many civic associations, and civic organizations' relationship with state structures remained complex and fraught. Without the means or independence to conduct programmatic activities, associations could become instruments of political parties who controlled institutions of the administrative state, rather than conduits of societal interests.

Social scientists observing Eastern Europe from the Americas in the late 1980s had drawn a clear distinction between state and society.[98] Autonomous and semiautonomous societal organizations had played an important role in weakening state socialism, and many analyses of civil society in Russia and Ukraine took a critical approach to the role the state might play in supporting civic engagement.[99] These analyses saw societal organizations as necessarily in opposition to the state.[100] Others observed that civil society was not, in this regional context, the exclusive domain of societal action.[101] Instead, it was a space in which state and societal actors interacted to produce government-organized NGOs,[102] state-funded civic organizations, and a variety of other hybrid forms of social association.[103] In such contexts, civil society could and often did imply partnership or another type of close relationship with state institutions or with international governance organizations.

Such partnership did not mean that such organizations served no social function. Rather, the specific way in which they were embedded in local and national political, social, and economic relationships differed from that of their counterparts in the West, some of which also received state support. When it came to funding from international sources, some felt the situation resembled that of a postcolonial polity, with highly fraught, power-laden, and complex relationships between local organizations and their supporting institutions in North America and elsewhere in Europe.[104] Against that backdrop of concerns about sovereignty, some in Russia and Ukraine saw a close relationship with state structures as lending legitimacy to their activities, rather than necessarily undermining that legitimacy. In this context, accusations that pro-regime demonstrations had been bought and paid for could readily be met with a shrug and "what about the support that other groups received?"

Neither Beasts of Burden nor Goats

What kinds of questions were people asking about Immortal Regiment, how did those questions frame the issues, and what are the political implications of those questions? It seemed nearly impossible, as Vladimir Putin marched at the head of the endless-seeming ranks of Immortal Regiment in Moscow in 2015, to imagine that other state representatives were not somehow involved in the movement. But had participants in Immortal Regiment, even those who may have received encouragement from superiors at work, really been actors playing a part? Were they, as in the lyrics of the band GreenJolly that had become the unofficial anthem of participants in Ukraine's Orange Revolution a decade before, "beasts of burden" or "goats"?[105]

The original meaning of the epithets in that protest song referred to Viktor Yanukovych's descriptions of his political opponents. In the Russophone prison slang that punctuated Yanukovych's speech as a politician, "goats" were prisoners who collaborate with the authorities. Protesters sang that they were children of Ukraine, not animals. This clearly articulated choice between collaborator or resisting subject echoed a dualism dominant in the scholarly literature. It framed interpretation in a way that generated enthusiasm for the movement but did not reflect the complex motivations for people's participation.

Where some observers and participants saw political theater, others saw an expression of grassroots politics. From one perspective, the co-opted movement was a mise-en-scène, a mere representation of civic engagement. From another, the movement continued to reflect sincere popular sentiment despite the involvement of the authorities. As a movement that provoked varying interpretations of its authenticity, Immortal Regiment illuminated complex relationships between state and society in contemporary Russia and disagreements about what constitutes real political participation.

In 2015, those who took Immortal Regiment as uniquely a social movement or expression of civic sentiment missed important aspects of the movement's broader meaning. As had been the case for many other demonstrations during this period, signs of payment and pressure were present in some processions. But those who viewed Immortal Regiment as an entirely co-opted symbol of state power likewise misapprehended its significance. Participants across Russia reported deep emotional engagement as they participated in the processions and as they prepared photographs to carry, connecting both with memories of their kin and family members who located, shared, and reproduced portraits for the marches.[106]

Participation in pro-regime demonstrations, after all, did not always translate into pro-regime behavior in other domains. In one study, only 70 percent of participants in pro-Putin demonstrations reported voting for Putin, and only 59 percent reported voting for United Russia.[107] Further, pro-regime demonstrations drove some people away from support for incumbents. As the political scientist Nikolai Petrov has argued, compelling people to stand out in the cold not only failed to encourage sympathy for the regime but also habituated people to using demonstrations as a way of solving problems.[108]

Immortal Regiment was no ordinary social movement. Its stated goals were affective and expressive: rather than seeking to achieve explicit policy goals, its activities sought to strengthen national bonds. Through people's participation in a series of discursive practices, it marked the boundaries of political community. As in most large gatherings of human beings, it encapsulated multiple genres in the same form. In 2015, Immortal Regiment was both *massovka* (a crowd scene) and an expression of individual sentiment.

In this respect, Immortal Regiment resembled examples of political theater elsewhere in post-Soviet space. The ambiguities associated with Immortal Regiment in 2015 were part of a broader historical and cultural landscape in which elements of the state and the social coexist in a complex, overlapping, and often vaguely defined equilibrium.[109]

Whether highly choreographed or improvised, political theater drew upon multiple constituencies: true believers, paid or pressured participants, and people who saw their interests as aligned with the political party under whose banner they stood, regardless of payment or pressure.[110] Some people fell into all these categories. Some understood the mechanisms of organization as signals of coercion or signs of authoritarian control, while many others saw only genuine feeling expressing itself, at long last, through a true grassroots movement.

In the case of Immortal Regiment, controversy about the nature of participation also distilled broader debates about representation: how do observers or participants distinguish between performance and the practice being performed, between signified and signifier? Imitation had long characterized aspects of politics in Russian politics. The eighteenth-century Crimean facades that, according to legend, were constructed by Prince Potemkin to impress Empress Catherine II in her travels on the peninsula after its annexation from the Ottoman Empire were but one early example of artifice in the region.

Historians have suggested Potemkin villages were more legend than reality. But debates about the veracity of the original story nonetheless crystallize the frictions and ambiguities embedded in concepts referring to gaps between external appearances and underlying realities.[111] Where should scholars draw the line between artifice and embellishment? Between embellishment and mere decoration? Wherein lies the distinction between deception and aspiration, or between artifice and representation? Where performance is persuasive, how do observers form judgments about what they are seeing?

In the practice of politics, these debates gained political salience over time. As observers came to use vocabularies associated with political theater to describe political institutions, including electoral practices and elite-led and elite-captured social movements, political analysis became bound up in disputes about which parties have the authority to define what is real or true.[112] Across the political spectrum, politicians and others increasingly referred to such concepts to accuse their opponents of inauthenticity.[113]

Some analyses of Russian politics have critiqued the failure to examine the effects of pro-regime demonstrations or the opinions of participants.[114] The sociologist Mischa Gabowitsch has critically observed that in the context of social movements in Russia, recent analysis has tended to view participation through the lens of coercion or state-led orchestration,[115] while the historian Stephen Kotkin has asked, "Must social movements be nonstate or anti-state to be 'real'?"[116]

As Vladimir Putin and five hundred thousand of his countrymen processed along Tverskoi Boulevard, where did society end and the state begin? For both observers of and participants in Immortal Regiment, answers to this question may have been far from obvious. Decades of scholarship in Russian history and politics have relied on clear distinctions between these two spheres, even while recognizing both their fusion during periods of totalitarian rule[117] and the necessarily shifting and contingent nature of their relationship.[118] Numerous recent studies have alluded to the problems engendered by this separation, and a small number of authors have attempted to conceptualize Russian political, economic, and social spheres in systemic terms, mirroring vernacular vocabularies of power.[119]

Yet amid the absence of a widely accepted alternative to conceptual categories of state and society, that analytical separation lingers, with theoretical frameworks used in scholarship positing distinct, opposing poles between which people might move. These frameworks are particularly open to interpretations that posit social behavior as either collaborative with or resistant to state agents. A small number of historians and anthropologists have taken a different tack,[120] but a version of this binary has dominated both studies of contemporary politics and Soviet historiography, especially of the Stalinist period: after decades of scholarship on totalitarianism that emphasized instruments of state repression and uncomplaining, long-suffering publics successfully socialized to those instruments, a revisionist turn posited not quiescent, but quietly resisting subjects.[121] Portrayals of those subjects, as the historian Anna Krylova and others have argued, may have reflected the preoccupations of the liberal democratic West even more than the self-understandings of Soviet subjects themselves.[122]

A focus on debates around ideal types—the collaborator, the resister—and what their presence may tell us about the nature of a political events may distract from the broader significance of those events. As previous chapters of this book have shown, most people who participate in political theater do so because of their economic circumstances. For many, the issue of whether or not to participate is easy to resolve; the answer is so obvious that this does not even trouble the mind as a question.

In such a context, attempts to determine the "true" nature of a performance pose considerable methodological and epistemological difficulty. More than that, is whether a performance "true" the right question? Not all political theater is obviously artifice, and participants in mass political action may be neither beasts of burdens nor goats, nor committed liberal subjects. But whether or which they are may be beside the point: the significance of contemporary political theater may lie elsewhere, not in the specific motivations or internal dispositions of its actors, but in the effects of performance on cast and audience alike.

In other words, if the questions we ask about political theater have to do with whether performance is false, or whether it is coerced, we may risk missing the point—and the politics—underlying the participation in the performance. Given that even people's own knowledge of their intentions can be murky and multiple, it may not be realistic to expect empirical resolution of questions about the authenticity of performance. Thinking about command performance in terms that emphasize adjudication of what is real or true may mean failing to take seriously the more complex motivations of actors on the stage.

Further, in the context of Russian politics, the very debate "Are state-led performances popular mobilizations or not?" may play into state-led efforts that cast doubt on the idea of a stable universe of facts.[123] The identification of this question as the key debate can be an example of reflexive control, the process by which a combatant sets the terms of decision-making such that his opponent voluntarily selects the desired outcome.[124] As Serguei Oushakine has observed in his analysis of Soviet dissident texts, even an apparently oppositional position can partake in and implicitly support regime goals because it "shared the symbolic field with the dominant discourse: it echoed and amplified the rhetoric of the regime, rather than positioning itself outside or underneath it."[125] In other words, the "real or not-real" debate is helpful to Kremlin dramaturges. It turns our attention away from the most important function of political theater in contemporary society: the production of ambiguity and, with it, the destabilization of people's sense of and trust in their own perceptions.

A Debilitating Level of Uncertainty

A short clip titled "Poor Americans" illustrates the doubt that political theater can introduce—doubt that can be both productive and, ultimately, dangerous for parties of power. In the summer of 2018, a group of Russian women of a certain age gather in a sunny courtyard. Before a camera, one woman begins to cry, covering her face with her palms and then wiping tears from her eyes. "Oh girls," she says, I feel so sorry for the Americans. The poor working people, they lost everything." Another woman comforts her: "Don't cry, everything will be fine. Putin will absolutely help them. He helps everyone, he will absolutely help the Americans too." The others agree, urging her not to be upset. She continues: "We hope so. . . . You watch on television—I sit and cry. I feel so bad for them."[126]

During the final moments of this scene of lamentation, the smallest, eldest woman, the video recording's protagonist, casts a brief glance toward the viewer. Her eyes flit to meet those of the onlooker, then she immediately looks back to the group. An attentive viewer may wonder: Is she an actor, and is this moment a brief break in the fourth wall? Is this irony, a sarcastic performance about the extent of the Russian president's power? Or a piece of poorly executed propaganda? Or is the elder simply a distraught person caught on video who has paused in her distress to notice a passerby?

Despite what most online commenters saw as the absurdity of the theme at the time and the awkward staging of the episode, the recording left room for a faint sliver of doubt as to its intended meaning. The women's interaction drew on established tropes of late twentieth-century Russian-American relations, reversing the condescension of pity some Americans had felt for Russians at times of economic crisis in the 1990s.[127] After all, at different times in American history, wells of emotion and empathy for Americans had been part of Soviet-era repertoires of international friendship. Following the assassination of President John F. Kennedy, widows in the Soviet Union were said to have sent Kennedy's bereaved wife letters of sympathy accompanied by coins in the envelopes. From a certain point of view, it was not out of the question that good-hearted provincial grandmothers might be concerned about the fate of people they had seen on television.

Analogous ambiguity had been present in some Soviet performances, but ambiguity served a different function then. During the late Soviet period, the form of parody known as *stiob* meticulously imitated official discourse. *Stiob* inhabited accepted forms of communication such that it was difficult to tell whether the performance was emulation or caricature. As the anthropologists Dominic Boyer and Alexei Yurchak have argued, in early twenty-first-century American culture, *The Colbert Report* exemplified a similar kind of embodiment. In late Soviet culture, ambiguity surrounding the meaning of the resulting performance left would-be critics of such performances on unsteady ground: was it praise or ridicule? This created a protective space for ironic critique of the regime.[128]

Contemporary command performances leave open a similar kind of doubt. Without knowledge of the inner worlds of participants—of all of the various, complex, and sometimes contradictory reasons human beings do things—who can say whether flag-waving, pro-regime protesters, pro-regime voters, or weeping grandmothers inhabit the form with sincere enthusiasm, irony (whether for the purposes of parody or safe disagreement), resignation, or something else?[129]

Analyzing *stiob*, Boyer and Yurchak wrote that rather than directly criticizing particular leaders or policies, *stiob* attacked official discourse at a deeper level. It did so in ways that direct critique could not accomplish. Parody "exposed an unspoken truth about late-socialist ideology: that the most important aspect of that ideology was to reproduce fixed forms and phraseology."[130] In this interpretation, form itself, not the content the form promoted, was the point. *Stiob* was an instrument of disenchantment, helping to precipitate "socialism's sudden and spectacular end."[131]

In today's politics, *stiob* traditions remain in the reservoir of interpretative frames available to those who participate in and watch performances of political theater. In his work on Strategy-31, a protest movement associated with the National Bolshevik Party and Another Russia, Mischa Gabowitsch highlights this possibility as he describes a young man who had traveled to the city of Cheliabinsk to participate in a gathering. Gabowitsch recounts his arrival, as the young man asks a member of the local Communist Party whether he belongs to Strategy-31. The "clever guy" responds, "We have come to defend the foundations of the Constitution of the Russian Federation."[132]

But in today's command performances, irony is not only, or not ultimately, an instrument of disenchantment. Instead, parties of power also benefit from ambiguity and doubt. Russian ideologist Vladislav Surkov's emphasis on narrative multiplicity as a tool of destabilization has produced systemic influence beyond the outcome of specific elections (or so he claims), interfering not only in elections, but also in people's minds.[133] The long-standing nondoctrinal, operational concept of nonlinear or hybrid warfare[134] popularized in recent years by Russian Armed Forces chief of staff General Valery Gerasimov likewise involves intentional ambiguity meant to "create a debilitating level of uncertainty."[135] Meanwhile, mirroring tactics used in Russian information warfare rely on mimesis in order to sow confusion.[136]

Political theater's logic of doubt and uncertainty tracks aspects of the Putin government's ideological work at home and abroad. Abroad, it may be reflected most strikingly in former president Donald Trump's campaign to discredit the official results of the 2020 American presidential elections. The theater of state recounts conducted by a private company functions as an instrument for delegitimizing ordinary public recounts under neutral supervision. Performances of democratic institutions, even where they are transparently performances, undermine those institutions because they confuse, introducing doubt about the authenticity of all institutions.

Contemporary political theater opens spaces of ambiguity and dual meaning. State-led performance and grassroots mobilization may be present within the same set of events, whether a march or an election. This means people can mistake grassroots political mobilization for state-led theater. Some might even conclude that opposition is a paid performance. For the dramaturge, this is a feature, not a bug. In some instances, as with Immortal Regiment, the result of this ambiguity is a debate about what is real.

Similar to late Soviet *stiob*, today's performances of political theater exist in mixed semiotic fields, living alongside the forms of political participation they seem to imitate. Imagine a pro-regime paid demonstration and a grassroots protest, each bearing banners for their cause, marching toward one another along the same street. Although participants in each may be dressed differently or belong to different age groups, from a distance the groups resemble one another. Because state-led political theater can so closely mirror the phenomena it seeks to portray, multiple, even conflicting interpretations of the same events are possible. As a result, audiences—and even sometimes participants—can never be entirely certain what, precisely, they are seeing or taking part in.

The simultaneous presence of both democratic institutions and regime-led political theater in the same semantic field thus can produce confusion and doubt. The mere practice of political theater can destabilize perceptions of political participation, producing ambiguity that can be used to discredit citizen engagement and open room for doubt as to the nature of any social mobilization.

Like *stiob*, an ironic relationship to command performance provides the participant something to hide behind, a way of avoiding declaring a position. In social environments characterized by mistrust, irony is more adaptive than sincerity. But even as a retreat from sincerity can mitigate risk, irony also can act as a shield for support of state-led or extremist ideologies. Contemporary extremist groups use ambiguity to spread their ideology while avoiding sanction. As Michiko Kakutani noted in *The Death of Truth*, the neo-Nazi *The Daily Stormer* style guide for websites instructs, "The unindoctrinated should not be able to tell if we are joking or not."[137] And experts in media and communication Alice Marwick and Rebecca Lewis have argued in their study of online extremism and manipulation that ironic use of fascist tropes can lead to the embrace of fascist ideologies.[138]

The hermeneutic polyphony of contemporary political theater highlights an important discontinuity with Soviet official culture. The historian Jan Plamper, writing of Stalin-era Soviet censorship practices, described concerted attempts on the part of the Soviet state to establish singularity (*odnoznachnost'*) and to rid semiotic fields of multiple meanings.[139] In Soviet contexts, clarity and singularity of meaning was a conscious goal of official performance and literature—even as the rigidity of ritual forms itself made possible multiple meanings.[140] Today's emphasis on multiplicity distinguishes contemporary political theater from its Soviet antecedents.

Further, contemporary political theater does not possess the rigidity of either high Stalinism or the late Soviet forms Yurchak described. Its form is flexible and often improvisational. What is required of participants is presence, not precise execution of a prescribed liturgy. As a result, state-led public demonstrations can provoke expressions of emotion that depart from the script, suggesting boredom, contempt, or anxiety. Such expressions are common and can be found in nearly every performance of contemporary political theater. In the Russian city of Voronezh in 2007, students of the history departments of the state university and pedagogical institute milled around a city square with medical workers and others compelled by their supervisors to participate. During the demonstration, a voice that listeners associated with Soviet-era public events boomed from the loudspeakers. The students laughed, provoking a middle-aged passerby to ask them if they were "smoking weed."[141] Videos posted in 2019 by opposition figure Aleksei Navalny's organization include similar examples from the city of Cheboksary and elsewhere.[142] Even as they engage in the politically significant act of obeying their local authorities' instructions, such participants are not acting "as if" they believed in leaders as cult figures, as in the protagonists of Lisa Wedeen's account of the ambiguities of authoritarian spectacle in Assad's Syria.[143] They are unresponsive to power-laden injunctions to smile.

At the same time, because of this multiplicity of affect and meaning, participation in command performances, like late Soviet *stiob*, can disguise the fragility of support for the regimes that stage performances. The dual or multiple meanings of performances for their participants can create a challenge for those who hope to gauge support for incumbent politicians. Widespread cooperation with state-led participation causes a signaling problem. People who assemble on the stage because of economic insecurity may or may not be pleased about their participation. Opposition to parties of power can spread unnoticed among participants, even as they may continue to read the script.

Conclusion
A New Social Contract

Twenty-five years after struggling university students had painted homegrown political slogans on Voronezh city walls, a new theater space opened its doors in the center of that city. The Nikitinsky advertised itself as an experimental repertory theater. Its small troupe of actors, describing themselves as having refused American models of profit-driven artistic production, planned to develop a repertoire as they performed.

In early July 2019, the Nikitinsky invited residents and guests of the city to attend a production that lasted six hours. Ticket holders could come and go as they pleased, viewing performances in progress in several staging areas throughout the theater. The performances would reflect on the meaning of freedom and choice (*vybor*)—specifically, "the big myth about choice." Participants were asked to consider the question "When and at what point in time are you truly making a conscious and free choice?" The company offered its own reflection: "We think that theater is that very territory of freedom. But even here the spectator sits in a seat and views that which the director proposes. You only chose the play: freedom ends there, becoming a spectre in reflection [*prizrak v otrazhenii*] in a simulacrum of freedom."[1]

While urging and teaching participants to think about the meaning of choice (*vybor*) outside the context of an election,[2] the troupe enacted constraints that continue to characterize contemporary politics. Twenty years of command performances had led to the gradual disappearance of the register of choice from official Russian political discourse, but the idea remained, circulating in other forms—here, on a traditional stage, at the center of the meaning of a play. Meanwhile, outside the physical confines of the theater house, in streets and city squares, in polling stations in schools, firehouses, municipal buildings, and village clubs, state agents regularly continued to draw people into command performances.

The message of the Nikitinsky play echoed an article by Putin chief ideologist Vladislav Surkov, published six months before in the daily *Nezavisimaia gazeta*.[3] Surkov depicted not Russia but Western democracies as the seat of political theater, arguing that the "illusion of choice is the most important of illusions, the crowning stunt of the western lifestyle in general and western democracy in part, which already long ago has been more devoted to the ideas of Barnum than to those of Cleisthenes." Surkov went on to describe his own vision of Russian society's refusal of this illusion and pursuit of sovereignty, followed by what he claimed was a "loss of interest in discussions about what democracy should be and whether in principle it should exist." Political theater had become not only a widespread practice, but also a metaphor that both regime and opposition used to advance their case.[4]

This Is Not Dictatorship

What should we call regimes dominated by the practice of command performances? Observers across the globe acknowledge the contradictions implicit in labels widely used to describe contemporary politics, like "illiberal democracy" or "state capitalism," or the analytical limitations and historical elisions of descriptors like "populism." In Russia, the economist Yevgeny Gontmakher asked at the end of 2019, "What stands in opposition to liberal democracy (with all of its shortcomings and problems)? What do we call this rival?" He suggested "Feudalism 2.0" as a name for liberal democracy's current rival.[5]

A positive consensus in response to this question has not emerged, but one thing is clear for many who live on the sands of democracy's low tide. On a Sunday afternoon in the summer of 2017, around a family table in a town in Viktor Orbán's Hungary, conversation turned to the current Hungarian government, where legislative tricks and constitutional reforms have tracked practices in Putin's Russia. As the assembled company debated how to categorize Orbán's style of rule, members of the generation that came of age just after World War II insisted, "We have known dictatorship. This is not dictatorship."[6]

This question of nomenclature is not a new dilemma. Twenty years earlier, writing of Russian young people's attempts to "practically orient themselves within a symbolic space that exceeds the limits of their personal imaginary," the anthropologist Serguei Oushakine identified what he called "post-Soviet aphasia": speechlessness in the face of radical political change. In his telling, speechlessness was accompanied not by silence, as anthropologists working in other contexts previously had observed, but by people's tenacious grip on symbolic elements associated with the Soviet order. Hanging on for dear life in the midst of radical and unexpected shifts, post-Soviet people clung to linguistic repertoires that were familiar to them—even as those repertoires no longer aligned with lived experience.[7]

Like Oushakine's interlocutors, observers of contemporary politics rely on recognizable categories of analysis to describe changing political orders in the twenty-first century. These include regime types such as democracy, authoritarianism, and hybrid regimes, as well as liberalism and its antipodes of conservatism, republicanism, illiberalism, and populism. Such concepts describe elite behavior, the design of institutions, and philosophies that inform contemporary leaders' tactical use of ideology. But they stop short of fully capturing how and where people today experience state power, or of clarifying lived relationships among political, social, and economic spheres. This particular gap between people's experience and the language of social science has implications for our understanding of politics. Russia and Ukraine are widely viewed as occupying different places in regime-type taxonomies. Yet key instruments of explicit political manipulation and control over most people's everyday lives, if not the frequency of their use, are similar in the two countries.

Analyzing the stagecraft and stage management of political theater in twenty-first-century Russia and Ukraine, we can see the local contours of a political shift that is prior to and deeper than regime change. This movement is not from democracy toward authoritarianism or the reverse, but from a relatively inclusive ideal of a social contract between citizens and the state to a politicization of the responsibilities of the state toward citizens. In this shift, membership in the polity based on loyalty to a set of ideals or identities gives way to membership based on fealty to local representatives of specific politicians. The sociologist Bálint Magyar has described the tip of this iceberg, emphasizing the capture of both state and business resources by a small number of families and networks of fictive kin.[8] The political economy of command performance shows that this transformation can extend to involve and affect entire societies.

By staging command performances, local state agents in Russia and Ukraine redefined fulfillment of basic human needs—warmth, light, ideas, health, payment for work—as delivery of privileges the state could provide or withhold based on whether or not people supported politicians or parties of power. For those involved, significant spheres of life came to be subject to a political quid pro quo. These seeds of populist logics of governance, planted around the turn of the millennium, gradually permitted the redefinition of the conceptual boundaries of the polity to include those loyal to leaders, rather than those loyal to countries or constitutions.

Typologies of comparative political analysis often assume that states enact regime types in a more or less uniform fashion across a given territory—even though it has long been understood that authoritarian regimes survive in part because of freedoms and other goods accorded to in-groups. While an emergent literature on subnational authoritarianism argues that subnational units within the same polity may be subject to different types of rule, and that authoritarianism may be constituted at the substate level,[9] this research still portrays regime type and territorial boundaries as coextensive, just at a lower level of administrative aggregation.

At first glance, the practice of political theater may seem to fit within such a framework. The practice of political theater is both strikingly uniform and unevenly distributed across Russia and Ukraine, and command performances operate in nearly identical fashion from one end of this expanse to the other. While the frequency and density of their use vary, the tools politicians use to incite participation seem relatively uniform across space. The institutional contexts for the models of stagecraft described here—factories, farms, hospitals, schools, universities, local government offices, and countless other contexts—are, from Uzhhorod, at Ukraine's boundary with Slovakia and the European Union, to Blagoveshchensk, a border city in Russia's Far East and gateway to China, virtually indistinguishable.

But despite this surprising uniformity in the mechanisms used to elicit participation in command performances, the availability of incentives that drive people to comply with demands to participate in political theater are neither evenly distributed across territory, nor relative to their distance from capital cities.[10] The great subnational spatial variety in whether and how people experience the institutionalized pressure of political theater points in a different analytical direction.[11]

In late twentieth- and early twenty-first-century Ukraine and Russia, the commodification and privatization of public goods opened up new spaces of economic risk. Local elites, given unfunded mandates by their superiors to deliver votes or other forms of political support, exploited those spaces. Today, people's access to income or production factors that can help them buy their way out of politicized public goods and services largely determines whether or not they become actors in that total system.

There are some regional regularities in the prevalence of political theater. As chapters 4 and 5 showed, these regularities track both changes over time in twenty-first-century privatization and decentralization and Soviet legacies of development, which concentrated people and industry in certain places.[12] As a result, political theater flourished in areas that maintained these concentrations and in new *monogorodok*, or company towns, where supervisors could hold people collectively responsible for their community's political behavior.[13] In other areas, changing patterns of municipal development dislodged some of the spatial-political legacies of Soviet planning. There, in rural areas where most people make a living from smallholder agriculture and remittance labor, in small towns with significant service sectors, and in suburbs, the coercion and persuasion that motivate some people's entrance onto the stage were individualized, private, selective, and partial.

Spatially inscribed differences are significant not least because variation in the availability of opportunities to pressure people can affect interpretation of electoral outcomes. In Ukraine, maps of election results during the early 2000s regularly seemed to suggest a divided and polarized country. In the west, voters cast ballots for EU-leaning candidates, while voters in the east and south skewed toward supposedly pro-Russia candidates. At the time, native speakers of the Ukrainian language were concentrated in western regions, while people who often spoke Russian in their daily lives lived in the east and south. Ethno-linguistic identity seemed to predict voting behavior, and observers interpreting those maps focused on that correlation. Ukrainian speakers were pro-European, the logic went, while Russian speakers felt loyalty to Moscow.[14]

Ukrainians' political behavior in the face of Russian aggression would later show that such inferences had been incorrect.[15] What those maps and their interpreters systematically had missed was the underlying political economy of political theater. In certain regions, those red and blue maps represented differences not so much in people's political beliefs as in structural opportunities to pressure people to vote—opportunities of which political parties aligned with presidents Leonid Kuchma and Viktor Yanukovych disproportionately availed themselves. In the industrialized east and south, where many people worked in factories or large farms or attended universities, the boundaries of many work communities overlapped with electoral precincts, and it was easy to bring people to the stage, regardless of their feelings about politics. The same was not true in the land-poor and less industrially developed regions of the west.

Mainly, variation in the practice of political theater does not follow state or administrative lines. It occurs at a much smaller scale. Across the

CONCLUSION

territories of Ukraine and the Russian Federation, people's experiences of interaction with state agents vary not only from region to region, but also from street to street and from household to household. This variation often depends on how local economic institutions interact with the state, and on their specific form of ownership. Some administrative regions are home to many more institutions that call citizens to participation than others, and some people in certain municipalities experience pressure at work, while others do not.

Outside the workplace, the spatially inscribed quality of coercion may disappear. As people leave their places of employment to return home, the identifiable contours separating workplaces where participation in political theater is required from those where it is not morph into a complex lacework in which those subject to coercion are connected to, and may live alongside, others who are not, as neighbors, family members, and friends. Even the immediate neighbors of block apartment buildings or village streets often do not share experiences of coercion or persuasion. Especially in urban areas, some people can be drawn into and their household economies deeply affected by requirements for participation in command performances, while others living nearby are left alone. Imagined as a map projection, people's involvement in command performances is a mottled surface with contours cutting through administrative regions, communities, and families.

Viewing the contours of power in this way, we can see at once expansive opportunities for particular techniques of control and the spotty, uneven use of these techniques. This vision of political power permits us to differentiate among individual experiences, allowing us to see how, as is the case in both Russia and Ukraine, some people may see themselves as living in a society where they have relative freedom, while others experience political control in most areas of their lives.

Because the tools of political theater's stagecraft are parasitic on existing social hierarchies, like those in families and workplaces, state agents can use these tools, leave them, then pick them up again—all without investing substantial resources in their reproduction. Opportunistic politicians can activate mechanisms of control, while others may let them lie temporarily dormant. In twenty-first-century Ukraine, command performances characterized electoral campaigns under Kuchma and Yanukovych but seemed to disappear from national politics under Yushchenko—even as they descended to the level of village council elections. During Yanukovych's second term as prime minister, performances once again came into widespread use at the national scale. The extent and intensity of their use can vary dramatically both from administration to administration and within periods of rule, leading, as the political scientist Henry Hale has argued, to the appearance of cyclical regime change.[16]

People's participation in political theater depends on those intermittent or episodic experiences of pressure. This leads to scattered constellations of experiences of domination, not a single vector of gradual change. Intermittence produces a different kind of fear from the fear usually associated with authoritarian power, where demands for command performance are consistently backed up by threats of physical violence. The price of leaving the theater can be economic insecurity, with ever more tenuous opportunities for employment and access to medical care, education, and necessary infrastructure. But sometimes supervisors do not follow through on threats, and in between elections, participants may live undisturbed. At those times, political theater can resemble the languid stretches of life in the summer cottages of Chekhov's plays, where nothing at all seems to happen.

People do not participate in political theater because of existing political preferences, but they do constitute new political identities through their participation. The communities that emerge from the practice of command performance are not defined by membership in an ethnic or religious group, deeply held convictions, programmatic support, or even by a relationship to place. Instead, participation in political theater traces places of vulnerability and exposure to certain kinds of economic pressure. Some people come to enjoy the full benefits of citizenship because of their loyalty to leaders, while others may find themselves excluded, disenfranchised, or impoverished because of their failure to cooperate.

Unlike regime-type concepts and other theoretical constructs that describe the politics of entire polities, political theater can prompt the development of groups whose boundaries are neither stably nor precisely spatially inscribed. The members of groups cohering around fealty to political elites and groups cohering around choice are not concentrated within the borders of particular states: the conceptual boundaries between them do not neatly correspond to territorial boundaries. Both groups may be found throughout Ukrainian and Russian society, and divisions between them follow no administrative maps. Instead, they cut jagged lines every which way through cities, neighborhoods, streets, and families.[17] Sometimes the practice of political theater may align publics in ways that may seem to coincide with the boundaries of certain kinds of demographic and socioeconomic spaces, as noted in the work of the geographer Natalya Zubarevich.[18] However, because they are produced both through ever-shifting structural constraints and local improvisations and learning, even these apparent boundaries are not stable.

At the same time, the evolution of new techniques and technologies inciting people to participation in command performance are hardening some of those boundaries. In Ukraine, the analyst Mykhailo Chaplyga and the political scientist Volodymyr Fesenko note that as expensive practices of vote buying continue to be used in close races, agitators and multi-level marketers likely will use ministerial databases to target potential supporters who receive pensions and government assistance.[19] Such a future could mean not only more explicit links between fidelity to incumbent politicians and access to social welfare and earned benefits, but also considerably greater opacity in the use of those links. Today, the transactions of political theater can be observed directly by those who take the time and trouble to do so. If the stage management of political theater migrates to the world of algorithms and cyber-intervention, it may be increasingly difficult to see and understand how portions of populations may come to be excluded from the demos and its benefits.

It can be tempting to view citizen mobilization in command performances in Russia and Ukraine as continuous with Soviet traditions of political theater. But the capture of state institutions and the politicization of bureaucracies for the private aims of politicians are better understood in the context of accelerating global processes of enclosure. The economic incentives that move citizens to participate in command performances show us that the dramaturgy and stage management of political theater may be properly understood as the logical political culmination of the privatization movements that began in the region at the end of the Soviet period. The practice of political theater has extended the life of those movements, expanding the local reach of the state and blurring the lines between state and society.

Far from Politics

If in the first years following the dissolution of the Soviet Union, the state had been nowhere to be found, its return in the twenty-first century was not limited to a strengthened executive apparatus, the expansion of security services,[20] the political alignment of private enterprises, and blurred lines between business interests and political power.[21] Its reach extended to the individuals who staffed public institutions and services, which incumbents transformed into instruments for creating loyalty to themselves personally.

The so-called garbage lustrations that swept across numerous regions of Ukraine in the autumn of 2014 followed a common liturgy, with such individuals as the targets. Participants describing themselves as anticorruption activists seized public servants by their arms and legs, brought them into municipal courtyards, and tossed them into dumpsters. On occasion, participants doused their targets with *zelenka*, the brilliant green antiseptic dye of mosquito-bitten Soviet childhood summers, damaging the eyes of the symbolically discarded.[22]

The targets of the lustrations were mainly people's deputies and others serving in government, but they also included a number of heads of hospital. Among these was Dr. Yaroslav Styranka, chief physician of a district hospital in the Ternopil' region. Activists associated with the nationalist Right Sector movement accused him of nepotism—the hospital's head midwife, who had presided over an unusual number of newborn deaths, was his wife—and he was known locally for buying votes for the Party of Regions.[23] But when, in mid-October, activists confronted Dr. Styranka at his desk, the doctor's first words of protest were not denial of these allegations. Instead, he insisted that the activists must be mistaken about the nature of his role. As an activist recorded the event, Dr. Styranka repeated, "I am not a public servant! I am not a public servant! [Ya ne derzhavnyi sluzhbovets'!]"[24]

Later, a Kremlin-sponsored film on the subject of garbage lustrations would describe the targets of the lustrations as "people who would seem to be far from politics," noting by way of example the chief physician of a military hospital some two hundred kilometers from Ternopil', in the city of Chernivtsi.[25] There, in early October, a Dr. Manolii Mihaichuk likewise had found himself seat-down in a dumpster pushed along a street by veterans of the Soviet war in Afghanistan who chanted "Shame!" while trailed by a few hundred participants in the action.[26]

The claim that the hospital's chief physician was "far from politics," and Dr. Stryanka's insistence that he was not a public servant, were ironic. Two decades of electoral manipulation had mobilized hierarchies within most public institutions, and the chief physician of any hospital would have been very close to politics indeed. People in such positions often were active participants in orchestrating, at the behest of regional leaders, the participation of subordinates and patients in electoral political theater.

In a process that paralleled aspects of the transformation of horizontal surveillance in Soviet society in the Khrushchev era,[27] state agents and interests had increasingly repopulated sites of social and economic reproduction. Command performances were not a mere symptom of the state's return: they were a key mechanism through which the administrative state reinserted itself into people's lives. In twenty-first-century Ukraine and Russia, political theater was the handmaiden of the expansion of state control. The practice of spectacle brought the state back into every sphere, rendering the face of power both local and personal.

From the standpoint of participants, the important players in the organization of political theater were not far-off bureaucrats or alien cadres. Instead, the sources of threats to entitlements and compensation were people known to them. The stage managers and stagehands of political theater were people's supervisors and colleagues, their community members—their priest, their neighbor, their mayor, the teachers of their children. Intermittently, these acted at the behest of national and regional leaders to organize command performances for parties of power, compelling and persuading people who depended on them in everyday life to participate in uncompetitive elections and other mises-en-scène. Because the face of pressure was local and personal, many extras in political theater could continue to appreciate national leaders—even as distance from Moscow or Kyiv did not mean distance from the state's warm embrace. Command performances changed what the state was, and for whom.

For actors and extras on the stage, the production managers and stagehands of political theater did not have singular, clear identities. While most people understood that political leaders and political parties stood behind efforts to coerce their participation, they did not see those who ensured compliance on the ground as always, exclusively, or even primarily state agents. Such individuals could serve in various roles simultaneously—as agents of the state, and as professionals.

These local regimes of coercion and persuasion obscured lines between state and society. Head doctors, like others in similar leadership roles, executed various functions. On most days, a chief physician was a doctor and administrator of health care providers. On occasion, still performing this role, he also would act as a servant of politicians, an agent of the state.

The context for this multiplicity of roles included not only the relatively recent history of Soviet electoral agitators,[28] but also the economic insecurity of previous decades. In order to manage the insecurity that followed the Soviet dissolution, postsocialist professionals had donned multiple hats,[29] maintaining access to multiple sources of income, cultivating numerous interwoven professional networks, and representing multiple, sometimes competing interests. In the academic world, some individuals with university or government positions also acted as officers of NGOs or businesses, or both. Because of such multiple sites of belonging—distinguished from the American "revolving doors" mainly by the simultaneity of different roles—it was not always clear what or whose interests an individual represented at any one time. To make things even more complicated, agents of the state could not be assumed to represent communal, rather than personal interests.

A recurring theme in people's lives in twenty-first-century Ukraine and Russia, as in most other places in the world, has been the progressive loss of access to jointly supplied or public goods—clean water, grazing land, pensions—to enclosure. If political and economic processes in the 1990s had been dominated by the privatization of farms and industry built by Soviet people, the twenty-first century brought redefinition: powerful actors situated at the nexus of politics and economic life identified things once regarded as shared or individual as now subject to appropriation and commodification. These included public spaces, personal data, and even instruments of governance.[30]

Politicians took advantage of these changes to hold ever-receding access to public goods hostage in return for performances of support at the ballot box or in the streets. Those performances then permitted politicians to continue policies and practices allowing further enclosure and capture of public goods. In processes of enclosure, the boundaries between private and public goods harden, even if they may remain in some sense "fuzzy."[31] Meanwhile, the zone of contact between state and society[32] became more fluid, more malleable.

In both Russia and Ukraine, people in positions of authority are activated in their role as state agents episodically, typically around elections and other moments in which visible support for parties of power is required. The rest of the time, they may have little or no obvious connection to state or party structures. In the dramaturgy of contemporary politics, we can imagine these connections as a flickering boundary around the state, including much larger and much smaller sets of individuals at different moments in time. Intermittent command performances can draw nearly anyone into a role as an actor or stagehand—an agent of the state—at any given moment. This risks destabilizing interpersonal trust even in periods between elections.

In certain ways, the transformation of state-society relations prompted by the practice of political theater may seem to resemble how statist models of politics theorize state-society relationships. In statist traditions of political analysis, boundaries between society and state blur because state actors also have private lives as part of society.[33] But in political theater, the obverse is true, as societal actors are drawn into collaboration with the state according to an uncertain timeline. The net effect can erase residual distinctions between state and societal actors. In Ukraine and Russia, for some of a certain age, this erasure can resonate with and activate memories of Soviet-era experiences, even as the sources of this shift are located in the post-Soviet period.

This book has focused on the experiences of people who participate in pro-regime performances and whose lives may not permit much choice or deliberation about doing so. But what does the state-society frontier look like from the perspective of those who publicly critique state dramaturgy? The view through this looking glass is remarkably similar. Masha Gessen, in their biographical account of five individuals in Putin's Russia, paints a picture of dissent that illustrates both the immanence of the state and the deep mutual imbrication in everyday life of those who do and do not publicly question their participation in command performances.

One of Gessen's dramatis personae is an organizer of Moscow's Bolotnaya demonstrations of 2012. Police confiscate from the organizer's apartment every last photograph she possesses of the life of her young son and her deceased mother, and she faces repeated interrogation and two years in prison. Her interrogations are two-way conversations. She and her questioner address each other with the informal you (*ty*). She knows her interrogator's supervisor personally: the supervisor is a woman whose family dacha is next to her own ex-husband's dacha. The two women—the one being investigated, and the supervisor of her interrogator—smoke together, and their young children play together. This immanence suffuses her experience of punishment for participation in a protest. Gessen writes of this organizer's persecution, "It sounded complicated, but it was so simple: she was passing to another side of existence easily, surrounded by familiar faces all the way."[34]

The immanence of state power is a familiar feature of totalitarian societies, where both horizontal networks and vertical hierarchies of surveillance and control suffuse everyday life.[35] In contemporary regimes practicing political theater, everyday economic relations are coordinated mainly by markets, and the repressive machinery of state power is a backup, rather than a primary tool for eliciting cooperation from society. However, for those who are drawn into performances, political theater may touch nearly every aspect of their lives. Meanwhile, for those situated elsewhere in the economy, in spaces less easily reached or of lesser interest to leaders, this may be not the case at all. Political theater can be a total system—but only for part of the population.

Is the Answer More Capitalism?

When Ukrainian presidential candidate Volodymyr Zelensky took the stage in Kyiv's Olympic Stadium in April 2019 to debate President Petro Poroshenko, he told the crowd, "I came here to break this system." The system to which Zelensky referred was not his country's institutions and laws, but the network of oligarchic power that ruled the country, binding political and economic interests, making public office available for private gain, and pulling millions of citizens into performances of democratic elections and public shows of support for incumbent politicians. Zelensky angrily confronted Poroshenko with a litany of questions that millions of Ukrainians wanted to ask their politicians: "How do you sleep at night? . . . Have you ever tried to live on a 1,500 hryven' [US$60] pension for even a month?!"[36] That year, presidential elections in Ukraine offered a choice. Zelensky's and his party's subsequent landslide victories crystallized Ukrainians' frustration.

Once he was in office, President Zelensky's policies reflected a common misreading of the situation: if public-sector ("budget") institutions and the incomplete privatization of resources such as agricultural land had impeded markets and left too much power over people's lives in the hands of the state, the solution must be more privatization and less state control. In this interpretation, the answer to abuses compelling public-sector workers to participate in command performances is further privatization and a smaller public sphere. In other words, if economic dependence on the state permits control by state agents, it should follow that less dependence would ease that control, allowing individuals greater autonomy. President Zelensky's answers to these problems followed a Hayekian logic, pushing an expanded bundle of property rights to agricultural land and firing thousands of public servants.[37]

But in and of itself, privatization does not offer protection against the politicization of services. Expanded privatization will not stop opportunistic politicians from mobilizing citizens for command performances. It will not close the theater. Instead, privatization changes who can be pressured and how. As numerous studies have shown, postsocialist privatization of industry and agriculture made people more, not less, dependent on local elites, and more willing to cooperate in their requests.[38] That dependence now expresses itself as submission to pressure to participate in political theater. More privatization may offer new possibilities for staging command performances. To the extent that people are obliged to submit to the politicization of basic services in order to maintain access to them, any sphere of economic activity—private or public—can become a possible means of political manipulation.

But what of existing public-sector institutions like schools and hospitals, frequent sites of recruitment for citizen participation in political theater? People working in the public sector are certainly the most vulnerable to pressure brought to bear by opportunistic incumbents. Pressure can be applied to any organization, institution, or company that receives state subsidies or preferential tax regimes or is subject to regulation. Yet fully eliminating possible avenues for pressure would mean cutting all regulatory and other ties between business and the state, a situation that does not and cannot exist in any modern polity.

Would improving wage levels more fully insulate publics from pressure campaigns? The problem here is that the possibility of pressure as it is used in Ukraine and Russia is not a disease of poverty. Numerous studies have shown an association between ordinary varieties of clientelism and poverty.[39] Yet, sometimes the relationship between how much money people make and whether they participate in machine politics is not linear, and this is the case in both Ukraine and Russia. The command performances described in this book require a minimum standard of living to function because people need to have something to lose. The tactics associated with political theater work best where people are employed or hold property on which they collect rents, where public transportation is present, where educational opportunities are available, and where access to health care is common. Pressure is not effective unless people normally expect to have access to these services. This means that people living in poverty or in places with undeveloped infrastructure can at times be *less* vulnerable to the use of certain electoral tactics than their middle-class cousins.

So what is to be done? For those who would like to see fewer command performances and more democratic engagement, if more privatization is not the answer, what kind of political economic order would shield people from being mobilized for political theater? Legislation prohibiting the use of executive authority for elections and election-related activities, enforced by an independent judiciary, could help prevent the capture of state institutions by political parties or politicians for private purposes, protecting citizens from the type of predation described in this book. Lasting solutions that provide for individual autonomy, however, will require not only robust measures protecting state bureaucracies from politicization, but also sustained efforts guaranteeing predictable universal basic livelihoods independent of people's expressed support for politicians.

But those who are more concerned with economic inequality than with democratic participation as such might ask different questions—and come to different conclusions—about the relative significance of the practice of political theater. For those allied with parties of power, the question might be not how to forestall command performances, but rather how to help people to see participation in expressions of support for parties of power as so intimately linked to their own economic interests that they understand their participation not as theater, but as programmatic support. This is the discursive move that Eastern European leaders who have grafted welfare regimes (long the provenance of the political left) to illiberal politics have made—and in many cases, have made successfully.

In the twenty-first century, not only industry, agriculture, and the service economy but also the administrative apparatus of the state itself are subject to attempts by powerful elites to capture resources. Even as scholars long have framed the contracting or outsourcing of state *functions* to private companies as part of enclosure, most still understand the use of public office for private gain as corruption—a state of exception, a departure from normal practice. But the capture of state *institutions* by parties of power imbricated in networks of oligarchic wealth also can be understood as part of broadening processes of enclosure.[40]

We can think of corruption in government as the extension of a global race to commodify and privatize all that can be named and assigned a value, including state offices. As the economist Yevgeny Gontmakher writes of Russia, "The state is quite simply privatized by a small group of people who occupy the formal positions of presidents, prime ministers, heads of department, governors, and mayors."[41] Rather than a Soviet throwback, this form of state capture is a hallmark and a condition of contemporary capitalism: an expression of total commodification, and an ultimate performance of political theater, as even those in the highest echelons of political power become actors playing assigned roles. No wonder, then, that those roles have come to include more public moments on the stage. When Vladimir Putin is photographed with a Siberian tiger or emerges from the Black Sea bearing an ancient amphora, he too is performing.[42] His performance offers the possibility of complicity for the bit players of command performances. The extras who populate pro-government demonstration crowds and whose ballots fill electoral urns can see clearly: even the president is drawn onto the stage.

Donald Trump Rents a Crowd

Twenty-first-century Ukraine and Russia, with their frayed systems of social welfare, their company towns and legacies of Soviet industrial policy,[43] their literate middle-income populations, and their entwined political and economic institutions and overlapping spheres of authority offered ideal conditions for politicians to stage political theater. Meanwhile, discursive legacies from the late Soviet period offered a ready-made set of practices—including an emphasis on form and performative, as opposed to literal, meanings of consent[44]—available for twenty-first-century politicians to use.

Soviet legacies offered props and tools for the practice of political theater in Russia and Ukraine, but those legacies are not required for its development elsewhere. Even in established democracies, a form of political theater that would be recognizable to many Russians and Ukrainians has begun to appear. In the United States, corporations and political parties on the political right fund so-called Astroturf movements—elite-led mobilization meant to look like grassroots activity. Political demonstrations showcase the enthusiasm of actors hired by the hour to express interest in issues and candidates.[45] Companies in cities with large numbers of aspiring actors, especially New York and Los Angeles, offer rental crowds to support politicians from mayoral candidates to, in the case of candidate Donald Trump, pretenders to the race for the American presidency.[46] In 2016, following a path reportedly trod by other New York politicians,[47] Trump's campaign initially engaged a casting company that issued a call several days before the candidate would announce his run for the presidency. The call offered fifty dollars in cash for three hours of work,[48] specifying that "we are looking to cast people for the event to wear T-shirts and carry signs and help cheer him in support of his announcement. We understand this is not a traditional 'background job,' but we believe acting comes in all forms."[49]

Paid demonstrations of the kind commonly seen in twenty-first-century Russia and Ukraine continued in the United States into the following year. In the final months of the presidential campaign, pro-Trump rallies organized by the Russian Internet Research Agency paid Americans to participate in demonstrations in multiple states, including Pennsylvania, Florida, and New York.[50]

The sociologist Edward Walker, who has studied related practices in the United States, argues that public affairs consultants who recruit citizens for paid participation in policy campaigns emphasize that mobilization is not effective, as "people on the receiving end can see right through it."[51] In post-Soviet space, political theater is effective precisely *because* people can see right through it: people understand perfectly well the power play involved in what they are being asked to do. Writing of spectacle in Syria under Hafez el-Assad, the political scientist Lisa Wedeen argued that the capacity to "compel people to say the ridiculous and to avow the absurd" both expressed and constituted the regime's power.[52] Knowing what is expected may be a legacy of Soviet-era politics, and that may slow the spread of political theater in the United States. But people's awareness that what they are doing or watching is performance does not necessarily make political theater less effective. On the contrary, it reminds people they have no say in writing the script.

Paid demonstrations are not the only element of post-Soviet-style political theater to be observed in American politics, and foreign intervention in elections is not the only way in which such tactics emerge. The political scientist Alexander Hertel-Fernandez has documented American companies' electoral pressure tactics, which use a brand of clientelism that closely resembles practices in Russia and Ukraine. He describes cases of workers in Ohio compelled to participate in a Republican political rally without pay during working hours, workers in Nevada threatened with possible job loss if President Obama were to be re-elected,[53] and a Florida time-share mogul who in 2000 pressured thousands of employees and "made sure everyone who was voting for Bush got to the polls."[54] In the 2016 presidential campaign, Trump adviser Paul Manafort attempted to create a back channel with the AFL-CIO in the hope of persuading the federation to limit union efforts to increase turnout in Michigan and Wisconsin.[55] These are not isolated instances: Hertel-Fernandez estimates that the proportion of American workers mobilized by their employers for political participation may reach 30 to 40 percent.

In the United States, the use of paid political activity by politicians poses some of the same risks of destabilizing knowledge regimes as it has in Ukraine and Russia. This can leave some open to the influence of disinformation campaigns. In October 2018, as several thousand people fleeing violence, poverty, and persecution in Central America made their way north in a coordinated group, President Donald Trump stood before campaign rallies. Making a gesture indicating the distribution of cash, he asked, "You know how the caravan started. Does everyone know what this means?"[56] Earlier that year, following the murder of seventeen people in a Parkland, Florida, high school, conspiracy theorists described surviving students as "crisis actors"[57]—people trained to play the role of victims for emergency services training simulations. Such theories became sufficiently prevalent that a staff member for a then member of the Florida state legislature and future congressional representative repeated the claim.[58] The CNN anchor Anderson Cooper interviewed Parkland student activist survivors about the accusation, prompting one student to address the claim directly: "I'm not a crisis actor."[59] In 2020, signaling belief in widespread performances of political theater in the United States, a sign at the annual pro-gun rally held on Martin Luther King Day in Richmond, Virginia, read "Bloomberg didn't pay me [to be here]."[60]

Where some people have personal experiences of remunerated or pressured participation, whispers of paid political activity can resonate with what they know of their own lives, making them more likely to believe similar claims about the lives of others. Efforts to make visible the architecture of "alternative narratives" can go some way toward addressing these risks,[61] but amid the practice of political theater the problem of resonance remains: some who believe these narratives are not simply consumers of disinformation, but people whose immanent experiences may give them reason to suspect others have been similarly treated.

Performances of political theater in the United States differ from their cousins in Russia and Ukraine in important ways, including their current primary use by corporations, rather than political parties,[62] as well as the fact that American middlemen draw upon professional actors, rather than visibly bored university students. But performances on US territory, while comparatively rare, do share an important feature with political theater in post-Soviet space: paid demonstrations can be nearly indistinguishable in appearance from unpaid gatherings. Actors hold signs, smile or shout, and even speak with journalists. Because of their formal similarity to grassroots activity, they create a dilemma for onlookers. Viewers aware of the existence and possibility of paid demonstrations may feel uncertain as to what it is they are seeing. Like the ambiguity generated through political theater in post-Soviet space, such uncertainty can destabilize people's confidence in their own perception and in the claims made by figures in positions of authority. This can strengthen the appeal of unsupported claims on the political right that voluntary and unremunerated mobilization is also paid. In other words, the existence of a few performances of political theater gives traction to suspicions and accusations of fakery elsewhere in the society.

Unlike democracy or authoritarianism, political theater need not be "the only game in town" to be politically consequential.[63] The portion of the electorate in the United States regularly engaged in workplace voter mobilization, Astroturf demonstrations, or outright vote buying is likely far smaller than it is in Russia or Ukraine. However, post-Soviet experiences have shown that the mere presence of the register of obligation as opposed to the register of choice in political participation can destabilize society-wide ways of thinking about politics. Given the decentralized design of American electoral institutions, even a small proportion of voters participating in political theater in one jurisdiction may be enough to make a difference in electoral outcomes at the federal level. Finally, although in post-Soviet space public institutions and their employees have been the main targets of party brokers, American experiences suggest that private-sector hierarchies can be effective as well.

There is every reason to think that there is room for the expansion of the practice of this type of political theater in the United States in future elections—especially where incumbent politicians embrace visions of politics that absolve government of responsibility to all people, as opposed to just their supporters. Existing guardrails in US politics may not be sufficient: between

2016 and 2020, members of the Trump administration openly and routinely ignored the Hatch Act, the law enacted in 1939 that, among other provisions, prohibits the use of executive-branch employees for political purposes.[64]

Overlapping political and economic authority are the sine qua non for the organization of command performances of democratic institutions. American social landscapes, dotted not with closely spaced Soviet-era industrial installations but with megachurches and other local total institutions, could prove fertile soil for the growth and spread of political dramaturgy. In the absence of consistent enforcement of the type of protections offered by the Hatch Act, people who worship, shop, find housing, open bank accounts, receive medical treatment, and educate their children under the umbrella of a single institution could find themselves voting according to the wishes of opportunistic or unscrupulous incumbent leaders as well.

Insofar as political theater is an aesthetic and political expression of an underlying political economy characteristic of the global shift from welfare to neoliberal capitalism, we can expect command performances to arise elsewhere, beyond Ukraine and Russia. Where democracy is staged, the social contract shifts to offer protection in return for political loyalty, and those who continue to engage in democratic contestation may find themselves excluded from the full benefits of membership in political communities. As mounting demographic and climate pressures make maintenance or reinstatement of universal social welfare a possibility only for the wealthiest of countries, the social contract of political theater may offer an attractive alternative to politicians: vote, or lose.

People who, like their Russian and Ukrainian contemporaries, have become disillusioned with executive overreach and corruption, the impotence of national legislatures, a system more responsive to capital than people, and for some, a frustrating absence of meaningful choice could receive such a turn positively. Paradoxically, abandoning the politics long associated with democratic elections and assembly to accept participation in command performances may satisfy those most in search of meaning in politics. For in political theater, everyone has a role.

NOTES

Introduction: Performances of Democracy

1. Serguei Alex. Oushakine, *The Patriotism of Despair: Nation, War, and Loss in Russia* (Ithaca, NY: Cornell University Press, 2009), 18.
2. Virág Molnár, "Street Art and the Contemporary Urban Underground: Social Critique or Coolness as Commodity?," New School for Social Research, 2016.
3. "Lozungovyi koshmar" [Slogan nightmare], *Voronezhskie vesti*, June 12, 1996, 4.
4. *Anekdoty s ulitsy Liziukova* 42–43 (Summer 1996): 12, 26.
5. M. M. Bakhtin, *The Dialogic Imagination*, ed. Michael Holquist, trans. C. Emerson and M. Holquist (Austin: University of Texas Press, 1981).
6. Alexei Yurchak, *Everything Was Forever, Until It Was No More: The Last Soviet Generation* (Princeton, NJ: Princeton University Press, 2005).
7. Oral testimony (hereafter OT), Yeltsin campaign worker, Voronezh, June 1996.
8. Scott Radnitz, *Weapons of the Wealthy: Predatory Regimes and Elite-Led Protests in Central Asia* (Ithaca, NY: Cornell University Press, 2010).
9. Studies focusing on resistance include Samuel Greene, *Moscow in Movement: Power and Opposition in Putin's Russia* (Redwood City, CA: Stanford University Press, 2015); Mischa Gabowitsch, *Protest in Putin's Russia* (Malden, MA: Polity, 2017); as well as work by Françoise Daucé, Regina Smyth, and Irina Soboleva, among others. Exceptions to this genre include Julie Hemment, *Youth Politics in Putin's Russia: Producing Patriots and Entrepreneurs* (Bloomington: Indiana University Press, 2015).
10. Dmitri Furman, "Imitation Democracies: The Post-Soviet Penumbra," *New Left Review* 54 (November–December 2008): 39.
11. Clifford Geertz, *Negara: The Theater State in Nineteenth-Century Bali* (Princeton, NJ: Princeton University Press, 1980); Georges Balandier, *Le pouvoir sur scènes* (Paris: Fayard, 2006).
12. The political scientist Nikolai Petrov wrote, "Institutions, while losing their role and content, aren't being eliminated entirely; their content is vanishing, but the outward shell remains in place. They are turning into decorative elements, pseudo-institutions, pale shadows of themselves." Nikolai Petrov, "The Political Design of Contemporary Russia," *Nezavisimaia Gazeta-Politika*, May 24, 2007 (*Johnson's Russia List* 2007, no. 121, May 29, 2007, no. 2).
13. Karen Petrone, *Life Has Become More Joyous, Comrades: Celebrations in the Time of Stalin* (Bloomington: Indiana University Press, 2000).
14. Ekaterina Schulmann, "Tsarstvo politicheskoi imitatsii," *Vedomosti*, August 15, 2014.
15. Jessica Allina-Pisano, *The Post-Soviet Potemkin Village: Politics and Property Rights in the Black Earth* (Cambridge: Cambridge University Press, 2008); Maxim

Trudolyubov, *The Tragedy of Property: Private Life, Ownership and the Russian State*, trans. Arch Tait (Malden, MA: Polity, 2018).

16. For controlled comparisons of post-Soviet political economy in these two states see Allina-Pisano, *Post-Soviet Potemkin Village*, and Stanislav Markus, *Property, Predation, and Protection: Piranha Capitalism in Russia and Ukraine* (Cambridge: Cambridge University Press, 2015). For relations between the two, see Paul D'Anieri, *Ukraine and Russia: From Civilized Divorce to Uncivil War* (New York: Cambridge University Press, 2019).

17. Volodymyr Zelensky, Facebook post, May 2, 2019, 10:34 a.m.

18. Thanks to Mariia Shynkarenko and Suzanne Wengle for this formulation.

19. But see Sharad Chari and Katherine Verdery, "Thinking between the Posts: Postcolonialism, Postsocialism, and Ethnography after the Cold War," *Comparative Studies in Society and History* 51, no. 1 (January 2009): 6–34; and Madina Tlostanova, "Can the Post-Soviet Think? On Coloniality of Knowledge, External Imperial and Double Colonial Difference," *Intersections: East European Journal of Society and Politics* 1, no. 2 (2015): 38–58.

20. Some recent work, including research on bureaucratic performance in Russia, has situated politics in a broader global context. See Ella Paneyakh, "Faking Performance Together: Systems of Performance Evaluation in Russian Enforcement Agencies and Production of Bias and Privilege," *Post-Soviet Affairs* 30, no. 2–3 (2014).

21. In its current usage, *imitatsiia*, like many other elements of the post-Soviet lexicon (especially with the abstract noun ending *-tsiia*) communicates not only poor imitation, but also foreignness. Analogous syncretic concepts communicate critique of foreign ideas: *dermokratiia, prikhvatizatsiia*.

22. Jessica Pisano, "Potemkin Villages," in *The Global Encyclopedia of Informality*, ed. Alena Ledeneva (London: University College London Press, 2017), 2:278–81.

23. See Ledeneva, *Global Encyclopedia of Informality*, 2 vols.

24. Clifford Geertz, "'From the Native's Point of View': On the Nature of Anthropological Understanding," *Local Knowledge: Further Essays in Interpretive Anthropology* (New York: Basic Books, 1983). The sociologist Rogers Brubaker and the historian Frederick Cooper offer another way of parsing analytical vocabularies, distinguishing between categories of practice and categories of analysis while acknowledging the close relationship between the two. Rogers Brubaker and Frederick Cooper, "Beyond 'Identity,'" *Theory and Society* 29, no. 1 (2000): 1–47.

25. Guy Debord, *La société du spectacle* (Paris: Gallimard, 1992).

26. Jeanne M. Penvenne, review of *Confronting Leviathan: Mozambique since Independence*, by Margaret Hall and Tom Young, *International Journal of African Historical Studies* 33, no. 1 (2000).

27. Emmanuel Terray, "Le climatiseur et la véranda," in *Afrique plurielle, Afrique actuelle: Homage à Georges Balandier* (Paris: Karthala, 1986).

28. Edward T. Walker, *Grassroots for Hire: Public Affairs Consultants in American Democracy* (New York: Cambridge University Press, 2014).

29. Alexander Hertel-Fernandez, *Politics at Work: How Companies Turn Their Workers into Lobbyists* (New York: Oxford University Press, 2018).

30. See Alena Ledeneva with Ružica Šimić Banović and Costanza Curro, "Telefonnoe pravo," in *The Global Encyclopedia of Informality*, ed. Alena Ledeneva (London: University College London Press, 2017), 2:457–59.

31. Steven Levitsky and Lucan A. Way, *Competitive Authoritarianism: Hybrid Regimes after the Cold War* (Cambridge: Cambridge University Press, 2010); Andreas Schedler, ed., *Electoral Authoritarianism: The Dynamics of Unfree Competition* (Boulder, CO: Lynne Rienner, 2006). The literature on formal and informal institutions, another place political scientists might look for ways to understand political theater, fits awkwardly around command performances, which involve structures and practices associated with both formal and informal institutions.

32. This book treats concepts somewhat differently from how they are often used in the study of politics. Here, concepts do not demarcate the boundaries of taxonomic categories, as regime types and other categories widely used in the study of politics usually do. Rather, following philosopher Étienne Balibar in his eponymous essay on the question, it treats concepts as productive sites and "crystallizations" of debate and dissensus: concepts exist to prompt debate, not to resolve it. Étienne Balibar, "Concepts," in *Political Concepts: A Critical Lexicon*, 2012, https://www.politicalconcepts.org/concept-etienne-balibar/.

33. Works that break through this conceptual problem include Henry Hale, *Patronal Politics: Eurasian Regime Dynamics in Comparative Perspective* (New York: Cambridge University Press, 2015); Dan Slater, "Democratic Careening," *World Politics* 65, no. 4 (2013): 729–63; and Gulnaz Sharafutdinova, *Political Consequences of Crony Capitalism inside Russia* (Notre Dame, IN: University of Notre Dame Press, 2010).

34. This substantial literature includes Henry Hale, "Explaining Machine Politics in Russia's Regions: Economy, Ethnicity, and Legacy," *Post-Soviet Affairs* 19, no. 3 (2003): 228–63. For Hungary and Romania, see Isabela Mares and Lauren E. Young, *Conditionality and Coercion: Electoral Clientelism in Eastern Europe* (New York: Oxford University Press, 2019).

35. Javier Auyero, *Poor People's Politics: Peronist Survival Networks and the Legacy of Evita* (Durham, NC: Duke University Press, 2000).

36. Viktor Pelevin, *Generation "P"* (Moscow: Vagrius, 1999); Andrew Wilson, *Virtual Politics: Faking Democracy in the Post-Soviet World* (New Haven, CT: Yale University Press, 2005); Peter Pomarantsev, *Nothing Is True and Everything Is Possible: The Surreal Heart of the New Russia* (New York: Public Affairs, 2014).

37. Sarah Birch, "Post-Soviet Electoral Practices in Comparative Perspective," *Europe-Asia Studies* 63, no. 4 (2011): 720–22; and Laura Adams, *The Spectacular State: Culture and National Identity in Uzbekistan* (Durham, NC: Duke University Press, 2010).

38. Yurchak, *Everything Was Forever*.

39. Bertolt Brecht, "The Modern Theater Is the Epic Theater: Notes to the Opera *Aufstieg und Fall der Stadt Mahagonny*" (1950), in *Brecht on Theatre: The Development of an Aesthetic*, ed. and trans. John Willett (New York: Hill & Wang, 1977), 33–42.

40. The use of this form in political contestation is, of course, not limited to post-Soviet space. See Augusto Boal, *Theater of the Oppressed* (New York: Theater Communications Group, 1993).

41. Elzbieta Matynia, *Performative Democracy* (Boulder: Paradigm Publishers, 2009).

42. V. B. Shklovsky, "Iskusstvo kak priiem," in *O Teorii prozy* (Moscow: Krug, 1925), 7–20.

43. Both Zelensky's formal political campaign and, in preceding years, the televised musical numbers of his troupe, Studio Kvartal-95, used both critique and catharsis to appeal to potential voters. Jessica Pisano, "Trump Says He Was Looking for Corruption in Ukraine—Where President Zelensky Was Known for Mocking Corruption in Ukraine," *Monkey Cage* (blog), *Washington Post*, November 14, 2019.

44. Jean Baudrillard, *Simulacres et simulation* (Paris: Galilée, 1981); Mikhail N. Epstein, *After the Future: The Paradoxes of Postmodernism and Contemporary Russian Culture* (Amherst: University of Massachusetts Press, 1995).

45. Epstein writes, "What is a key to Soviet hyperreality and makes it similar to Baudrillard's Western high-tech culture is that not only do ideological icons refer to no substantially existing actuality but the icons' signifier and signified do not interact. . . . The lack of depth or even apparent depth means the impossibility of interpretation, that is, something hidden that can be teased out and revealed. Since everything is equal only to itself, meaning becomes impossible" (337). Edith Clowes proposes a double hermeneutic in response, asking, "Has the term [postmodernism] caught on so fast because it is the latest fad from the West or because it suggests a cultural condition that is somehow close to Russians' own post-Soviet experience?" Clowes, "Simulacrum as S(t)imulation? Postmodernist Theory and Russian Cultural Criticism," *Slavic and East European Journal* 39, no. 3 (Autumn 1995): 334.

46. Thomas Seifrid, "'Illusion' and Its Workings in Modern Russian Culture," *Slavic and East European Journal* 45, no. 2 (2001): 205–6, referencing P. A. Florensky, *Mnimosti v geometrii* (Moscow: Pomor'e, 1922), 214.

47. See Erving Goffman, *The Presentation of the Self in Everyday Life* (New York: Anchor Books, 1959).

48. On this intellectual tradition see Anna Krylova, "The Tenacious Liberal Subject in Soviet Studies," *Kritika: Explorations in Russian and Eurasian History* 1 (2000): 119–46, and Gulnaz Sharafutdinova, "Was There a 'Simple Soviet' Person? Debating the Politics and Sociology of 'Homo Sovieticus,'" *Slavic Review* 78, no. 1 (2019): 173–95.

49. Lisa Wedeen, "Acting 'as If': Symbolic Politics and Social Control in Syria," *Comparative Studies in Society and History* 40, no. 3 (July 1998): 503–23.

50. Oleg Kharkhordin, *The Collective and the Individual in Russia: A Study of Practices* (Berkeley: University of California Press, 1999).

51. On social and affective dimensions of contemporary Russian politics, see Gulnaz Sharafutdinova, *The Red Mirror: Putin's Leadership and Russia's Insecure Identity* (New York: Oxford University Press, 2020) and Samuel A. Greene and Graeme B. Robertson, *Putin v. the People: The Perilous Politics of a Divided Russia* (New Haven: Yale University Press, 2019).

52. See Viacheslav Morozov, "Uneven Worlds of Hegemony: Towards a Discursive Ontology of Societal Multiplicity," *International Relations*, April 2021.

53. Maria Panova, "ZAMERZAIEM!," *Pravda*, January 2010, no. 2.

54. Caroline Humphrey, *The Unmaking of Soviet Life: Everyday Economies after Socialism* (Ithaca, NY: Cornell University Press, 2002); Brian Taylor, *State Building in Putin's Russia: Policing and Coercion after Communism* (New York: Cambridge University Press, 2011), chap. 1.

55. Gerald M. Easter, *Capital, Coercion, and Postcommunist States* (Ithaca, NY: Cornell University Press, 2012).

56. Alena V. Ledeneva, *Can Russia Modernise? Sistema, Power Networks and Informal Governance* (Cambridge: Cambridge University Press, 2013).

57. Exceptions include Hale, *Patronal Politics*; Bálint Magyar, *A Magyar Maffiaállam anatómiája* (Budapest: Noran Libro Kiadó, 2015); Ledeneva, *Can Russia Modernise?*; Myron J. Aronoff and Jan Kubik, *Anthropology and Political Science: A Convergent Approach* (Oxford: Berghahn Books, 2012); Aleksandr Volkov and Aleksandr Privalov, *Skelet nastupaiushchego: Istochniki i dve sostavnye chasti biurokraticheskogo kapitalizma v Rossii* (Saint Petersburg: Piter, 2008).

58. In the first instance see Ledeneva, *Can Russia Modernise?* In the second, see Stanislav Markus, *Property, Predation, and Protection*. Un-disaggregated categories—state and business—dominated analysis of the wide-scale reconfiguration of property rights attribution after 2000, with redistribution first cast as renationalization of goods privatized during the 1990s. For example, Anders Aslund, "The Folly of Renationalization," *Moscow Times*, May 23, 2006, posted on website of Peterson Institute for International Economics, www.piie.com, accessed February 16, 2017.

59. On the Ukrainian state as palimpsest see Tanya Richardson, "The Terrestrialization of Amphibious Life in a Danube Delta 'Town on Water,'" *Suomen Anthropologie* 43, no. 2 (Summer 2018): 3–29.

60. For example, Aleksei Zudin, "Gosudarstvo i biznes v Rossii: Evoliutsiia modeli vzaimootnoshenii," *Neprikosnovennyi zapas*, no. 6, 2006. See Andrew Barnes, *Owning Russia: The Struggle over Factories, Farms, and Power* (Ithaca, NY: Cornell University Press, 2006).

61. Timothy Mitchell, "The Limits of the State: Beyond Statist Approaches and Their Critics," *American Political Science Review* 85, no. 1 (1991): 78.

62. Akhil Gupta, *Red Tape: Bureaucracy, Structural Violence, and Poverty in India* (Durham, NC: Duke University Press, 2012); Laurence Jacobs and Desmond King, *The Unsustainable State* (Oxford: Oxford University Press, 2009); James C. Scott, *The Art of Not Being Governed: An Anarchist History of Upland Southeast Asia* (New Haven, CT: Yale University Press, 2009); Aradhana Sharma and Akhil Gupta, *The Anthropology of the State: A Reader* (Oxford: Blackwell, 2006).

63. James T. Sparrow, William J. Novak, and Stephen W. Sawyer, *Boundaries of the State in US History* (Chicago: University of Chicago Press, 2015), 3.

64. Writing on the use of clear analytical differentiations between state and society in rural Kyrgyzstan, the anthropologist Madeleine Reeves notes, "As ethnographic work has shown, what is important is often who comes to take on the person of the state . . . and can they successfully maintain a claim to its authority?" Madeleine Reeves, review of *Weapons of the Wealthy: Predatory Regimes and Elite-Led Protests in Central Asia*, by Scott Radnitz, *Central Asian Survey*, February 2013. Stanislav Markus makes a similar point in *Property, Predation, and Protection*.

65. Galia Ackerman, "Entretien avec Dimitri Fourman. De Gorbatchev à Poutine: Les illusions perdues," *Politique internationale* 109 (Autumn 2005): 253–73, and Dmitri Furman, "Imitation Democracies: The Post-Soviet Penumbra," *New Left Review* 54 (November–December 2008): 29–47; Ledeneva, *Can Russia Modernise?*

66. Jessica Allina-Pisano, "Sub Rosa Resistance and the Politics of Economic Reform: Land Redistribution in Post-Soviet Ukraine," *World Politics* 56, no. 4 (July 2004): 554–81.

67. Bryn Rosenfeld, *The Autocratic Middle Class: How State Dependency Reduces the Demand for Democracy* (Princeton, NJ: Princeton University Press, 2020).

68. See Humphrey, *Unmaking of Soviet Life*.

69. Anna M. Grzymala-Busse, *Redeeming the Communist Past: The Regeneration of Communist Parties in East Central Europe* (New York: Cambridge University Press, 2002). The performances in this book are thus distinct from the performative practices at the core of politics where the administrative state is absent or diminished, as in Lisa Wedeen's *Peripheral Visions: Publics, Power, and Performances in Yemen* (Chicago: University of Chicago Press, 2008).

70. Jessica Allina-Pisano, "Social Contracts and Authoritarian Projects in Post-Soviet Space: The Use of Administrative Resource," *Communist and Post-Communist Studies* 43, no. 4 (2010): 373–82; Timothy Frye, John Reuter, and David Szakonyi, "Political Machines at Work: Workplace Mobilization and Electoral Subversion in Russia," *World Politics* 66, no. 2 (April 2014): 195–228; Timothy Frye, John Reuter, and David Szakonyi, "Hitting Them with Carrots: Voter Intimidation and Vote Buying in Russia," *British Journal of Political Science* 49, no. 3 (July 2019): 857–81.

71. On the former, see Dominic Boyer and Alexei Yurchak, "American Stiob: Or, What Late-Socialist Aesthetics of Parody Reveal about Contemporary Political Culture in the West," *Cultural Anthropology* 25, no. 2 (2010): 179–221.

1. Researching Political Theater

1. Interview with the author, Moscow, June 1994.

2. Anne Lounsbery, *Life Is Elsewhere: Symbolic Geography in the Russian Provinces, 1800–1917* (Ithaca, NY: Cornell University Press, 2019).

3. Frederick Cooper and Anne Stoler, eds., *Tensions of Empire: Colonial Cultures in a Bourgeois World* (Berkeley: University of California Press, 1997), and Peter Sahlins, *Boundaries: The Making of France and Spain in the Pyrenees* (Berkeley: University of California Press, 1991). And see Jane Burbank and Frederick Cooper, *Empires in World History: Power and the Politics of Difference* (Princeton, NJ: Princeton University Press, 2011).

4. Jill Lepore, *New York Burning: Liberty, Slavery, and Conspiracy in Eighteenth-Century Manhattan* (New York: Vintage Books, 2005), xv.

5. Stein Rokkan, *Citizens, Elections, Parties* (Oslo: Universitetforlaget, 1970); see also Richard Snyder, "Scaling Down: The Subnational Comparative Method," *Studies in Comparative International Development* 36, no. 1 (Spring 2001): 93–110.

6. Jessica Allina-Pisano, *The Post-Soviet Potemkin Village: Politics and Property Rights in the Black Earth* (Cambridge: Cambridge University Press, 2008), 23–24.

7. Timothy Frye, John Reuter, and David Szakonyi, "Political Machines at Work: Workplace Mobilization and Electoral Subversion in Russia," *World Politics* 66, no. 2 (April 2014): 195–228.

8. See Irina V. Soboleva, "Peer Pressure in Contentious Mobilization" (Columbia University, 2017).

9. See Timothy J. Colton and Henry E. Hale, "The Putin Vote: Presidential Electorates in a Hybrid Regime," *Slavic Review* 68, no. 3 (Fall 2009): 473–503; Daniel Treisman, "Presidential Popularity in a Hybrid Regime: Russia under Yeltsin and Putin," *American Journal of Political Science* 55, no. 3 (2011): 590–609; Timothy Frye, Scott Gehlbach, Kyle L. Marquardt, and Ora John Reuter, "Is Putin's Popularity Real?," *Post-Soviet Affairs* 33, no. 1 (January 2017): 1–15.

10. For advantages of participant-observation over interview-based research see Jessica Allina-Pisano, "How to Tell an Axe Murderer: An Essay on Ethnography, Truth, and Lies," in *Political Ethnography: What Immersion Contributes to the Study of Power*, ed. Edward Schatz (Chicago: University of Chicago Press, 2009), 53–73.

11. A. I. Ahram and Paul Goode, eds., "Observing Autocracies from the Ground Floor," special issue, *Social Science Quarterly* 97, no. 4 (2016): 823–33.

12. Matthew Desmond, *Evicted: Poverty and Profit in the American City* (New York: Broadway Books, 2016), 317–18.

13. On the role of humor in Russian political protest see Jennifer G. Mathers, "Even the Toys Are Demanding Free Elections: Humour and the Politics of Creative Protest," in *Cultural Forms of Protest in Russia*, ed. Birgit Beumers, Alexander Etkind, Olga Gurova, and Sanna Turoma (London: Routledge, 2018), 105–19. And see contributions in Neringa Klumbytė and Gulnaz Sharafutdinova, eds., *Soviet Society in the Era of Late Socialism, 1964–1985* (Lanham, MD: Lexington Books, 2013).

14. In the United States, Steven Stoll's *Ramp Hollow: The Ordeal of Appalachia* (New York: Hill & Wang, 2018).

15. David Ost, *The Defeat of Solidarity: Anger and Politics in Postcommunist Europe* (Ithaca, NY: Cornell University Press, 2005).

16. Katherine J. Cramer, *The Politics of Resentment: Rural Consciousness in Wisconsin and the Rise of Scott Walker* (Chicago: University of Chicago Press, 2016).

17. Arlie Russell Hochschild, *Strangers in Their Own Land: Anger and Mourning on the American Right* (New York: New Press, 2016); Carol Anderson, *White Rage: The Unspoken Truth of Our Racial Divide* (New York: Bloomsbury, 2016); Nancy Isenberg, *White Trash: The 400-Year Untold History of Class in America* (New York: Viking, 2016).

18. Charles Lindblom, *Politics and Markets: The World's Political-Economic Systems* (New York: Basic Books, 1977).

2. History of the Form

1. Video, accessed June 10, 2013, http://www.youtube.com/watch?v=mr9RX_qnwFA&feature=grec_index.

2. Irina Petrovskaya, "Tvortsy vselenskoi pokazukhi," *Izvestiia*, December 24, 2010, 8.

3. Lenta.ru, "'Zloveshchego' kardiologa iz Ivanovo vyzvali v prokuraturu," last modified December 17, 2010, http://lenta.ru/news/2010/12/17/procur.

4. Igor' Karmazin, "Pravdorub Khrenov," *Moskovskii komsomolets*, December 18, 2010, 1.

5. Evgenii Sazonov, "Kardiolog Ivan Khrenov: 'Ya tol'ko potom ponial, chto mne zvonil Putin!'" *Komsomol'skaia pravda*, last modified December 17, 2010, https://www.kp.ru/daily/24610/779769/.

6. Vitalii Petrov, "Obratnyi zvonok," *Rossiiskaia gazeta*, December 20, 2010, 2.

7. One of the videos of this episode, titled "Putin i obkurennaia devushka" (Putin and the stoned girl), from February 2, 2008, was viewed more than 9.5 million times on YouTube: https://www.youtube.com/watch?v=RlCrAmQEUdk.

8. Karmazin, "Pravdorub Khrenov."

9. Alena V. Ledeneva, *Russia's Economy of Favors: Blat, Networking, and Informal Exchange* (Cambridge: Cambridge University Press, 1998).

10. János Kornai, *The Socialist System: The Political Economy of Communism* (Princeton, NJ: Princeton University Press, 1991).

11. Ledeneva, *Russia's Economy of Favors*, and Elena Osokina, *Our Daily Bread: Socialist Distribution and the Art of Survival in Stalin's Russia, 1927–1941*, ed. Kate Transchel, trans. Kate Transchel and Greta Bucher (Armonk, NY: M. E. Sharpe, 2001).

12. Joseph Berliner, *Factory and Manager in the USSR* (Cambridge, MA: Harvard University Press, 1957).

13. Mikhail Zadornov, "Blagodarnost' (Otkrytoe pis'mo general'nomu sekretariu)," *Teatr*, no. 3 (March 1988): 189–90.

14. Viktor Pelevin, *Omon Ra* in *Zhizn' nasekomykh* (Moscow: Vagrius, 1999), 21–152.

15. Anna Krylova, "Saying 'Lenin' and Meaning 'Party': Subversion and Laughter in Soviet and Post-Soviet Society," in *Consuming Russia: Popular Culture, Sex, and Society since Gorbachev*, ed. Adele Marie Barker (Durham, NC: Duke University Press, 1999), 252.

16. For example, "Peskov: Rassuzhdaiushchie o brezhnevizatsii Putina nichego ne znaiut o genseke, on byl pliusom dlia strany," *Gazeta.Ru*, last modified October 4, 2011, http://www.gazeta.ru/news/lenta/2011/10/04/n_2037898.shtml#p2.

17. Mikhail Zadornov, "Bud' gotov!," video, last modified November 24, 2011, https://www.youtube.com/watch?v=qLNQVuPLoiU.

18. On that nostalgia see Viktor Pelevin, *Generation "P"* (Moscow: Vagrius, 2001).

19. Lenta.ru, "'Zloveshchego' kardiologa iz Ivanovo vyzvali v prokuraturu," last modified December 27, 2010, http://lenta.ru/news/2010/12/17/procur.

20. Nancy Shields Kollmann, *Kinship and Politics: The Making of the Muscovite Political System, 1345–1547* (Stanford, CA: Stanford University Press 1987), 8, 150, and Kollmann, "The Façade of Autocracy," in *Reinterpreting Russian History: Readings 860s–1860s*, ed. Daniel H. Kaiser and Gary Marker (New York: Oxford University Press, 1994). See also Donald Ostrowski, "The Façade of Legitimacy: Exchanges of Power and Authority in Early Modern Russia," *Comparative Studies in Society and History* 44, no. 3 (July 2002): 534–63, as well as Nicholas Henshall, *The Myth of Absolutism: Change and Continuity in Early Modern Monarchy* (London: Longman, 1992), and Henshall, "The Myth of Absolutism," *History Today* 42 (June 1992): 40–47.

21. Nancy Shields Kollmann, *By Honor Bound: State and Society in Early Modern Russia* (Ithaca, NY: Cornell University Press, 1999), and Marshall Poe, "Russian Despotism: The Origins and Dissemination of Early Modern Commonplace" (PhD diss., University of California, Berkeley, 1993).

22. For example, Victor Lieberman, ed., *Beyond Binary Histories: Re-imagining Eurasia to c. 1830* (Ann Arbor: University of Michigan Press, 1999).

23. Thomas Seifrid, "'Illusion' and Its Workings in Modern Russian Culture," *Slavic and East European Journal* 45, no. 2 (2001): 205–6.

24. Seifrid, 205–15.

25. Priscilla Roosevelt, *Life on the Russian Country Estate: A Social and Cultural History* (New Haven, CT: Yale University Press, 1995), and Yuri Lotman, "Theater and Theatricality in the Order of Early Nineteenth Century Culture," in *Semiotics and*

Structuralism: Readings from the Soviet Union, ed. Henryk Baran (White Plains, NY: International Arts and Sciences, 1974), 33–63.

26. Seifrid, "'Illusion,'" 206–7.

27. Seifrid, 206–7, citing Uspenskii, "Historia Sub Specie Semioticae," in Baran, *Semiotics and Structuralism*, 64–75, and V. M. Zhivov, "Kul′turnye reformy v sisteme preobrazovanii Petra I," in *Iz istorii russkoi kul′tury*, vol. 3, *XVII-nachalo XVIII veka*, ed. A. D. Koshelev (Moscow: Shkola, 1996), 528–83.

28. See Stephen E. Hanson, *Time and Revolution: Marxism and the Design of Soviet Institutions* (Chapel Hill: University of North Carolina Press, 1997).

29. Representative of the Committee of Voters of Ukraine, interview with the author, Kharkiv, July 13, 2006.

30. Mikhail Epstein, "The Origins and Meaning of Russian Postmodernism," in *After the Future: The Paradoxes of Postmodern and Contemporary Russian Culture* (Amherst: University of Massachusetts Press, 1995), 196.

31. Epstein, 191.

32. Ivan Sergeevich Aksakov, "Vse sushchestvuet u nas—budto by," *Den′*, no. 48, November 30, 1863.

33. Astolphe de Custine, *La Russie en 1839*, vol. 3 (Brussels: Ligaran, 2015). As cited in Epstein, "Origins and Meaning of Russian Postmodernism," 191.

34. For views from Eastern European travelers abroad see the three-part series edited by Wendy Bracewell and Alex Drace-Francis, *East Looks West*, vol. 1, *Orientations: An Anthology of East European Travel Writing, ca. 1550–2000*; vol. 2, *Under Eastern Eyes: A Comparative Introduction to East European Travel Writing on Europe*; and vol. 3, *A Bibliography of East European Travel Writing in Europe* (Budapest: Central European University Press, 2008).

35. *Murzilki*'s musical parodies, together with summaries of the news items upon which they comment, can be heard at Avtoradio, last modified April 29, 2021, http://www.avtoradio.ru/murzilki.

36. Oleg Lomovoi, "Kardiolog Khrenov rasskazal vsiu pravdu Putinu," 2011. Lyrics to parody of "Dvazhdy dva chetyre." Original text and video may be viewed at Avtoradio, accessed June 10, 2013, http://www.avtoradio.ru/?an=ml_parody_page&uid=142960.

37. In one rendition of the song, which was written by M. Pliatskovskii and V. Shainskii, Eduard Khil′ leads members of Bolshoi Detskii Khor in a staged classroom performance: video, accessed June 10, 2013, http://www.youtube.com/watch?v=u5DPEg1lp3s.

38. Evgeniia Suprycheva, "Korrespondent 'KP' proveril: Mnogo li pravdy v tom, chto rasskazal Putinu doktor Khrenov," *Komsomol′skaia pravda*, December 28, 2010, 10.

39. Oleg Alalykin, "Aktual′no: Dialogii v studii." Interview with Ivan Khrenov, video, last modified December 17, 2010, http://www.youtube.com/watch?v=twsyrZP5u5w.

40. Evgenii Sazonov, "Kardiolog Ivan Khrenov: 'Tol′ko posle razgovora ya ponial, chto mne zvonil glava pravitel′stva!," *Komsomol′skaia pravda*, December 20, 2010, 5.

41. Radio Mayak, "Pokazukha v Rossii," video, last modified December 17, 2010, http://www.youtube.com/watch?v=jygrov-aYmA.

42. Video on http://rutube.ru/tracks/3914531.html?r=68c136a55b5027036f646 aisefef63dof, accessed June 10, 2013.

43. Radio Mayak, "Pokazukha v Rossii."

44. Radio Mayak, "Pokazukha v Rossii."

45. Alexei Yurchak, "Soviet Hegemony of Form: Everything Was Forever, until It Was No More," *Comparative Studies in Society and History* 45, no. 3 (July 2003): 486.

46. See also Alena Ledeneva, "Open Secrets and Knowing Smiles," *East European Politics and Societies* 25, no. 4 (November 2011): 720–36.

47. Igor' Karmazin, "Pravdorub Khrenov," *Moskovskii komsomolets*, December 18, 2010, 1.

48. As Žižek notes, following Sloterdijk's *Critique of Cynical Reason* (1989, 33): Slavoj Žižek, *The Sublime Object of Ideology* (London: Verso, 1989).

49. Václav Havel, "The Power of the Powerless," in *The Power of the Powerless: Citizens against the State in Central-Eastern Europe*, by Václav Havel et al. (Armonk, NY: M. E. Sharpe, 1985), 25.

50. Havel, 39–40.

51. Havel, 38.

52. Havel, 39.

53. Linda Cook, *The Soviet Social Contract and Why It Failed: Welfare Policy and Workers' Politics from Brezhnev to Yeltsin* (Cambridge, MA: Harvard University Press, 1993); Kate Brown, *Plutopia: Nuclear Families, Atomic Cities, and the Great Soviet and American Plutonium Disasters* (Oxford: Oxford University Press, 2015).

54. Suprycheva, "Korrespondent 'KP' proveril," 10.

55. Suprycheva.

56. Natal'ia Boiarkina, "Chto vy nas 'lechite'?," *Argumenty i fakty*, March 9, 2011, 40.

57. Tat'iana Smol'iakova and Marina Gritsiuk, "Ivanovo deistvo," *Rossiiskaia gazeta*, December 28, 2010, 1.

58. Suprycheva, "Korrespondent 'KP' proveril," 10.

59. Alalykin, "Aktual'no: Dialogii v studii."

60. See Melissa Locker, "John Oliver Uses a Gun and *The Sopranos* to Get You to Care about Local News," Time.com, last modified July 3, 2017, http://time.com/4843463/john-oliver-local-news-last-week-tonight/.

61. Owen Matthews and Anna Nemtsova, "Moscow's Phony Liberal," *Newsweek*, February 25, 2010. See also Brian Whitmore, "The Pokazukha Liberalization," Radio Free Europe / Radio Liberty, last modified March 8, 2010, https://www.rferl.org/a/The_Pokazuka_Liberalization/1978031.html.

62. Aleksandra Beluza, "Potemkinskie golosa," *Izvestiia*, December 29, 2010, 12.

3. Setting the Stage

1. Bernice Q. Madison, *Social Welfare in the Soviet Union* (Stanford, CA: Stanford University Press, 1956).

2. See Eliot Bernstein's intervention, "Gratuitous Violence and Gratuitous Acts: Defining *Bespredel*," https://www.aatseel.org/100111/pdf/program/2005/abstracts/bornstein.htm.

3. "Direktor shkoly iz Brianskoi oblasti beseduet s uchenikami o Naval'nom i likhikh 90-x," https://www.youtube.com/watch?v=00MoQ6UqAjU, last modified

March 18, 2017, accessed April 4, 2017, and viewed 75,925 times as of that date. A search on Yandex shows numerous uploads and tens of thousands of views, including on Russian-language social media platforms such as Odnoklassniki.

4. Gulnaz Sharafutdinova, "Russia's Struggle over the Meaning of the 1990s and the Keys to Kremlin Power," PONARS Eurasia Policy Memo no. 592, May 2019.

5. On "zombies" see Viktor Pelevin, "Zombifikatsiia. Opyt sravnitel'noi antropologii," 1990, http://pelevin.nov.ru/pov/pe-zombi/1.html; Eliot Borenstein, "The Talking Dead: Articulating the 'Zombified' Subject under Putin," unpublished manuscript, accessed July 19, 2016, https://sllc.umd.edu/sites/sllc.umd.edu/files/The%20Talking%20Dead_3.pdf.

6. For another approach to this dilemma see Gulnaz Sharafutdinova, *The Red Mirror: Putin's Leadership and Russia's Insecure Identity* (New York: Oxford University Press, 2020).

7. Michel Foucault, "What Is an Author?," in *Language, Counter-memory, Practice*, ed. Donald F. Bouchard (Ithaca, NY: Cornell University Press, 1977), 113–38.

8. Alaina Lemon, "Sympathy for the Weary State? Cold War Chronotypes and Moscow Others," *Comparative Studies in Society and History* 51, no. 4 (2009): 832–64.

9. Edward Schatz, ed., *Political Ethnography: What Immersion Contributes to the Study of Power* (Chicago: University of Chicago Press, 2009).

10. Robin Wagner-Pacifici and Iddo Tavory offer a caution regarding analytical empathy: "Politics as a Vacation," *American Journal of Cultural Sociology* 5, no. 3 (2017): 307–21.

11. Anton Pavlovich Chekhov, "Student," *Russkie vedomosti*, 1894.

12. "Conversation about Being Forced into Empathy," from "Dialektik auf dem Theater," in reference to Horace's *Ars Poetica*, in *Brecht on Theater: The Development of an Aesthetic*, ed. and trans. John Willett (New York: Farrar, Hill & Wang, 1992), 271.

13. Lemon, "Sympathy for the Weary State?"

14. On Russian hagiographical traditions see Jessica Pisano, "Constructed Lives: Author as Saint in the Soviet Literary Biographical Museum" (AB thesis, Harvard University, 1993), http://id.lib.harvard.edu/alma/990046486380203941/catalog.

15. Jacques Le Goff, *Faut-il vraiment découper l'histoire en tranches?* (Paris: Seuil, 2014).

16. David M. Woodruff, *Money Unmade: Barter and the Fate of Russian Capitalism* (Ithaca, NY: Cornell University Press, 1999); Paul Seabright, ed., *The Vanishing Rouble: Barter Networks and Non-monetary Transactions in Post-Soviet Societies* (Cambridge: Cambridge University Press, 2000); and Clifford G. Gaddy and Barry William Ickes, *Russia's Virtual Economy* (Washington, DC: Brookings Institution, 2002).

17. John J. Stephan, *The Russian Far East: A History* (Stanford, CA: Stanford University Press, 1996).

18. Katherine Verdery, "Fuzzy Property: Rights, Power, and Identity in Transylvania's Decollectivization," in *Uncertain Transition: Ethnographies of Change in the Postsocialist World*, ed. Michael Burawoy and Katherine Verdery (Lanham, MD: Rowman & Littlefield, 1999), 53–81.

19. Valerie Sperling, *Organizing Women in Contemporary Russia: Engendering Transition* (Cambridge: Cambridge University Press, 1999).

20. The author's research in Voronezh in 1996, 1997–98, and 2000, in Moscow and Leningrad / Saint Petersburg in 1991, 1992, 1994, 1996, 1997, and 1998, and in Ukraine in 1992 and 1999–2000 inform this and following sections. See also Joma Nazpary, *Post-Soviet Chaos: Violence and Dispossession in Kazakhstan* (London: Pluto, 2002). Some specific local details, such as the ambiance on the Voroshilova Street bus, draw on the author's firsthand experience.

21. Francine du Plessix Gray, *Soviet Women: Walking the Tightrope* (New York: Doubleday, 1990).

22. Lewis H. Siegelbaum, *Cars for Comrades: The Life of the Soviet Automobile* (Ithaca, NY: Cornell University Press, 2008); Corinna Kuhr-Korolev, "Women and Cars in Soviet and Russian Society," in *The Socialist Car: Automobility in the Eastern Bloc*, ed. Lewis H. Siegelbaum (Ithaca, NY: Cornell University Press, 2011), 186–203.

23. On meanings and legal issues surrounding metal doors in post-Soviet apartment buildings see Aurore Chaigneau, *Le droit de propriété en mutation: Essai à la lumière du droit russe* (Paris: Dalloz, 2008).

24. Pension arrears for this period are documented in the regional press. For example, "40 protsentov pozhilykh liudei v oktiabre ostalis' bez pensii," *Kommuna*, November 4, 1995, 1; Hartmut Lehmann, Jonathan Wadsworth, and Alessandro Acquisti, "Grime and Punishment: Job Insecurity and Wage Arrears in the Russian Federation," *Journal of Comparative Economics* 27 (1999): 565–617; Vladimir Gimpelson and Douglas Lippoldt, *The Russian Labor Market: Between Transition and Turmoil* (Lanham, MD: Rowman & Littlefield, 2001), 125–44.

25. Deniz Yükseker, "Shuttling Goods, Weaving Consumer Tastes: Informal Trade between Turkey and Russia," *International Journal of Urban and Regional Research* 31, no. 1 (March 2007): 60–72.

26. Alena V. Ledeneva, *Russia's Economy of Favors: Blat, Networking, and Informal Exchange* (Cambridge: Cambridge University Press, 1998).

27. Regarding the complexities of sheep breeding in another national context see James Rebanks, *The Shepherd's Life: A Tale of the Lake District* (London: Penguin Books, 2015).

28. Oral testimony, district department of economic planning, Kharkiv region, January 10, 2000.

29. On infrastructure see Stephen J. Collier, *Post-Soviet Social: Neoliberalism, Social Modernity, Biopolitics* (Princeton, NJ: Princeton University Press, 2011).

30. Jessica Allina-Pisano, "Opting Out under Stalin and Khrushchev: Post-war Sovietization in a Borderlands Magyar Village," *Problems of Post-Communism* 58, no. 1 (January–February 2011): 58–66.

31. See Jessica Allina-Pisano, *The Post-Soviet Potemkin Village: Politics and Property Rights in the Black Earth* (Cambridge: Cambridge University Press, 2008), 176.

32. Allina-Pisano, *Post-Soviet Potemkin Village*.

33. David M. Woodruff, "It's Value That's Virtual: Bartles, Rubles, and the Place of Gazprom in the Russian Economy," *Post-Soviet Affairs* 15, no. 2 (1999): 130–48.

34. Vadim Volkov, *Violent Entrepreneurs: The Use of Force in the Making of Russian Capitalism* (Ithaca, NY: Cornell University Press, 2002), and Federico Varese, *The Russian Mafia: Private Protection in a New Market Economy* (Oxford: Oxford University Press, 2001).

35. On nonmonetary employee compensation in the 1990s see Simon Commander and Richard Jackman, "Firms and Government in the Provision of Benefits in Russia," and Irina Tratch and Andreas Wörgötter, "The Enterprise Social Wage in the Transitional Economy of Ukraine," in *Enterprise and Social Benefits after Communism*, ed. Martin Rein, Barry L. Friedman, and Andreas Wörgötter (Cambridge: Cambridge University Press, 1997), 95–114 and 261–83; Michael McFaul, "The Political Economy of Social Policy Reform in Russia: Ideas, Institutions, and Interests," in *Left Parties and Social Policy in Postcommunist Europe*, ed. Linda Cook, Mitchell A. Orenstein, and Marilyn Rueschemeyer (Boulder, CO: Westview, 1999), 221. On post-Soviet nonmonetary exchange systems see David Woodruff, *Money Unmade: Barter and the Fate of Russian Capitalism* (Ithaca, NY: Cornell University Press, 2000), and Gaddy and Ickes, *Russia's Virtual Economy*.

36. *Bogatye tozhe plachut* (*Les ricos también lloran*) was shown on state television from November 1991. The show was broadcast twice daily during the workweek from December 1991 to July 1992.

37. On mortality in the 1990s see Giovanni Andrea Cornia and Renato Paniccia, "The Transition Mortality Crisis: Evidence, Interpretation, and Policy Responses," in *The Mortality Crisis in Transitional Economies*, ed. Giovanni Andrea Cornia and Renato Paniccia (Oxford: Oxford University Press, 2000), 3–37; Elizabeth Brainerd and David M. Cutler, "Autopsy on an Empire: Understanding Mortality in Russia and the Former Soviet Union," *Journal of Economic Perspectives* 19 (2005): 107–30; Vladimir M. Shkolnikov et al., "Mortality Reversal: The Story So Far," *Hygiea Internationals: An Interdisciplinary Journal for the History of Public Health* 4, no. 1 (2004): 29–80; Vladimir M. Shkolnikov, Martin McKee, and David A. Leon, "Changes in Life Expectancy in Russia in the Mid-1990s," *Lancet* 357 (2001): 917–21.

38. On Russian banking sector reform and the economic crash of 1998 see Juliet Johnson, *A Fistful of Rubles: The Rise and Fall of the Russian Banking System* (Ithaca, NY: Cornell University Press, 2000).

39. Ian McAllister and Stephen White, "'It's the Economy, Comrade!' Parties and Voters in the 2007 Russian Duma Election," *Europe-Asia Studies* 60, no. 6 (2008): 931–57; A. V. Makarkin, "Vybory v ramkakh kontrakta," *Pro et contra*, no. 1 (January–February 2008); Henry E. Hale, Michael McFaul, and Timothy J. Colton, "Putin and the 'Delegative Democracy' Trap: Evidence from Russia's 2003–04 Elections," *Post-Soviet Affairs* 20, no. 4 (2004): 285–319; Stephen White and Ian McAllister, "Putin and His Supporters," *Europe-Asia Studies* 55, no. 3 (May 2003): 383–99; Stephen White and Ian McAllister, "The Putin Phenomenon," *Journal of Communist Studies and Transition Politics* 4, no. 24 (2008): 604–28.

40. Hale and Colton write, "These findings suggest that for voting, the change that mattered most between 2000 and 2004 was a general optimism regarding the economy and the government's ability to do something about it rather than the immediate experience or observation of positive change," Henry Hale and Timothy J. Colton, "The Putin Vote: The Demand Side of Hybrid Regime Politics," 16, paper prepared for presentation at the conference "The Frontiers of Political Economics," Higher School of Economics, Moscow, May 29, 2009.

41. Katherine Verdery and Caroline Humphrey, eds., *Property in Question: Value Transformation in the Global Economy* (Oxford: Berg, 2004).

42. M. N. Afanas'ev, *Klientelizm i Rossiiskaia Gosudarstvennost'* (Moscow: Moskovskii obshchestvennyi nauchnyi fond, 2000).

43. See Michael Johnston, "Patrons and Clients, Jobs and Machines: A Case Study of the Uses of Patronage," *American Political Science Review* 73, no. 2 (June 1979): 385–98.

44. On clientelism in Latin American contexts see Alberto Diaz-Cayeros, Federico Estévez, and Beatriz Magaloni, *Strategies of Vote Buying: Democracy, Clientelism and Poverty Relief in Mexico*, and Mariela Szwarcberg, *Mobilizing Poor Voters: Machine Politics, Clientelism, and Social Networks in Argentina* (Cambridge: Cambridge University Press, 2005).

45. Jessica Allina-Pisano, "Social Contracts and Authoritarian Projects in Post-Soviet Space: The Use of Administrative Resource," *Communist and Post-Communist Studies* 43, no. 4 (2010): 373–82. For elsewhere in Eastern Europe see Isabela Mares and Lauren E. Young, *Conditionality and Coercion: Electoral Clientelism in Eastern Europe* (New York: Oxford University Press, 2019).

46. See Timothy Frye, Ora John Reuter, and David Szakonyi, "Hitting Them with Carrots: Voter Intimidation and Vote Buying in Russia," *British Journal of Political Science* 49, no. 3 (July 2019): 857–81.

47. Valerii Vyzhutovich, "Lichnoe mnenie. Pamiati kandidata o demokratii," *Novye Izvestiia*, June 15, 2006.

48. Allina-Pisano, *Post-Soviet Potemkin Village*.

49. A parallel can be observed in the United States following adoption of the Trump administration's tax reform bill in 2018. When House Speaker Nancy Pelosi described resulting increases in take-home pay for many workers as "crumbs" in comparison to the windfalls for wealthy individuals, she was widely criticized for not understanding the importance of even modest bonuses for many.

50. János Kornai, *The Socialist System: The Political Economy of Communism* (Princeton, NJ: Princeton University Press, 1992), 110–30.

51. Andrew Barnes, *Owning Russia: The Struggle over Factories, Farms, and Power* (Ithaca, NY: Cornell University Press, 2006), and Susanne Wengle, *Post-Soviet Power: State-Led Development and Russia's Marketization* (New York: Cambridge University Press, 2015).

52. Mark G. Field, "A Comment on the Russian Health Crisis," *Eurasian Geography and Economics* 46, no. 7 (2005): 5; N. M. Rimashevskaia and I. V. Korkhova, "Poverty and Health in Russia," *Sociological Research* 43, no. 3 (2004): 26; L. L. Rybakovskii, O. D. Zakharova, A. E. Ivanova, and T. A. Demchenko, "Russia's Demographic Future," *Russian Social Science Review* 45, no. 3 (2004): 21; Stephen K. Wegren, *Russia's Policy Challenges: Security, Stability and Development* (New York: M. E. Sharpe, 2003); Arturas Tereskinas, "Men and Social Suffering in Contemporary Lithuania," *Anthropology of East Europe Review* 28, no. 1 (Spring 2010): 23–39. On Soviet semiotic fields and male experience, Lilya Kaganovsky, *How the Soviet Man Was Unmade: Cultural Fantasy and Male Subjectivity under Stalin* (Pittsburgh: University of Pittsburgh Press, 2008).

53. Valerie Sperling, *Organizing Women in Contemporary Russia: Engendering Transition* (New York: Cambridge University Press, 1999).

54. Sue Bridger and Rebecca Kay, "Gender and Generation in the New Russian Labor Market," in *Gender, Generation, and Identity in Contemporary Russia*, ed. Hilary Pilkington (London: Routledge, 1996); Alessandra Stanley, "With Prostitution Booming, Legalization Tempts Russia," *New York Times*, March 3, 1998; Yu. F. Florinskaia,

"Trudovaia migratsiia iz malykh rossiiskikh gorodov kak sposob vyzhivaniia," *Sotsiologicheskie issledovaniia* 6 (2006): 79–87.

55. Sunnee Billingsley, "The Post-Communist Fertility Puzzle," *Population Research Policy Review* 29, no. 2 (April 2010): 193–231.

56. Caroline Humphrey, *The Unmaking of Soviet Life: Everyday Economies after Socialism* (Ithaca, NY: Cornell University Press, 2002).

57. Jessica Allina-Pisano and Eric Allina-Pisano, "'Friendship of Peoples' after the Fall: Violence and Pan-African Community in Post-Soviet Moscow," in *Africa in Russia, Russia in Africa: 300 Years of Encounters*, ed. Maxim Matusevich (Trenton, NJ: Africa World, 2006), 175–98.

58. André Simonyi, "Waiting for the Cows to Come Home: A Political Ethnography of Security in a Complex World; Explorations in the Magyar Borderlands of Contemporary Ukraine" (PhD diss., University of Ottawa, 2013).

59. Nora Dudwick, Elizabeth Gomart, and Alexandre Marc, with Kathleen Kuehnast, *When Things Fall Apart: Qualitative Studies of Poverty in the Former Soviet Union* (Washington, DC: World Bank, 2003).

60. Linda J. Cook, "Brezhnev's 'Social Contract' and Gorbachev's Reforms," *Soviet Studies* 44, no. 1 (1992): 37–56.

61. Serguei Alex. Oushakine, "In the State of Post-Soviet Aphasia: Symbolic Development in Contemporary Russia," *Europe-Asia Studies* 52, no. 6 (2000): 991–1016.

62. Boris Grebenshchikov, "Poezd v ogne," 1988.

63. Jessica Allina-Pisano, "How to Tell an Axe Murderer: An Essay on Ethnography, Truth, and Lies," in *Political Ethnography: What Immersion Contributes to the Study of Power*, ed. Edward Schatz (Chicago: University of Chicago Press, 2009), 66–71.

64. Donald J. Trump, Inauguration speech, Washington, DC, January 20, 2017.

65. Henry Hale, "Explaining Machine Politics in Russia's Regions: Economy, Ethnicity, and Legacy," *Post-Soviet Affairs* 19, no. 3 (July–September 2003); Grigorii V. Golosov, "Russia's Regional Legislative Elections, 2003–2007: Authoritarianism Incorporated," *Europe-Asia Studies* 63, no. 3 (May 2011): 397–414; Kimitaka Matsuzato, "Authoritarian Transformations of the Mid-Volga National Republics: An Attempt at Macro-Regionology," *Journal of Communist Studies and Transition Politics* 20, no. 2 (June 2004).

66. The author thanks Tat'iana Zhurzhenko for this insight, made around a seminar table in 2005 as we discussed an embryonic version of this project. See also Kelly McMann, *Economic Autonomy and Democracy: Hybrid Regimes in Russia and Kyrgyzstan* (New York: Cambridge University Press, 2006).

4. Staging Performances

1. This chapter draws on participant-observation research and unstructured interviews conducted by the author between 1999 and 2014. Interactions with interlocutors took place in the language of their choice (Russian, Ukrainian, and Hungarian).

2. Stephen White, Richard Rose, and Ian McAllister, *How Russia Votes* (Chatham, NJ: Chatham House, 1997); Timothy J. Colton, *Transitional Citizens: Voters and What Influences Them in the New Russia* (Cambridge, MA: Harvard University

Press, 2000); Michael McFaul, "Russia's 1996 Presidential Elections," *Post-Soviet Affairs* 12, no. 4 (1996): 318–50; Ted Brader and Joshua A. Tucker, "The Emergence of Mass Partisanship in Russia, 1993–1996," *American Journal of Political Science* 45, no. 1 (January 2001): 69–83; Marko Bojcun, "The Ukrainian Parliamentary Elections in March–April 1994," *Europe-Asia Studies* 47, no. 2 (March 1995): 229–49; Taras Kuzio, "The 1994 Parliamentary Elections in Ukraine," *Journal of Communist Studies and Transition Politics* 11, no. 4 (1995): 335–61.

3. L. Tarasova, "Nemaie chasu ochikuvaty," *Slobids'kyi krai*, January 29, 2000, 1.

4. Rishennia konstytutsiinoho sudu Ukrainy 27 bereznia 2000 roku no. 3-rp/2000, *Sprava* no. 1-26/2000, accessed November 28, 2016, http://www.ccu.gov.ua/docs/410.

5. A. Molchanov, "Informatsionnoe soobshchenie 'Odesskogo Memoriala' o mitinge, posviashchennom vseukrainskomu referendumu," *Prava Liudyny v Ukraini. Informatsiinyi portal Kharkivs'koi pravozakhysnoi hrupy*, December 27, 2000, Khpg.org, accessed February 24, 2017.

6. Sarah Birch, "The Presidential Election in Ukraine, October 1999," *Electoral Studies* 21 (2002): 339–63.

7. This approach was present in the 1999 presidential elections in some regions. Council of Europe Ad Hoc Committee to Observe the Presidential Elections in Ukraine (October 31 and November 14, 1999), Doc. 8603, December 21, 1999; Kimitaka Matsuzato, "All Kuchma's Men: The Reshuffling of Ukrainian Governors and the Presidential Election of 1999," *Post-Soviet Geography and Economics* 42, no. 6 (2001): 416–39. For Russia see Henry Hale, "Explaining Machine Politics in Russia's Regions: Economy, Ethnicity, and Legacy," *Post-Soviet Affairs* 19, no. 3 (2003); Grigorii V. Golosov, "Machine Politics: The Concept and Its Implications for Post-Soviet Studies," *Demokratizatsiya: The Journal of Post-Soviet Democratization* 21, no. 4 (Fall 2013): 459–80; Vladimir Gel'man and Sergei Ryzhenkov, "Local Regimes, Sub-national Governance and the 'Power Vertical' in Contemporary Russia," *Europe-Asia Studies* 63, no. 3 (May 2011): 449–65.

8. "Pro pidsumky vseukrains'koho referendumu 16 kvitnia 2000 roku," Tsentral'na vyborcha komisiia, Povidomlennia vid 25 kvitnia 2000, last modified April 25, 2000, http://zakon0.rada.gov.ua/laws/show/n0002359-00.

9. E. Zakharov, "Chto zavtra otnimut? A my—otdadim," reporting official figures broadcast by radio in *Prava Liudyny v Ukraini. Informatsiinyi portal Kharkivs'koi pravozakhysnoi hrupy*, December 27, 2000, Khpg.org, accessed February 24, 2017.

10. "Zahal'noderzhavnyi vyborchyi okruh. Rezul'taty holosuvannia 14.11.1999 roku," Cvk.gov.ua, accessed November 28, 2016.

11. Yurii Murashov and Yevhen Dykyi, "Vsenarodnyi referendum 16.04.2000—fars, shcho vidkydaie demokratychni peretvorennia v Ukraini na desiatyrichchia nazad," *Prava Liudyny v Ukraini. Informatsiinyi portal Kharkivs'koi pravozakhysnoi hrupy* 4, accessed July 7, 2014, http://khpg.org.ua.index.php?id=977920235.

12. Klub Veselykh i Nakhodchivykh, LTL, Kharkiv, April 13, 2000.

13. Alena Ledeneva, "Open Secrets and Knowing Smiles," *East European Politics and Societies* 25, no. 4 (November 2011): 720–36.

14. Murashov and Dykyi, "Vsenarodnyi referendum 16.04.2000," 2, accessed July 7, 2014, http://khpg.org.ua.index.php?id=977920235.

15. L. Tarasova, "Referendum: Dumka narodu," *Slobids'kyi krai*, January 25, 2000, 1.
16. Oral testimony (OT), numerous sites in the city of Kharkiv and Kharkiv region, March and April 2000.
17. Murashov and Dykyi, "Vsenarodnyi referendum 16.04.2000," 3, accessed July 7, 2014, http://khpg.org.ua.index.php?id=977920235.
18. Evidence presented here is drawn from the author's observations and conversations in the region in the months leading up to and following the referendum, in subsequent years, and from published and unpublished analyses of the referendum. Conversations took place in district-level and regional-level land offices, among private farmers and local NGOs, on former state and collective farms, and with students at three universities. For more on the research for this book see chapter 1.
19. OT, Kharkiv district, March 29, 2000.
20. Murashov and Dykyi, "Vsenarodnyi referendum 16.04.2000," 3.
21. Murashov and Dykyi, "Vsenarodnyi referendum 16.04.2000," 3.
22. "Shcho dorozhche: Referendum chy diiezdatnyi parlament?," *Slobids'kyi krai*, March 11, 2000, 1; L. Lohvynenko, "Starshi hovoryly za molodshykh," *Slobids'kyi krai*, April 18, 2000.
23. V. Dzereviaho, "'Initsiatyva' kerivnykiv deiakykh ustanov u Kharkovi," *Prava Liudyny v Ukraini. Informatsiinyi portal Kharkivs'koi pravozakhysnoi hrupy*, December, 27, 2000, Khpg.org, accessed February 24, 2017.
24. Endorsements appeared in print and other media. Between January and April, a Kharkiv regional newspaper ran several dozen endorsements of the referendum project that used identical talking points.
25. B. Moskal'ov, "Vyhidno dlia narodu," *Slobids'kyi krai*, February 1, 2000, no. 12–13, 1, and H. Konopel'tsev, "U molodi svidomyi vybir," *Slobids'kyi krai*, April 15, 2000, 2.
26. L. Lohvynenko, "U tsei chas—nahorodam osoblyva tsina," *Slobids'kyi krai*, April 13, 2000, 1, and "Vslukhatysia v holos narodu," *Slobids'kyi krai*, April 6, 2000, 2.
27. "Dzerkalo hromads'koi dumky," *Slobids'kyi krai*, March 28, 2000, 1.
28. OT, Kharkiv, March–April 2000.
29. Field research notes, Chuhuiv, Kharkiv region, April 15, 2000.
30. OT, Kolomats'kyi raion, Kharkiv region, April 6, 2000.
31. "Zaiava hromadianyna Ukrainy Ye. Khoduna Holovi Tsentral'noi vyborchoi komisii p. Riabtsiu," *Prava Liudyny v Ukraini. Informatsiinyi portal Kharkivs'koi pravozakhysnoi hrupy*, December 27, 2000, Khpg.org/977920714, accessed September 9, 2021.
32. OT, Kharkiv Regional State Administration, April 4, 2000.
33. OT, Kharkiv National University, March 29, 2000.
34. Murashov and Dykyi, "Vsenarodnyi referendum 16.04.2000," 3.
35. E. Zakharov, "Chto zavtra otnimut? A my—otdadim," reporting official figures broadcast by radio in *Prava Liudyny v Ukraini. Informatsiinyi portal Kharkivs'koi pravozakhysnoi hrupy*, December 27, 2000, Khpg.org, accessed February 24, 2017.
36. OT, village council official, Kharkiv district, Kharkiv region, March 31, 2000.
37. Postanova Tsentral'noi vyborchoi komisii, March 9, 2000, no. 29, "Pro koshtorys na pidhotovku ta provedennia vseukrains'koho referendumu za narodnoiu

initsiatyvoiu 16 kvitnia 2000 roky," and no. 39, "Pro zatverdzhennia koshtorysiv vydatkiv na pidhotovku ta provedennia vseukrains'koho referendumu za narodnoiu initsiatyvoiu 16 kvitnia 2000 roku," TsDAVO, f. 5225, op. 2.

38. OT, Kharkiv district, March 31, 2000.
39. OT, Kharkiv district land tenure office official, March 31, 2000.
40. OT, Kolomatskyi district, April 6, 2000.
41. "A u Vinnytsi tak," *Prava Liudyny v Ukraini. Informatsiinyi portal Kharkivs'koi pravozakhysnoi hrupy*, December 27, 2000, Khpg.org, accessed February 24, 2017.
42. "Referendum neobkhidnyi!," February 10, 2000.
43. F. Mohish, "Dlia yednosti politychnykh syl," *Novyny Zakarpattia*, February 1, 2000.
44. I. Chopovdia, "Vlada i profspilky: Spivpratsia posyliuiet'sia," *Novyny Zakarpattia*, March 11, 2000.
45. M. Horba, E. Popovych, and V. Prykhod'ko, "Shist' konstruktyvnykh 'tak' narodnykh demokrativ Zakarpattia na shist' pytan' referendumu," *Novyny Zakarpattia*, February 29, 2000; M. Horba, "Dialoh mizh vladoiu i narodom," *Novyny Zakarpattia*, March 7, 2000.
46. V. Pan'kovych, "Tverdishe staty na shliakh utverdzhennia narodovladdia," and I. Lupych, "Vidpovidal'nist' u vsikh—odnakova," *Novyny Zakarpattia*, January 25, 2000.
47. I. Hanych, "Sprava ne v kil'kosti," *Novyny Zakarpattia*, March 2, 2000.
48. N. Maik, "Pered zakonom usi maiut' buty rivnymy," *Novyny Zakarpattia*, February 3, 2000.
49. N. Tehza, "Nash vybir—chitkyi kurs i tverda pozytsiia," *Novyny Zakarpattia*, January 18, 2000, and in the same issue, "Zvernennia lideriv oblasnykh orhanizatsii politychnykh partii Ukrainy bloku 'Nash vybir—Leonid Kuchma!'"
50. V. Pan'kovych, ". . . Shchob parlament zakonodavcho pidkripliuvav khid reform," *Novyny Zakarpattia*, February 3, 2000; "Vyiznyi den' deputata," *Novyny Zakarpattia*, February 19, 2000; V. Pan'kovych and I. Slyvka, "Reformy—u ploshchynu konkretyky," *Novyny Zakarpattia*, February 22, 2000; P. Turianytsia, "Na zasadakh derzhavotvorennia," *Novyny Zakarpattia*, March 11, 2000.
51. Yu. Sadvari, "Krok do prohresyvnykh i vyrishal'nykh zmin u suspil'stvi," *Novyny Zakarpattia*, March 2, 2000.
52. M. Lizanets', "Ya tverdo perekonanyi, shcho plebistsyt provodyty potribno," *Novyny Zakarpattia*, March 2, 2000.
53. "Zadlia konsolidatsii suspil'stva," *Novyny Zakarpattia*, March 4, 2000.
54. "Prezydentu Ukrainy Leonidovi Kuchmi," and I. Usta and M. Palinchak, ". . . Sluzhyty Bohu i narodu," *Novyny Zakarpattia*, January 29, 2000.
55. V. Kravchuk, "Proiavliaiut' odnostainist'," *Novyny Zakarpattia*, March 2, 2000.
56. M. Zozulynets', "Zoseredytysia na realizatsii rehional'nykh problem," *Novyny Zakarpattia*, March 7, 2000.
57. I. Husti, "Holos narodu—'za,'" *Novyny Zakarpattia*, January 1, 2000; V. Telichko, "Viriu u zdorovyi hluzd nashoho narodu," *Novyny Zakarpattia*, January 1, 2000, 5.
58. E.g., I. Slyvka, "Nam neobkhidna konsolidatsiia zusyl'," *Novyny Zakarpattia*, February 8, 2000.

59. M. Rosokha, "Kozhen . . . povynen vidpovidaty personal'no," *Novyny Zakarpattia*, February 29, 2000.

60. M. Pavliuk, "Osvitiany oblasti—za referendum," *Novyny Zakarpattia*, January 1, 2000, 5

61. Kateryna Popova, "Z viroiu v maibutnie," *Novyny Zakarpattia*, March 7, 2000.

62. "Za shchaslyve maibutnie nashykh ditei," *Novyny Zakarpattia*, February 19, 2000.

63. "Vsenarodna initsiatyva, shcho proiniala rozum i sertse," *Novyny Zakarpattia*, February 19, 2000.

64. "Shliakhom suspil'noho prohresu ta demokratii," *Novyny Zakarpattia*, March 7, 2000. Also I. Myhalyna, "Dovesty do lohichnoho kintsia," *Novyny Zakarpattia*, February 19, 2000.

65. For example, M. Mehesh, head of initiative group no. 8 and director of Uzhhorod ZOSh no. 1; I. Husti, "Holos narodu—'za,'" January 1, 2000.

66. OT, Uzhhorod, May 2004.

67. Volodymyr Martin, "Smert' rektora UzhNU—zapytannia bez vidpovidei," *Dzerkalo Tyzhnia*, July 2, 2004.

68. OT, Uzhhorod, May 2004.

69. "Zakarpatskaia mafia: Udar shchupal'tsem spruta. Malen'koe pogranichnoe Zakarpat'e ispokon vekov slavilos' svoimi kurortami, mineral'nymi vodami i peizazhami. A v khronikakh," From-ua.com, May 16, 2005, accessed September 9, 2021.

70. The day of Slyvka's funeral, a colleague whom other academic colleagues had identified as a security services representative insisted I meet with him. Over lunch in an otherwise empty restaurant, he dramatically prolonged the conversation, keeping me at the table until the funeral was over.

71. Vasilii Gertsanich, "Na Zakarpat'e idet 'boi' za Uzhgorodskii natsional'nyi universitet," UA-Reporter.com, August 20, 2009, accessed February 27, 2017.

72. Stepan Tsaregorodtsev, "Zakarpatskii gubernator posle smerti rektora UzhNU Slivki pribiraet universitet pod sebia," Obkom, July 8, 2004, obkom.net.ua, accessed February 27, 2017.

73. Political scientist Vladimir Gel'man explains how contemporary neopatrimonial uses of the power vertical across sectors differ from Soviet-era practices: "The Vicious Circle of Post-Soviet Neopatrimonialism in Russia," *Post-Soviet Affairs* 32, no. 5 (2016): 455–73.

74. Jessica Allina-Pisano, "Social Contracts and Authoritarian Projects in Post-Soviet Space: The Use of Administrative Resource," *Communist and Post-Communist Studies* 43, no. 4 (2010): 1–10; Regina Smyth, Anton Sobolev, and Irina Soboleva, "A Well-Organized Play: Symbolic Politics and the Effect of the Pro-Putin Rallies," *Problems of Post-Communism* 60, no. 2 (March/April 2013): 24–39.

75. Alena V. Ledeneva, "Telephone Justice in Russia," *Post-Soviet Affairs* 24, no. 4 (2008); Alena V. Ledeneva, *Can Russia Modernise? Sistema, Power Networks and Informal Governance* (Cambridge: Cambridge University Press, 2013); Kathryn Hendley, "'Telephone Law' and the 'Rule of Law': The Russian Case," *Hague Journal on the Rule of Law* 1 (2009): 241–62.

76. Jessica Allina-Pisano, *The Post-Soviet Potemkin Village: Politics and Property Rights in the Black Earth* (Cambridge: Cambridge University Press, 2008).

77. The protest song "Razom nas bahato, nas ne podolaty," written by Roman Kalyn, Roman Kostiuk, and Mykola Kulinich, that became the anthem of Ukraine's 2004 "Orange Revolution" refers to these understandings; Ledeneva, "Open Secrets and Knowing Smiles," 720–36.

78. E.g., a report of written, rather than telephoned instructions following Russia's annexation of Crimea. "Moskovskie shkoly poluchili raznariadki k 'putingu' 18 marta," Grani.ru, last modified March 17, 2015, http://grani.ru/Politics/Russia/m.239186.html.

79. GOLOS report, 20–21, last modified November 2, 2011, 5009-golos-zayavlenie-1-02-11-2011-gosduma-pdf.pdf.

80. Committee of Voters of Ukraine, "Report on the Pre-election Environment, September 16–October 3, 2004," October 8, 2004.

81. GOLOS report, 22.

82. "Vybory: Administrativnyi resurs v deistvii," November 11, 2011, Biznes-klass Arkhangel'sk, accessed July 28, 2014, http://www.bclass.ru/vlast-i-obschestvo/vibori-administrativniy-resurs-v-deystvii.

83. Committee of Voters of Ukraine, "Report on the Pre-presidential Election Environment, July 2004," August 12, 2004.

84. Anna Abakunova, "Today on December 2, 2013, in Dnipropetrovsk, a Meeting of 5000 People Was Convened to Support the President," *Ukrains'ki novyny*, December 3, 2013, translated by Nykolai Bilaniuk for UKL.

85. Tatiana Zhurzhenko, *Borderlands into Bordered Lands: Geopolitics of Identity in Post-Soviet Ukraine* (Stuttgart: Ibidem Verlag, 2010); Committee of Voters of Ukraine, "Report on the Pre-election Environment," September 1–15, 2004.

86. Committee of Voters of Ukraine, "Report on the Pre-election Environment," September 13, 2004.

87. See Mischa Gabowitsch, *Protest in Putin's Russia* (Cambridge, MA: Polity, 2017), and Samuel A. Greene, *Moscow in Movement: Power and Opposition in Putin's Russia* (Stanford, CA: Stanford University Press, 2014).

88. OT, Kharkiv, July 2006.

89. Among hundreds of such reports see Oleksandr Palii, "Falsyfikatsiia vyboriv-2004: Yak orhanizovuvavsia 'pidrakhui,'" *Ukrains'ka Pravda*, last modified November 15, 2005, http://www.pravda.com.ua/articles/2005/11/15/3017827/.

90. Oleksandr Burmahin and Natalia Kozarenko, "Shcho take adminresurs, abo yak 'pidstavliaiut'sia' slukhniani kerivnyky," March 2, 2002, accessed July 14, 2014, http://www.uapravo.org/text.php?id=56.

91. GOLOS report, 22.

92. Loren Graham, *The Ghost of the Executed Engineer: Technology and the Fall of the Soviet Union* (Cambridge, MA: Harvard University Press, 1996).

93. See Alena V. Ledeneva, *How Russia Really Works: The Informal Practices That Shaped Post-Soviet Politics and Business* (Ithaca, NY: Cornell University Press, 2006), 91–114.

94. Nadia Druzhynina, "Deputy Candidate Kozachenko Accuses Authorities of Intimidating Voters in Poltava Region: Bread Denied to Voters Who Refuse to Sign Statement to Support Authorities," *Ukrainian News*, June 18, 2004.

95. For example, OT, Kharkiv, 2000; Committee of Voters of Ukraine, "Report on the Pre-election Environment," September 1–15, 2004.

96. For example see "Vybory: Administrativnyi resurs v deistvii," Biznes-klass Arkhangel'sk, accessed July 28, 2014, http://www.bclass.ru/vlast-i-obschestvo/vybory-administrativniy-resurs-v-deystvii; Elena Nikol'skaia, "Samye rasprostranennye narusheniia na vyborakh," Utro.ru Politika, accessed February 2, 2016, http://www.webcitation.org/66qz7cAgc; "Kuplennyi vybor," RIO, accessed October 2, 2012.

97. "Nachal'nik poprosil sfotografirovat' biulleten' s galochkoi v nuzhnom meste?," Rostislav Zhuravlev, Ekho Moskvy, last modified September 29, 2011, http://echo.msk.ru/blog/nazbol_rost/816421-echo/.

98. For example, see "Kak golosovat' za Edinuiu Rossiiu. Instruktsiia: Chto delat', esli tebia zastavliaiut golosovat' za Edinuiu Rossiiu," last modified October 28, 2011, https://youtu.be/7z6_SXvznlY.

99. For Ukraine see "Skoro vybory. Kak zarabotat' na prodazhe golosa, sokhraniv dostoinstvo (instruktsiia)," Zakarpattya.net, last modified July 23, 2012, http://zakarpattya.net.ua/Blogs/98707-Skoro-v%D1%8Bbor%D1%8B.-Kak--zarabotat-na-prodazhe-holosa-sokhranyv-dostoynstvo-ynstruktsyia.

100. "Kak golosovat' za Edinuiu Rossiiu. Instruktsiia: Chto delat', esli tebia zastavliaiut golosovat' za Edinuiu Rossiiu," last modified October 28, 2011, https://youtu.be/7z6_SXvznlY.

101. Jessica Allina-Pisano, "Sub Rosa Resistance and the Politics of Economic Reform: Land Redistribution in Post-Soviet Ukraine," *World Politics* 56, no. 4 (July 2004): 554–81.

102. On detecting practices of falsification see Mikhail Myagkov, Peter C. Ordeshook, and Dimitri Shakin, *The Forensics of Election Fraud: Russia and Ukraine* (Cambridge: Cambridge University Press, 2009).

103. On symbioses of household and enterprise economies see Gavin Kitching, "The Revenge of the Peasant? The Collapse of Large-Scale Russian Agriculture and the Role of the Peasant 'Private Plot' in That Collapse, 1991–97," *Journal of Peasant Studies* 26, no. 1 (1998), and Allina-Pisano, *Post-Soviet Potemkin Village*, 175–76.

104. Sergei Chernov, "Conscripts' Relatives Fear They'll Be Sent to Ukraine amid Alleged Coercion," *Moscow Times*, January 29, 2015.

105. Yuliia Kysel'ova, "Znovu pro fal'syfikatsii: Ryzyky dlia holosuvannia i test na zrilist'," *Telekrytyka*, March 14, 2006.

106. In addition to the sources cited for specific examples here, this section also draws on analysis of findings published in a number of reports, among them those of the Committee of Voters of Ukraine (October 2001–March 2002, August 12, 2004, September 1–5, 2004, and September 13, 2004) and GOLOS.

107. An earlier version of this argument appears in Allina-Pisano, "Social Contracts and Authoritarian Projects in Post-Soviet Space."

108. This is the most documented type of coercion. Among many other examples see Steve Gutterman, "Candidate Claims Fraud in Sochi Mayoral Vote," Associated Press, April 27, 2009.

109. In a well-known example, the European University of Saint Petersburg temporary closed after assessment of fire risk. Faculty members thought it was about a European Commission grant on election monitoring. See Luke Harding, "Russia Shuts University That Displeased Putin," *Guardian*, last modified February 12, 2008, http://www.theguardian.com/world/2008/feb/12/russia. Other references to

the fifty-two fire violations discovered at EUSP that year include Galina Stolyarova, "Education: A Terrible Thing to Waste," *Transitions Online*, April 3, 2008.

110. Committee of Voters of Ukraine, Report on the Pre-election Environment, 2004, September 1–15, 2004.

111. Druzhynina, "Deputy Candidate Kozachenko Accuses Authorities of Intimidating Voters in Poltava Region."

112. "Vybory: Administrativnyi resurs v deistvii," Biznes-klass Arkhangel'sk, last modified November 11, 2011, http://www.bclass.ru/vlast-i-obschestvo/vibori-administrativniy-resurs-v-deystvii.

113. Paul Martin Sacks, *The Donegal Mafia: An Irish Political Machine* (New Haven, CT: Yale University Press, 1976).

114. OT, meeting of regional private farmers' association, Kharkiv, 1999.

115. For a related but contrasting argument that, in the context of property law, identifies roots in Soviet traditions of jurisprudence see Aurore Chaigneau, *Le droit de propriété en mutation. Essai à la lumière du droit russe* (Paris: Dalloz, 2008).

116. Requirements for loyalty toward the center as a condition of access to service provision also were expressed through urban development projects. See Daniela Zupan, Vera Smirnova, and Amanda Zadorian, "Governing through *stolichnaya praktika*: Housing Renovation from Moscow to the Regions," *Geoforum* 120 (2021) 155–64. In the context of Soviet modernity see Nikolai Ssorin-Chaikov, "Hobbes' Gift," in *Two Lenins: A Brief Anthology of Time* (Chicago: University of Chicago Press, 2017), 95–120.

117. Thanks to Sergei Kukharenko for this point.

5. Improvisation

1. This chapter draws on field research in the region conducted by the author between 2004 and 2014. Research visits in nine of the eleven years lasted from a few weeks to a few months.

2. Sherrill Stroschein, *Ethnic Struggle, Coexistence, and Democratization in Eastern Europe* (Cambridge: Cambridge University Press, 2012).

3. Rogers Brubaker, *Nationalism Reframed: Nationhood and the National Question in the New Europe* (New York: Cambridge University Press, 1996).

4. For example, oral testimony (OT), Zakarpattia, Ukraine, July 2008.

5. OT, Berehove, Zakarpattia, August 2008.

6. OT. Conversations in Zakarpattia frequently turned around this theme in 2008, 2009, and 2010.

7. This theme was a perennial topic of conversation among Hungarian speakers in Zakarpattia until Euromaidan. OT, Zakarpattia, 2004, 2007, 2008, 2009, 2010, 2011, 2012. Their complaints closely tracked those of some Russian-speaking Ukrainians in Crimea during the same period: OT, 2009.

8. OT, Zakarpattia, August 2010, September 2011.

9. André Simonyi, "Waiting for the Cows to Come Home: A Political Ethnography of Security in a Complex in a Complex World; Explorations in the Magyar Borderlands of Contemporary Ukraine" (PhD diss., University of Ottawa, 2013).

10. Svetlana Dorosh, "Iskazheny li rezul'taty vyborov v Zakarpat'e," BBC Ukraine, last modified November 4, 2015, https://www.bbc.com/ukrainian/ukraine_in_russian/2015/11/151104_ru_s_transcarpathia_election_results.

11. Tom Balmforth, "Ukraine's Euromaidan Drives Up Price of . . . Illegal Vote Buying," Radio Free Europe / Radio Liberty, October 27, 2014, and Ioulia Shukan, "La circonscription de no. 102: Le terrain de jeux pour enfants comme ersatz de confiance," November 9, 2014, carnets de terrain de Ioulia Shukan, Carnetsdeterrain. wordpress.com.

12. OT, Zakarpattia, June 2014.

13. On subsequent iterations of vote buying in the region, "Iskazheny li rezul'taty vyborov v Zakarpat'e?," BBC Ukraiina, last modified November 4, 2015, https://www.bbc.com/ukrainian/ukraine_in_russian/2015/11/151104_ru_s_transcarpathia_election_results.

14. Vechernii kvartal, last modified March 23, 2019, https://www.youtube.com/watch?v=vov6IoovpVs.

15. "Skoro vybory. Kak zarabotat' na prodazhe golosa, sokhraniv dostoinstvo (instruktsiia)," last modified February 23, 2012, https://zakarpattya.net.ua/Blogs/98707-Skoro-v%D1%8Bbor%D1%8B.-Kak.

16. OT, Zakarpattia, June 2014.

17. Jessica Allina-Pisano, "From Iron Curtain to Golden Curtain: Remaking Identity in the European Union Borderlands," *East European Politics and Societies* 23, no. 2 (May 2009): 266–90.

18. On the reproduction of social discourse as personal narrative see Jessica Allina-Pisano, "How to Tell an Axe Murderer: An Essay on Ethnography, Truth, and Lies," in *Political Ethnography: What Immersion Contributes to the Study of Power*, ed. Edward Schatz (Chicago: University of Chicago Press, 2009), 53–73.

19. Jessica Allina-Pisano, "Sub Rosa Resistance and the Politics of Economic Reform: Land Redistribution in Post-Soviet Ukraine," *World Politics* 56, no. 4 (July 2004): 554–81.

20. Stephen Deets, "The Hungarian Status Law and the Specter of Neomedievalism in Europe," *Ethnopolitics* 7, no. 2–3 (2008): 195–215.

21. Field notes, Zakarpattia, 2004, and subsequent years.

22. Allina-Pisano, "From Iron Curtain to Golden Curtain."

23. Allina-Pisano, "From Iron Curtain to Golden Curtain."

24. OT, Mali Selmentsi, August 2010.

25. OT, Astei-Beregsurány, July 2008.

26. OT, Astei-Beregsurány, July 2008.

27. OT, Zakarpattia, June 2014.

28. OT, Zakarpattia, June 2014.

29. This phenomenon has been amply documented across postsocialist space in Europe and Eurasia. See, among others, Jessica Allina-Pisano, *The Post-Soviet Potemkin Village: Politics and Property Rights in the Black Earth* (Cambridge: Cambridge University Press, 2008); Katherine Verdery, *The Vanishing Hectare: Property and Value in Postsocialist Transylvania* (Ithaca, NY: Cornell University Press, 2003); Caroline Humphrey, *Marx Went Away—but Karl Stayed Behind* (Ann Arbor: University of Michigan Press, 1999).

30. "Perebuvannia pershoho zastupnyka Holovy Verkhovnoii Rady Ukrainy Viktora Medvedchuka v Zakarpatti," *Novyny Zakarpattia*, February 24, 2000.
31. OT, Zakarpattia, May 2004.
32. Simonyi, "Waiting for the Cows to Come Home."
33. For an account of contemporary village-police relations see also Simonyi, "Waiting for the Cows to Come Home."
34. Sunday homily in Hungarian at a Greek Catholic church, Zakarpattia, August 2011. Another book could be written about the sermons delivered in this village and their relationship to the rise of Fidesz and support for Orbán among transborder Hungarians. During fieldwork I normally participated in Ukrainian and Hungarian Mass at a Greek Catholic church but also attended Lutheran services.
35. OT and interviews with parish priests and KMKSZ representatives, Uzhhorods′kyi district and Chop, Zakarpattia, 2010–2012.
36. André Simonyi, "Émergence: Un village en Transcarpatie et ses trois églises," in *Les religions et les modernités politiques*, ed. André Simonyi and Martin Poeti (Montréal: Presses de l'université de Montréal, forthcoming 2022).
37. OT, Zakarpattia, August 2011.
38. Field notes, Uzhhorods′kyi district, Zakarpattia, 2012.
39. Ilona Lechner, "A szülők arra kérik a politikusokat és a hivatalnokokat, hogy szeptember 1-jén ne menjenek az iskolákba," Kárpátalja.ma, last modified August 19, 2017.
40. OT, Zakarpattia, August 2010 and July 2011. Accounts of shareholders, a farm mechanic, and retired milkmaid, respectively.
41. OT, Zakarpattia, June 2014.
42. Field notes, Zakarpattia, July 2011.
43. OT, Zakarpattia, August 2010.
44. OT, Zakarpattia, May 2004.
45. Allina-Pisano, "From Iron Curtain to Golden Curtain," 266–90.
46. OT, Zakarpattia, July 2007; Allina-Pisano, "From Iron Curtain to Golden Curtain."
47. Simonyi, "Waiting for the Cows to Come Home."
48. OT, Zakarpattia, August 2010.
49. OT, Zakarpattia, August 2010.
50. For example, Zakarpattia regional state archive (DAZO), 47.1.380 (1944).
51. See also Simonyi, "Waiting for the Cows to Come Home."
52. OT, Zakarpattia, August 2011.
53. Loren Graham, *The Ghost of the Executed Engineer: Technology and the Fall of the Soviet Union* (Cambridge, MA: Harvard University Press, 1996).
54. OT, Zakarpattia, June 2014.
55. OT, Zakarpattia, June 2014.
56. OT, Zakarpattia, June 2014.
57. "Potik bizhentsiv v krainu-susidku Zakarpattia zrostaie," *Novyny Zakarpattia*, February 9, 2015.
58. "U Zakarpatti obureni vyhadkamy Lavrova pro mobilizatsiiu za national′noiu oznakoiu," Radio Svoboda, January 30, 2018.
59. OT, Zakarpattia, June 2014.
60. OT, Zakarpattia, June 2014.
61. OT, Zakarpattia, June 2011.

62. OT, Zakarpattia, June 2014.

63. "VHO 'Komitet vybortsiv Ukraiiny' vydav zvit po dniu holosuvannia," last modified October 29, 2012, 12, https://www.cvu.dn.ua/ru/news/vgo-komitet-viborciv-ukrayini-vidav-zvit-po-dnyu-golosuvannya.

64. OT, Zakarpattia, August 2011.

65. On Baloha's influence in the region see Piotr Żochowski and Tadeusz Iwański, "Zakarpattia—Together, But Separated," accessed April 17, 2018, https://www.osw.waw.pl/en/publikacje/osw-commentary/2015-09-30/zakarpattia-together-separated.

66. OT, Zakarpattia, May 2004 and subsequent years.

67. Field notes, Zakarpattia, July 2011.

68. Field notes, Zakarpattia, June–October 2011.

69. Allina-Pisano, *Post-Soviet Potemkin Village*.

70. OT and field notes, Zakarpattia, March 2011.

71. Snizhana Rusyn, "U tsyhans'komu tabori v zakarpats'kyi Ivanivtsi zhyve tysiacha liudei," Zakarpattia onlain, accessed April 7, 2018, www.zakarpattya.net.ua.

72. Iryna Uzlova, "Tsyhan Yanukovych," Ukraina Moloda, last modified January 30, 2013, http://www.umoloda.kiev.ua/number/2215/116/78867; "Zakarpats'komu Yanukovychu vzhe vypovnylosia 2 rochky," Mukachevo.net, accessed April 7, 2018, http://mukachevonet/ua/news/view/53460. Years later, just a few kilometers away, a baby would be named for President Zelensky. Yevhen Kizilov, "Malen'kyi D'opiosh Zelens'kyi: z'iavylysia detail pro novonarodzhenoho tezku prezydenta," *Ukraiins'ka Pravda*, last modified June 18, 2020, http://www.pravda.com.ua/news/2020/06/18/7256248.

73. See tongue-in-cheek video reportage, "Yanukovich zhivet v tsyganskom tabore na Zakarpat'e: On zdes' avtoritet," last modified January 13, 2014, https://censor.net.ua/video_news/266225/yanukovich_jivet_v_tsyganskom_tabore_na_zakarpate_on_zdes_avtoritet_video.

74. "Obiednana opozytsiia zaiavliaie pro systemni porushennia v roboti vyborchyh dil'nyts' na Zakarpatti," Zakarpatpost.net, February 10, 2012.

75. For example, Ivan Kolodii, "Nestikavi vybory na Zakarpatti," *L'vivs'ka hazeta*, no. 56, March 28, 2006.

76. "Kuplenyi vybir," rionews.com.ua, last modified, October 2, 2012.

77. "VHO 'Komitet vybortsiv Ukrainy' vydav zvit po dniu holosuvannia," last modified October 29, 2012, https://www.cvu.dn.ua/ru/news/vgo-komitet-viborciv-ukrayini-vidav-zvit-po-dnyu-golosuvannya.

78. For discussion of this point see Oleg Tkachuk, "Vybory-2019: Kak budut pokupat' golosa izbiratelei i v kakuiu summu eto oboidetsia," vesti-ukr.com, January 11, 2019, accessed May 9, 2019.

79. Studies that regard this problem through the lens of electoral fraud likewise find spatial variation. See Robert G. Moser and Allison C. White, "Does Electoral Fraud Spread? The Expansion of Electoral Manipulation in Russia," *Post-Soviet Affairs* 33, no. 2 (March 2017): 85–99.

80. OT, Zakarpattia, June 2014.

6. Meanings of Participation

1. For an account of this and episodes of Ukraine's "Revolution of Dignity" see Ioulia Shukan, *Génération Maïdan. Vivre la crise ukrainienne* (Paris: L'Aube, 2016).

2. For example, "Na Evromaidani blyz'ko 200 tysiach liudei khorom zaspivaly himn Ukrainy," *Novyny Kyieva* na 1+1-TSN.ua, December 14, 2013. "Okean El'zy, kontsert na Evromaidani," EspresoTV, last modified December 15, 2013, https://www.youtube.com/watch?v=MfUvKkz579Q.

3. Segodnia.ua, "Zamgossekretaria SShA razdala na Maidane khleb," *Russia Today*, accessed December 11, 2013, https://www.youtube.com/watch?v=JHXu5GBorXo; BBC News Ukraiina, "Nuland pryhostyla maidanivtsiv pechyvom," last modified December 11, 2013, https://www.youtube.com/watch?v=nWKVHp1G56o.

4. "Zamgossekretaria SShA razdala liudiam na Maidane khleb i pechen'e," Kanal Ukraina; "Nuland i Paiett na Maidane razdaiut pechen'e aktivistam i silovikam," nbnews, accessed May 13, 2016, nbnews.com.ua/ru/news/107673; "Zamgossekretaria SShA razdala mitinguiushchim na Maidane khleb i pechen'e," last modified December 11, 2013, https://www.mk.ru/social/article/2013/12/11/958167-zamgossekretarya-ssha-razdala-mitinguyuschim-na-maydane-hleb-i-pechene.html.

5. Interview with Christiane Amanpour on CNN International's "Amanpour," posted on US State Department website, accessed April 21, 2014, iipdigital.usembassy.gov/st/English/texttrans/2014/04.

6. For example, "Zamgossekretaria SShA razdaet liudiam na Maidane pechen'e i bulochki," Segodnia.ua, accessed May 13, 2016, http://Segodnia.ua/politics/news/zamgossekretarya-ssha-razdaet-lyudyam-na-maydane-pechene-i-bulochki-481921.html.

7. Alexandr Maksimenko, "Sandwiches Are Symbol of Sympathy to Ukrainians at Maidan: Nuland," Sputnik, accessed December 18, 2013, http://sputniknews.com/politics/20141218/1015963186.html.

8. "U.S. Point Person on Ukraine Crisis," CNN, accessed July 7, 2016, http://edition.cnn.com/TRANSCRIPTS/1404/25/ampr.01.html.

9. "MID Ukrainy: Nuland razdavala uchastnikam Maidana imenno pechen'e," RIA Novosti, last modified February 9, 2016, http://ria.ru/world/20160219/1377330507.html. Similar coverage was carried elsewhere. For example, "V Kieve utochnili assortiment razdavavshikhsia Nuland na Maidane produktov," Lenta.ru, last modified February 19, 2016, https://lenta.ru/news/2016/02/19/cookiesnuland/.

10. Aleksandra Sergomasova, "Razdavavshaia pechen'e na Maidane Nuland sobralas' na Ukrainu," TV Center, last modified May 4, 2021, https://www.tvc.ru/news/show/id/210179.

11. See "Kto tam spriatalsia za blok. Politicheskaia kukhnia v deistvii," accessed September 10, 2015, http://vmestezp.org/novosti/zaporozhe/4002-kto-tam-spryatalsya-za-blok-politicheskaya-kuhnya-v-deystvii.html.

12. For a post-Maidan example see Vitalii Chervonenko, "Chernigovskie vybory: Den'gi, grechka, i Saakashvili," BBC Ukraina, last modified July 21, 2015, https://www.bbc.com/Ukrainian/ukraine_in_Russian/2015/07/150721_ru_s_chernihiv_election_new.

13. Emily S. Channell-Justice, "'We're Not Just Sandwiches': Europe, Nation, and Feminist (Im)Possibilities on Ukraine's Maidan," *Signs: Journal of Women in Culture and Society* 42, no. 3 (2017): 717–41.

14. IIP Digital, US Department of State text and transcripts, April 23, 2014, interview with Christiane Amanpour, accessed May 11, 2016, iipdigital.usembassy.gov/st/english/texttrans/2014/04.

15. See Valerie J. Bunce and Sharon L. Wolchik, *Defeating Authoritarian Leaders in Postcommunist Countries* (New York: Cambridge University Press, 2011); Joshua A. Tucker, "Enough! Electoral Fraud, Collective Action Problems, and Post-Communist Colored Revolutions," *Perspectives on Politics* 5, no. 3 (September 2007): 535–51; Lucan Way, "The Real Causes of the Color Revolutions," *Journal of Democracy* 19 (July 2008): 55–69; Mark Beissinger, "An Interrelated Wave," *Journal of Democracy* 20, no. 1 (January 2009): 74–77; and Paul D'Anieri, ed., *Orange Revolution and Aftermath: Mobilization, Apathy, and the State in Ukraine* (Washington, DC: Woodrow Wilson Center and Johns Hopkins University Press, 2010).

16. "Zhena Viktora Yanukovicha schitaet, chto vo vremia aktsii na Maidane Nezavisimosti razdaiut amerikanskie valenki i nakolotye narkotikami apel'siny," Ukrainskaia Pravda, last modified November 30, 2004, http://www.pravda.com.ua/rus/news/2004/11/30/4383455/.

17. Ivan Krastev, "Ukraine's Easy Work," *World Affairs Journal*, accessed June 16, 2016, http://www.worldaffairsjournal.org/blog/ivan-krastev/ukraines-easy-work; Richard Boudreaux, "Bucks Populi: Making Democracy a Going Concern in Kiev: Rent-a-Crowd Entrepreneurs Find People Fast to Cheer or Jeer for $4 an Hour," *Wall Street Journal*, February 5, 2010.

18. Grigorii Yudin, "Vybory protiv golosovaniia," *Vedomosti*, March 2, 2012.

19. Frederic C. Schaffer, *Democracy in Translation: Understanding Politics in an Unfamiliar Culture* (Ithaca, NY: Cornell University Press, 2000).

20. Henry Hale, "The Myth of Mass Russian Support for Autocracy: The Public Opinion Foundations of a Hybrid Regime," *Europe-Asia Studies* 63, no. 8 (2011): 1357–75.

21. Scholars have noted the significance of loyalty in how social scientists evaluate elections, as well as the dual meaning of Russian elections generally. See Mariia Zavadskaia and Vsevolod Bederson, "Kto i kak otsenivaet vybory: Osobennosti ekspertnogo kachestva regional'nykh vyborov 13 sentiabria 2015 goda v Rossii," *Mir Rossii* 27, no. 3 (2018): 82–106. Nikolai Grishin has suggested that elections serve as a release valve and to index public opinion: "The Meaning of Elections in the Russian Federation," *European Politics and Society* 16, no. 2 (2015): 194–207.

22. Natalya Roudakova, *Losing Pravda: Ethics and the Press in Post-Truth Russia* (Cambridge: Cambridge University Press, 2017), 6.

23. Numerous commentators and sociologists attest to the timing of this shift. Vladimir Rimskii, "Otnoshenie rossiian k institutu vyborov," Radio Svoboda, last modified November 17, 2011, https://www.svoboda.org/a/24394759.html.

24. Aleksandra Glukhova, "Triumf 'Slugi naroda,'" *Kommuna*, April 5, 2019.

25. Gulnaz Sharafutdinova, "Was There a 'Simple Soviet' Person? Debating the Politics and Sociology of 'Homo Sovieticus,'" *Slavic Review* 78, no. 1 (2019): 173–95, as well as Samuel Greene, "Homo Post-Sovieticus: Reconstructing Citizenship in Russia," *Social Research: An International Quarterly* 86, no. 1 (2019): 181–202.

26. Erving Goffman, *The Presentation of the Self in Everyday Life* (New York: Anchor Books, 1959).

27. A critical analysis of this vocabulary may be found in William Jay Risch, "Who's Laughing Now? What Volodymyr Zelensky's Presidential Win May Mean for Ukraine Studies," *NewsNet: News of the Association for Slavic, East European and Eurasian Studies* 59, no. 3 (June 2019): 2–7.

28. Timothy Frye, Scott Gehlbach, Kyle Marquardt, and Ora John Reuter, "Is Putin's Popularity Real?," *Post-Soviet Affairs* 33, no. 1 (2017): 1–15.

29. James C. Scott, *Weapons of the Weak: Everyday Forms of Peasant Resistance* (New Haven, CT: Yale University Press, 1985), and *Domination and the Arts of Resistance: Hidden Transcripts* (New Haven, CT: Yale University Press, 1990).

30. Alexei Yurchak, "Soviet Hegemony of Form," *Comparative Studies in Society and History* 45, no. 3 (2003): 480–510.

31. Alexei Yurchak, *Everything Was Forever, Until It Was No More* (Princeton, NJ: Princeton University Press, 2005), 23.

32. See Gulnaz Sharafutdinova and Neringa Klumbyte, eds., *Soviet Society in the Era of Late Socialism, 1965–1984* (Lanham, MD: Lexington Books, 2012).

33. On monarchical tropes in contemporary Russian politics see Natalia Mamonova, "Naïve Monarchism and Rural Resistance in Contemporary Russia," *Rural Sociology* 81, no. 3 (2016): 316–42.

34. Irina Soboleva and Regina Smyth, "Peer Pressure, Protest Dynamics, and Democratic Commitment," Working Paper, 2017.

35. "Sotsiologiia: Krizis doveriia," *Novaya Gazeta*, accessed July 10, 2015, www.novayagazeta.ru/politics/51942.html.

36. "Strana vybiraet dostoinykh," *Ogonek*, June 26, 1973.

37. Benedict Anderson, *Imagined Communities: Reflections on the Origin and Spread of Nationalism* (London: Verso, 1983).

38. "Vybory bez vybora [Elections without a choice]. Chitateli 'Gubernii' vspominaiut, kak golosovali v sovetskie gody," Guberniia, accessed October 4, 2017, https://www.gubernia74.ru/articles/society/21044.

39. Victor Zaslavsky and Robert J. Brym, "The Functions of Elections in the USSR," *Soviet Studies* 30 (1978): 362–71.

40. Lisa Wedeen advances a related argument about Syria under Hafez al-Assad in *Ambiguities of Domination: Politics, Rhetoric, and Symbols in Contemporary Syria* (Chicago: University of Chicago Press, 1999).

41. Rasma Karklins, "Soviet Elections Revisited: Voter Abstention in Noncompetitive Voting," *American Political Science Review* 80, no. 2 (June 1986): 449–70.

42. Henry N. Brailsford, *How the Soviets Work* (New York: Vanguard, 1927). As quoted in Howard R. Swearer, "The Functions of Soviet Local Elections," *Midwest Journal of Political Science* 5, no. 2 (May 1961): 129–49. Also see Richard M. Scammon, "Why the Russians Bother with Elections," *New York Times Magazine*, April 6, 1958, 14, 63–64.

43. Alsu Tagirova, "Elections: A Feedback Mechanism in the Soviet Union?," *Sources and Methods*, last modified March 12, 2018, https://www.wilsoncenter.org/blog-post/elections-feedback-mechanism-the-soviet-union, accessed November 29, 2018. Tagirova references documents in the Presidential Archive of the Republic of Kazakhstan, f. 708, op. 42, d. 308, 38–41.

44. Most of the literature on Russian and Ukrainian elections in the 1990s takes this position. Even literature on post-Soviet electoral clientelism proceeds from a baseline assumption that during this period, most people understood elections as being about choice. Some see this frame as predominant up through and including the election of Vladimir Putin to his first term as president. See Timothy J. Colton

and Michael McFaul, *Popular Choice and Managed Democracy: The Russian Elections of 1999 and 2000* (Washington, DC: Brookings Institution, 2003).

45. "Vybory: Analizy, prognozy. V urne lezhalo . . . zerkalo," *Kommuna*, December 21, 1995, 1.

46. A. Glukhova, dotsent VGU, "Tri neschast'ia rossiiskoi demokratii," *Kommuna*, October 3, 1995, 3.

47. "Komu byt' vo glave Voronezha. Obrashcheniie predstavitelei tvorcheskoi intelligentsii k izbirateliam g. Voronezha," *Kommuna*, December 9, 1995, 1.

48. V. Volodin, "Kazhdyi golos mozhet stat' reshaiushchim," *Kommuna*, December 16, 1995, 1.

49. V. Kordov, "Zavtra—vybory. Idi! I smotri ne oshibis'," *Komuna*, December 16, 1995, 1.

50. V. Rakhmanin, "Vybory: Klany i partii," *Kommuna*, December 14, 1995, 3.

51. V. Kordov, "Obzor pisem v 'Kommunu.' Prostoi chelovek v bol'shoi politike," *Kommuna*, December 15, 1995, 1.

52. "Slovo izbirateliam," *Kommuna*, December 9, 1995, 3.

53. *Kommuna*, October 10, 1995, 1.

54. *Kommuna*, October 25, 1995, 1.

55. Beatriz Magaloni, *Voting for Autocracy: Hegemonic Party Survival and Its Demise in Mexico* (Leiden: Cambridge University Press, 2006); Jennifer Gandhi and Ellen Lust-Okar, "Elections under Authoritarianism," *Annual Review of Political Science* 12, no. 1 (2009): 403–22.

56. Yana Gorokhovskaia, "What It Takes to Win When the Game Is Rigged: The Evolution of Opposition Electoral Strategies in Moscow, 2012–2017," *Democratization* 26, no. 6 (2019): 975–92.

57. Barbara Geddes, *How Dictatorships Work: Power, Personalization, and Collapse* (Cambridge: Cambridge University Press, 2018), 129–53; Georgy Egorov and Konstantin Sonin, "Dictators and Their Viziers: Endogenizing the Loyalty-Competence Trade-Off," *Journal of the European Economic Association* 9, no. 5 (2011): 903–30.

58. E.g., Ora John Reuter and Graeme Robertson, "Subnational Appointments in Authoritarian Regimes: Evidence from Russian Gubernatorial Appointments," *Journal of Politics* 74, no. 4 (2012): 1023–37.

59. Nikolai Grishin, "The Meaning of Elections in the Russian Federation," *European Politics and Society* 16, no. 2 (2015): 194–207.

60. Ariel Ahram and Paul Goode, "Researching Authoritarianism in the Discipline of Democracy," *Social Science Quarterly* 97, no. 4 (2016): 834–49.

61. Patrick Chabal and Jean-Pascal Daloz, *Culture Troubles: Politics and the Interpretation of Meaning* (Chicago: University of Chicago Press, 2006).

62. Oleg Kharkhordin, "What Is the State? The Russian Concept of *Gosudarstvo* in the European Context," *History and Theory* 40 (May 2001): 206–40, and Oleg Kharkhordin, *Republicanism in Russia: Community before and after Communism* (Cambridge, MA: Harvard University Press, 2018).

63. "'Ya gosudarev chelovek i obiazana otdat' svoi grazhdanskii dolg.' Izbirateli na Podmoskovnykh uchastkakh o tom, zachem oni progolosovali za 'Edinuiu Rossiiu' i LDPR," *Novaia gazeta*, September 19, 2016.

64. E. A. Kulagina, "Politicheskaia kul'tura rossiian: Motivatsiia uchastiia i neuchastiia v vyborakh (na primere vyborov v Gosudarstvennuiu dumu)," *Monitoring obshchestvennogo mneniia: Ekonomicheskie i sotsial'nye peremeny* 4, no. 84 (2007): 22.

65. A major online educational platform highlights a lesson on the theme "Elections are my civic duty'": https://infourok.ru/klassniy-chas-na-temuviborimoy-grazhdanskiy-dolg-1174843.html, accessed June 1, 2021.

66. K. Heorhiiev, "Iak vyrishyt' narod-tak i bude!," *Slobids'kyi krai*, April 18, 2000, 1.

67. Vlad Kovleiskii, "Prodannyi golos, ili urna dlia nigilista," *Moskovskii komsomolets*, September 23, 1999.

68. "Zirky ne zalyshylysia v storoni pid chas vyboriv i vykonaly svii hromadians'kyi obov'iazok," last modified April 2, 2019, https://ukr.media/culture/389081.

69. "'Braty uchast' u vyborakh—nash hromadians'kyi obov'iazok,' Mytropolyt Iosaf," last modified April 10, 2019, https://news.church.ua/2019/04/10.

70. Nikolai Starykh, "'Voiny kopromatov' ne budet?," *Kommuna*, October 12, 2007; "Na vstreche Prezidenta s doverennymi litsami byli i Kommunovtsy," *Kommuna*, February 13, 2004.

71. Ol'ga Rudenko, "Deputat v svoem okruge. Dal slovo—derzhi," *Kommuna*, October 24, 2003.

72. Petr Chalyi, "Deputat za rabotoi. Proshchai, pechnoi dymok nad kryshei," *Kommuna*, October 24, 2003.

73. Vladimir Volodin, "Golosovat' nado za deputatov, sposobnykh otstaivat' interesy naroda," *Kommuna*, November 14, 2003.

74. "Glas naroda. Voronezhtsy—o vyborakh v gosudarstvennuiu Dumu," *Kommuna*, November 14, 2003.

75. Volodin, "Golosovat' nado za deputatov, sposobnykh otstaivat' interesy naroda."

76. Aleksei Nakvasin, "Vybory-2003. Glavnyi administrativnyi resurs—poriadochnost'," *Kommuna*, November 20, 2003.

77. "Opros. Pust' kazhdyi sam reshaet," *Kommuna*, January 27, 2004.

78. "Opros. Pust' kazhdyi sam reshaet"; Nikolai Starykh, "Vybory. 'Razbudit' molodogo izbiratelia," *Kommuna*, October 26, 2007.

79. Ol'ga Rudenko, "Za chestnye vybory—na dele," *Kommuna*, October 24, 2003.

80. Nakvasin, "Vybory-2003. Glavnyi administrativnyi resurs—poriadochnost'."

81. "Na temu vyborov. Mezhdu pravdoi i 'chernym' piarom," *Kommuna*, March 6, 2004.

82. "Vybory-2003. Po Voronezhu vovsiu letaiut lipovye listki," *Kommuna*, October 18, 2003.

83. Aleksandr Sysoev, "Dolg politika—rastit' patriotov," *Kommuna*, November 20, 2003.

84. Vasilii Chernousov, "Pravo na vybor," *Kommuna*, November 10, 2007.

85. Novogodnee obrashchenie k grazhdanam Rossii, last modified December 31, 2018, www.kremlin.ru/events/president/news/59629.

86. Ksenia Zubacheva, interview with Timothy J. Colton, "Memo from Valdai: Treat Russia Like a Normal Country with Its Own Interests," Russia Direct, last modified October 23, 2015, https://russia-direct.org/qa/memo-valdai-treat-russia-normal-country-its-own-interests.

87. On a more tightly controlled variation on this theme see Laura Adams, *The Spectacular State: Culture and National Identity in Uzbekistan* (Durham, NC: Duke University Press, 2010).

88. See Masha Gessen's discussion of Yuri Levada's well-known *Sovietskii Prostoi Chelovek* in *The Future Is History: How Totalitarianism Reclaimed Russia* (New York: Riverhead Books, 2017), 60–66. These antinomies, they write, "required Homo Sovieticus to fragment his consciousness to accommodate both of the contradictory positions . . . [to] hold two contradictory beliefs at the same time. These beliefs ran on parallel tracks, and so long as the tracks indeed did not cross, they were not in conflict" (61).

89. But see Brian D. Taylor, *The Code of Putinism* (New York: Oxford University Press, 2018) and Marlene Laruelle, *Is Russia Fascist? Unraveling Propaganda East and West* (Ithaca: Cornell University Press, 2021).

90. Aurore Chaigneau, *Le droit de propriété en mutation. Essai à la lumière du droit russe* (Paris: Dalloz, 2008), 84.

91. On compartmentalization of public and private patriotic repertoires in Russia see J. Paul Goode, "Humming Along: Public and Private Patriotism in Putin's Russia," in *Everyday Nationhood: Theorising Culture, Identity and Belonging after Banal Nationalism*, ed. Michael Skey and Marco Antonsich (London: Palgrave Macmillan, 2017), 121–46.

92. Alena V. Ledeneva, *Russia's Economy of Favors: Blat, Networking, and Informal Exchange* (Cambridge: Cambridge University Press, 1998).

93. Cosmina Tanasoiu, "Homo Post-communistus: Portrait of a Character in Transition," *Perspectives on European Politics and Society* 14, no. 4 (2013): 599–612.

94. Bertolt Brecht, "The Modern Theater Is the Epic Theater: Notes to the Opera *Aufstieg und Fall der Stadt Mahagonny*" (1950), in *Brecht on Theater: The Development of an Aesthetic*, ed. and trans. John Willett (New York: Hill & Wang, 1977), 37.

95. Petrov, "Putingi i mitingi," Slon, accessed November 16, 2015, http://slon.ru/russia/putingi_i_mitingi_742378.xhtml.

96. Mischa Gabowitsch, "Are Copycats Subversive? Strategy-31, the Russian Runs, the Immortal Regiment, and the Transformative Potential of Non-hierarchical Movements," *Problems of Post-Communism* 65, no. 5 (2018): 297–314.

7. States of Ambiguity

1. See Mischa Gabowitsch, "Are Copycats Subversive? Strategy-31, the Russian Runs, the Immortal Regiment, and the Transformative Potential of Non-hierarchical Movements," *Problems of Post-Communism* 65, no. 5 (2016): 307, and Svetlana Boym, *Another Freedom: The Alternative History of an Idea* (Chicago: University of Chicago Press, 2010).

2. For accounts of the development of this movement see Gabowitsch, "Are Copycats Subversive?," 307, and Ivan Kurilla, "Memory of the War and Other Memories in Russia, 2019," *PONARS Eurasia*, last modified May 8, 2019, http://www.ponarseurasia.org/point-counter/article/memory-war-and-other-memories-russia-2019.

3. Françoise Daucé, *Une paradoxale oppression: Le pouvoir et les associations en Russie* (Paris: CNRS éditions, 2013); Graeme B. Robertson, *The Politics of Protest in*

Hybrid Regimes: Mapping Dissent in Post-Communist Russia (Cambridge: Cambridge University Press, 2011).

4. Thanks to fellows at the Institute for Advanced Study at Central European University for discussion of an early version of this chapter and argument in fall 2015.

5. Maksim Hanukai, "Resurrection by Surrogation: Spectral Performance in Putin's Russia," *Slavic Review* 79, no. 4 (Winter 2020): 800–824; Anya Bernstein, "Love and Resurrection: Remaking Life and Death in Contemporary Russia," *American Anthropologist* 118, no. 1 (2016): 12–23. On war memorialization, for example, Julie Fedor, Markku Kangaspuro, Jussi Lassila, and Tatiana Zhurzhenko, eds., *War and Memory in Russia, Ukraine, and Belarus* (Cham, Switzerland: Palgrave Macmillan Memory Studies, 2017); and Shaun Walker, *The Long Hangover: Putin's New Russia and the Ghosts of the Past* (Oxford: Oxford University Press, 2018), 21–42.

6. Mischa Gabowitsch, "Russia's Arlington? The Federal Military Memorial Cemetery near Moscow," paper presented at the conference "Russian Politics beyond the Kremlin," Yale University, November 4, 2016.

7. See video, last modified May 9, 2015, https://www.youtube.com/watch?v=IOb0YTcWZFY; video, last modified May 12, 2012, https://www.youtube.com/watch?v=Z06pR01MUhg; video, last modified May 13, 2012, https://www.youtube.com/watch?v=Go6iejoBdbc.

8. "Ob aktsii 'Bessmertnyi polk' izvestno podavliaiushchemu bol'shinstvu rossiian," Ekho Moskvy, May 22, 2015.

9. Moypolk, accessed September 23, 2015, http://moypolk.ru/eto-est-nash-bessmertnyy-osnovnye-voprosy-k-istorii-bessmertnogo-polka.

10. Moypolk, last modified April 29, 2021, http://moypolk.ru/ustav-polka.

11. Moypolk, last modified April 29, 2021, http://moypolk.ru/ustav-polka.

12. Moypolk, last modified April 29, 2021, http://moypolk.ru/ustav-polka.

13. On Soviet treatments of the war see Nina Tumarkin, *The Living and the Dead: The Rise and Fall of the Cult of World War II in Russia* (New York: Basic Books, 1994). Many of the films to which today's participants had been exposed were produced in the 1970s and 1980s. Some of those most widely viewed included *Letiat zhuravli* (1957), *Oni srazhalis' za rodinu* (1975), *My iz budushchego* (2008), *Zvezda* (2002), *V avguste 44-go* (2001), *Podvig razvedchika* (1947), *Brestskaia krepost'* (2010), *Zhenia, Zhenechka i "Katyusha"* (1967), *Kukushka* (2002), and *Dva boitsa* (1943).

14. Moypolk, accessed October 2, 2015, http://moypolk.ru/eto-est-nash-bessmertnyy-osnovnye-voprosy-k-istorii-bessmertnogo-polka.

15. Parts of the permanent exhibition, some of which date to the mid-1990s, may be viewed at https://www.warmuseum.kiev.ua/.

16. See Serguei Alex. Oushakine, *The Patriotism of Despair: Nation, War, and Loss in Russia* (Ithaca, NY: Cornell University Press, 2009), 51. See also Ries's discussion of a "community of shared suffering": Nancy Ries, *Russian Talk: Culture and Conversation during Perestroika* (Ithaca, NY: Cornell University Press, 1997), 87.

17. Olga Shevchenko, "A Sea of Moving Faces: The Visual Politics of the Immortal Regiment Movement," paper presented at the annual meeting of ASEEES, Boston, December 6–9, 2018.

18. Video, accessed August 3, 2015, https://www.youtube.com/watch?v=DnJPfZCuZJ0.

19. Video, accessed September 23, 2015, https://www.youtube.com/watch?v=foXc8M9fomU.

20. "Amurskaia oblast': 'Bessmertnyi polk' iz shkol'nikov i russko-kitaiskii saliut v Den' Pobedy," last modified May 7, 2015, http://moypolk.ru/news/amurskaya-oblast-bessmertnyy-polk-iz-shkolnikov-i-russko-kitayski.

21. Riavrn, last modified May 9, 2015, http://riavrn.ru/news/uchastniki-aktsii-bessmertnyy-polk-pronesli-po-voronezhu-fotografii-voevavshikh-rodnykh/.

22. See video, last modified May 11, 2015, https://www.youtube.com/watch?v=TDggZ-_SxIw&index=169&list=PLOLvyeJJ1Jk0-SgzKrI7MOH65b2QsScF2.

23. "Russian Reporters 'Attacked at Secret Soldier Burials,'" BBC News, last modified August 27, 2014, www.bbc.com/news/world-europe-28949582.

24. See Pal Kosto, "Symbol of the War—but Which One? The St George Ribbon in Russian Nation Building," *Slavonic and East European Review* 94, no. 4 (October 2016): 660–701.

25. See Mischa Gabowitsch, "Etnographiia Dnia Pobedy," *Neprikosnovennyi zapas* 3, no. 101 (2015): 109.

26. Andrei Okara, "Den' Pobedy kak informatsionnaia duel' Moskvy i Kieva (zametki)," Ekho Moskvy, accessed September 28, 2015, http://m.echo.msk.ru/blogs/detail.php?ID=1552514.

27. Serguei Alex. Oushakine, "Performative Objects: How Things Do Things without Words," in *Russian Performances: Word, Object, Action*, ed. Julie A. Buckler, Julie A. Cassiday, and Boris Wolfson (Madison: University of Wisconsin Press, 2018), 54–63.

28. On divergent meanings and interpretations that had emerged in the Ukraine-Russia borderlands see Tetiana Zhurzhenko, "'Chuzha viina' chy 'spil'na Peremoha'? Natsionalizatsiia pam'iati pro Druhu svitovu viinu na ukraino-rosiis'komu prykordonni," *Ukraina moderna*, no. 18 (2011): 100–26.

29. Examples of this locution in Ukrainian media in 2014 are numerous. For example, see comments section on "ATO Na Vostoke Ukrainy 2 maia, Gorod Nikopol," May 2, 2014, City-nikopol.com.ua/3373-ato-na-vostoke-ukrainy-2-maya-foto-video-obnovlyaetsya.html.

30. On interpretations of these events and the roles of ethnic identity see Henry E. Hale, Oxana Shevel, and Olga Onuch, "Believing Facts in the Fog of War: Identity, Media and Hot Cognition in Ukraine's 2014 Odesa Tragedy," *Geopolitics* 23, no. 4 (September 2018): 851–81.

31. "Bessmertnyi polk! Gozman vs Karaulov. Skandal v studii!," video, accessed October 12, 2015, https://www.youtube.com/watch?v=P3hNjF5PE2U.

32. The identity of the man in the photograph carried by the president later became an object of minor controversy. For example, Maksim Bakulev, "'Bessmertnyi polk.' Chei portret nes Putin?," newsBabr.com, accessed February 2, 2016, http://newsbabr.com/msk/?IDE=135646.

33. Video, accessed October 6, 2015, https://www.youtube.com/watch?v=D0PV56MFexc.

34. As reported on website of the movement Moypolk, accessed September 21, 2015, http://moypolk.ru/moskva-v-kolonne-polka-vyshli-bolee-300-tysyach-chelovek.

35. Jessica Allina-Pisano, "How to Tell an Axe Murderer: An Essay on Ethnography, Truth, and Lies," in *Political Ethnography: What Immersion Contributes to the Study of Power*, ed. Edward Schatz (Chicago: University of Chicago Press, 2009), 68–70.

36. Moypolk, accessed September 21, 2015, http://moypolk.ru/buturlinovka-voronezhskaya-oblast-bessmertnyy-polk-dlya-pokazuhi-ili-pochemu-v-kolonny-polka-ne; Zoia Koshik, "K pamiati naroda—s uvazheniem," *Stroitel'stvo i Nedvizhimost' v Voronezhskom raione*, no. 22 (723), May 28–June 3, 2015.

37. Moypolk, accessed September 21, 2015, http://moypolk.ru/v-sele-ilinka-habarovskogo-kraya-v-kolonnu-polka-vpervye-vstali-60-chelovek.

38. Oleg Lur'e, "'Bessmertnyi polk.' Tekhnologia feikov i bol'shie den'gi," Ekho Moskvy, last modified May 11, 2015, http://echo.msk.ru/blog/oleg_lurie/1546.508-echo/.

39. For example, https://www.youtube.com/watch?v=PjK-tyIXz1E, accessed May 11, 2015.

40. Maria Snegovaya, Facebook discussion thread on "Slov nyet. 'Bessmertnyi polk'—napolovinu feik. V printsipe, nichego novogo, no, vse ravno, zhut', konechno," last modified May 10, 2015, http://www.kasparov.ru/material.php?id=554F9AAE21954. Others observed that the presence of schoolchildren was a sign of state-led activity. On generationally defined experiences of protest see Svetlana Erpyleva, "'Na mitingi ia ne khodil, menia roditeli ne otpuskali': Vzroslenie, zavisimost' i samostoiatel'nost' v depolitizirovannom kontekste," in *Politika apolitichnykh: Grazhdanskie dvizheniia v Rossii 2011–2013 godov* (Moscow: Novoe literaturnoe obozrenie, 2015), 106–40.

41. Evgenii Kiselev, "Moe 9 maia. Posleslovie ko Dniu Pobedy," last modified May 11, 2015, http://echo.msk.ru/blog/kiselev/1546320-echo/.

42. Ksenia Larina, Ekho Moskvy, https://www.youtube.com/watch?v=1drlmGPgEiQ.

43. Dmitrii Gordon on Victory Day celebrations, last modified May 6, 2019, https://www.youtube.com/watch?v=QUxDadsabqQ.

44. Andrei Okara, "Den' Pobedy kak informatsionnaia duel' Moskvy i Kieva (zametki)," Ekho Moskvy, accessed September 28, 2015, http://m.echo.msk.ru/blogs/detail.php?ID=1552514.

45. Boris Romanov, "Kak Stalin otmenil den' Pobedy v 1947 godu," www.proza.ru/2010/05/11/32, last modified May 11, 2010.

46. For biographical note and interview see Ol'ga Yarusova, "Vladislav Gubskii: 'Studenty—oni kak deti,'" *Alma Mater. Gazeta Tomskogo Gosudarstvennogo Universiteta*, no. 2574, last modified January 29, 2015, http://almamater.tsu.ru/show_story.phtml?nom=2574&s=6747.

47. Vladislav V. Gubskii, "Zhurnalistskaia initsiativa 'Bessmertnyi polk' v aspekte formirovaniia grazhdanskogo obshchestva," *Zhurnalistskii ezhegodnik* 1 (2012): 58.

48. Gabowitsch, "Etnografiia Dnia Pobedy."

49. Moypolk, accessed September 21, 2015, http://moypolk.ru/node/316780.

50. Moypolk, accessed September 23, 2015, http://moypolk.ru/eto-est-nash-bessmertnyy-osnovnye-voprosy-k-istorii-bessmertnogo-polka.

51. Viacheslav Kozlov, Natal'ia Korchenkova, "'Bessmertnyi polk' ne khochet v shtat. Avtory obshchestvennoi initsiativy prosiat ogradit' ikh ot biurokratii i politiki," *Kommersant*, last modified May 29, 2015, http://kommersant.ru/doc/2736209.

52. "Vladimir Putin predostereg ot biurokratizatsii aktsii 'Bessmertnyi polk,'" Ekho Moskvy, last modified May 29, 2015, http://echo.msk.ru/news/1557174-echo.html. See also gazeta.ru and previous day's report on Ekho, "Prezident Putin vyskazal ozabochennost' i predostereg ot biurokratizatsii initsiativy 'Bessmertnyi polk,'" Ekho Moskvy, last modified May 28, 2015, http://echo.msk.ru/news/1557052-echo.html.

53. Mark Morjé Howard, *The Weakness of Civil Society in Post-Communist Europe* (Cambridge: Cambridge University Press, 2003).

54. See, for example, Samuel A. Greene, *Moscow in Movement: Power and Opposition in Putin's Russia* (Redwood City, CA: Stanford University Press, 2014); Mischa Gabowitsch, *Protest in Putin's Russia* (Cambridge: Picador, 2016); Boris Gladarev, "Istoriko-kulturnoe nasledie Peterburga: Rozhdenie obshchestvennosti iz dukha goroda," in *Ot obshchestvennogo k publichnomu*, ed. Oleg Kharkhordin (Saint Petersburg: EUSP, 2011), 69–304; and Oleg Kharkhordin on the *Zhivoi gorod* movement in Kharkordin, *Republicanism in Russia: Community before and after Communism* (Cambridge, MA: Harvard University Press, 2018).

55. Boris Zhukov, "Sotsial'no-ekologicheskii Soiuz" ("l'Union socio-écologique") 2004, as quoted in Daucé, *Une paradoxale oppression*, 27.

56. Daucé, *Une paradoxale oppression*.

57. Tatiana Barchunova, "Siberian Immortal Regiment Deployment in Moscow, or How Regional Grassroots Initiatives Are Appropriated by Kremlin Patriotic Education Program," paper presented at the conference "Russian Politics beyond the Kremlin," Yale University, November 4, 2016.

58. Gabowitsch, "Are Copycats Subversive?," 14.

59. See Nikolai Petrov, "Putingi i mitingi," Slon.ru, last modified February 6, 2012, http://slon.ru/russia/putingi_i_mitingi_-742378.xhtml.

60. Scott Radnitz, *Weapons of the Wealthy: Predatory Regimes and Elite-Led Protests in Central Asia* (Ithaca, NY: Cornell University Press, 2010); Robertson, *Politics of Protest in Hybrid Regimes*.

61. See Regina Smyth, Anton Sobolev, and Irina Soboleva, "A Well-Organized Play: Symbolic Politics and the Effect of the Pro-Putin Rallies," *Problems of Post-Communism* 60, no. 2 (March–April 2013): 26.

62. For example, Marina Zateichuk, Elizaveta Surnacheva, Tonia Samsonova, and Nikolai Dzis'-Voinarovskii, "Skol'ko liudei khodiat na mitingi? A na 'putingi'?," Slon, last modified June 6, 2012. See also Julia Ioffe, "Protest and Pretend in Moscow," *New Yorker*, last modified February 4, 2012, https://www.newyorker.com/news/news-desk/protest-and-pretend-in-moscow.

63. "Poll: Half of Ukrainians Don't Support Kyiv Euromaidan," *Kyiv Post*, last modified December 30, 2013, http://www.kyivpost.com/content/ukraine/poll-half-of-ukrainians-dont-support-kyiv-euromaidan-rb-334469.html.

64. Oral testimony (OT), June 2014, Zakarpattia.

65. Jessica Allina-Pisano, "Legitimizing Facades: Civil Society in Post-Orange Ukraine," in *Orange Revolution and Aftermath: Mobilization, Apathy, and the State in Ukraine*, ed. Paul D'Anieri (Washington, DC: Woodrow Wilson Center and Johns Hopkins University Press, 2010), 229–53.

66. OT, Kharkiv Regional State Administration, July 2006.

67. Anna Abakunova, "Today on December 2, 2013, in Dnipropetrovsk, a Meeting of 5000 People Was Convened to Support the President," *Ukrains'ki novyny*, December 3, 2013, translated by Nykolai Bilaniuk for UKL.

68. OT, June 2014, Zakarpattia.

69. Presidential decree no. 355/2007, "Pro dostrokove prypynennia povnovazhen' Verkhovnoii Rady Ukrainy ta pryznachennia pozacherhovykh vyboriv," April 26, 2007.

70. Allina-Pisano, "Legitimizing Facades."

71. E.g., Viktor Stepanenko and Yaroslav Pylynskyi, eds., *Ukraine after the Euromaidan* (Bern: Peter Lang, 2015).

72. Mark R. Beissinger, "Structure and Example in Modular Political Phenomena: The Diffusion of Bulldozer/Rose/Orange/Tulip Revolutions," *Perspectives on Politics* 5, no. 2 (June 2007): 259–76; Valerie J. Bunce and Sharon L. Wolchik, "Favorable Conditions and Electoral Revolutions," *Journal of Democracy* 17, no. 4 (2006): 5–18; Taras Kuzio, "Civil Society, Youth, and Societal Mobilization in Democratic Revolutions," *Communist and Post-Communist Studies* 39 (2006): 365–86.

73. Andrew Wilson, *Virtual Politics: Faking Democracy in the Post-Soviet World* (New Haven, CT: Yale University Press, 2005); Jessica Allina-Pisano, "Klychkov i Pustota: Post-Soviet Bureaucrats and the Production of Institutional Facades," in *What Is Soviet Now?*, ed. Thomas Lahusen and Peter Solomon (London: LIT Verlag, 2007), 40–56.

74. Stephen Boykewich, "Protests for Hire in Former Soviet World," Agence France-Presse, May 9, 2007. For a firsthand description of travel from Donetsk to protest in Kyiv see Oleksandr Chernenko, "'Goluboi' vagon," *Fokus*, no. 16, accessed April 23, 2007, http://focus.in.ua/article/12596.html.

75. See Valerie Bunce and Sharon Wolchik, *Defeating Authoritarian Leaders in Postcommunist Countries* (New York: Cambridge University Press, 2011).

76. Ioulia Shukan, "Orchestrating a Protest Movement to Conduct a Revolution," and Tammy Lynch, "Building a Revolution: Elite Choice and Opposition Tactics in Pre-Orange Ukraine," both in *Orange Revolution and Aftermath: Mobilization, Apathy, and the State*, ed. Paul D'Anieri (Washington, DC: Woodrow Wilson Center and Johns Hopkins University Press, 2010); Mark Beissinger, *Nationalist Mobilization and the Collapse of the Soviet State* (Cambridge: Cambridge University Press, 2002).

77. Shukan, "Orchestrating a Protest Movement."

78. Ioulia Shukan, "The Orange Revolution: Reflections about a Successful Strategy of Collective Action," *Institut d'Études Politiques de Paris*, 2006, 10.

79. Inna Vedernikova, "Profsoiuz: Iz karmana 'sovka' na skovorodku kapitala?," *Zerkalo nedeli*, December 17, 2005.

80. Kateryna Shchotkina, "Kul'turna polityka: 'Tretii'—zaivyi?," *Dzerkalo tyzhnia*, July 13–19, 2002.

81. Michael W. Foley and Bob Edwards, "Beyond Tocqueville: Civil Society and Social Capital in Comparative Perspective," *American Behavioral Scientist* 42, no. 1 (September 1998): 12; James Coleman, *Foundations of Social Theory* (Cambridge, MA: Harvard University Press, 1990); Robert D. Putnam, *Making Democracy Work: Civic Traditions in Modern Italy* (Princeton, NJ: Princeton University Press, 1993); and Robert D. Putnam, *Bowling Alone: The Collapse and Revival of American Community* (New York: Simon & Schuster, 2000).

82. Valerie Sperling, *Organizing Women in Contemporary Russia: Engendering Transition* (Cambridge: Cambridge University Press, 1999).

83. Shchotkina, "Kul'turna polityka."

84. In 2000, the efforts of the leaders of the Kharkiv regional farmers' organization to collect dues from members frequently resulted in frustration. OT, Kharkiv region, 2000.

85. Shchotkina, "Kul'turna polityka."

86. Robertson, *Politics of Protest in Hybrid Regimes*; Elizabeth Plantan, "Not All NGOs Are Created Equal: Selective Repression and Civil Society in Russia and China," paper presented at the workshop "Citizens and the State in Authoritarian Regimes: Comparing Mass Politics and Policy in China and Russia," University of Notre Dame, March 10, 2017.

87. Panel presentation, "The State of the Civil Society and Human Rights in Russia," Central European University, Budapest, December 8, 2015.

88. Shchotkina, "Kul'turna polityka."

89. See Greene, *Moscow in Movement*.

90. Pavel Arsen'ev, "Grazhdanskoe obshchestvo vliiatel'naia sila. Dlia togo, chtoby ono moglo vypolniat' svoiu funktsiiu, neobkhodimo finansirovanie iz nezavisimykh ot vlasti istochnkov," *Nezavisimaia gazeta*, April 12, 2001.

91. Author field notes, Kolomats'kyi District, Kharkiv oblast, April 6, 2000.

92. Vitalii Kulik, "'Grantoed' pod mikroskopom," website of Hromads'ki initsiatyvy u vyborakh, accessed January 17, 2006, http://vybir.cpe.org.ua/articles/item_21.html.

93. Anatolii Gritsenko, "Ataka vlasti na 'grantoedov,'" *Zerkalo nedeli*, December 13, 2003.

94. OT, Kharkiv Regional State Administration, July 2006. Jessica Allina-Pisano, "Legitimizing Facades: Civil Society in Post-Orange Ukraine," in *Orange Revolution and Aftermath: Mobilization, Apathy, and the State in Ukraine*, ed. Paul D'Anieri (Washington, DC: Woodrow Wilson Center and Johns Hopkins University Press, 2010), and Stanislav Markus, "Sovereign Commitment and Property Rights: The Case of Ukraine's Orange Revolution," *Studies in Comparative International Development* 51, no. 4 (June 2015).

95. Author's interview with a district official, Kharkiv oblast, July 2006.

96. OT, head of organization, Kharkiv, July 2006.

97. For example, Jo Crotty, Sarah Marie Hall, and Sergej Ljubownikow, "Post-Soviet Civil Society Development in the Russian Federation: The Impact of the NGO Law," *Europe-Asia Studies* 66, no. 8 (2014): 1253–69.

98. See Stephen Kotkin's analysis of the complexities of the relationship between the concepts state and society in Jan Gross's early work, revisiting the meaning of the Soviet proposition *"Gosudarstvo—eto my!"* in "The State—Is It Us? Memoirs, Archivists, and Kremlinologists," *Russian Review* 61, no. 1 (January 2002): 35–51.

99. Here it may be useful to differentiate between what Foley and Edwards describe as "polemical and heuristic" uses of the concept of civil society. Arguably, visions of civil society advanced in the English-language literature on Eastern European politics frequently fell into the former category. Foley and Edwards, "Beyond Tocqueville," 5–20.

100. Grzegorz Ekiert and Jan Kubik, *Rebellious Civil Society: Popular Protest and Democratic Consolidation in Poland, 1989–1993* (Ann Arbor: University of Michigan Press, 1999).

101. Jean L. Cohen and Andrew Arato, *Civil Society and Political Theory* (Cambridge, MA: MIT Press, 1994).

102. David Abramson, "A Critical Look at NGOs and Civil Society as a Means to an End in Uzbekistan," *Human Organization* 58, no. 3 (1999): 244.

103. Alexandra Hrycak, "Foundation Feminism and the Articulation of Hybrid Feminisms in Post-Socialist Ukraine," *East European Politics and Societies* 20, no. 1 (2006): 69–100.

104. Timothy Mitchell, *Rule of Experts: Egypt, Techno-Politics, Modernity* (Berkeley: University of California Press, 2002).

105. Andrii Mykhalko, ed., *Pisennyi vinok: Ukrains'ki narodni pisni* (Kyiv: Krynytsia, 2007), accessed April 29, 2021, http://nashe.com.ua/source/30.

106. Shevchenko, "Sea of Moving Faces."

107. Smyth, Sobolev, and Soboleva, "Well-Organized Play," 31.

108. Petrov, "Putingi i mitingi."

109. Kharkordin, *Republicanism*.

110. Irina Soboleva and Regina Smyth, "Peer Pressure, Protest Dynamics, and Democratic Commitment," Working Paper, 2017.

111. Aleksandr M. Panchenko, "'Potemkinskie derevni' kak kul'turnyi mif" in *Russkaia istoriia i kul'tura: Raboty raznykh let* (Saint Petersburg: Yuna 1999), 462–75.

112. Allina-Pisano, "How to Tell an Axe Murderer," 53–73.

113. E.g., Maksim Grigor'ev, *Fake-Struktury: Prizraki rossiiskoi politiki* (Moscow: Evropa, 2007), 22.

114. Smyth, Sobolev, and Soboleva, "Well-Organized Play," 29.

115. Gabowitsch, "Are Copycats Subversive?," 1.

116. Stephen Kotkin, "From Overlooking to Overestimating Putin's Authoritarianism," *Slavic Review* 68, no. 3 (Fall 2009): 550.

117. Jan Gross, "A Note on the Nature of Soviet Totalitarianism," *Soviet Studies* 34, no. 3 (1982): 367–76; Stephen Kotkin, "The State—Is It Us? Memoirs, Archives, and Kremlinologists," *Russian Review* 61, no. 1 (2002): 35–51.

118. Oleg Kharkhordin, "What Is the State? The Russian Concept of *Gosudarstvo* in the European Context," *History and Theory* 40 (May 2001): 206–40.

119. Alena V. Ledeneva, *Can Russia Modernise? Sistema, Power Networks and Informal Governance* (Cambridge: Cambridge University Press, 2013); Henry E. Hale, *Patronal Politics: Eurasian Regime Dynamics in Comparative Perspective*, Problems of International Politics (Cambridge: Cambridge University Press, 2014); Stanislav Markus, *Property, Predation, and Protection: Piranha Capitalism in Russia and Ukraine* (Cambridge: Cambridge University Press, 2015).

120. Kate Brown, *Plutopia: Nuclear Families, Atomic Cities, and the Great Soviet and American Plutonium Disasters* (Oxford: Oxford University Press, 2013), and "Gridded Lives: Why Kazakhstan and Montana Are Nearly the Same Place," *American Historical Review* 106, no. 1 (February 2001): 17–48; Daniel Mark Vyleta, "City of the Devil: Bulgakovian Moscow and the Search for the Stalinist Subject," *Rethinking History* 4, no. 1 (2000): 37–53.

121. Sheila Fitzpatrick, *Stalin's Peasants: Resistance and Survival in the Russian Village after Collectivization* (Oxford: Oxford University Press, 1996).

122. Anna Krylova, "The Tenacious Liberal Subject in Soviet Studies," *Kritika: Explorations in Russian and Eurasian History* 1, no. 1 (Winter 2000): 119–46.

123. Michiko Kakutani, *The Death of Truth: Notes on Falsehood in the Age of Trump* (New York: Tim Duggan Books, 2018), 147.

124. For an overview see Timothy L. Thomas, "Russia's Reflexive Control Theory and the Military," *Journal of Slavic Military Studies* 17 (2004): 237–56.

125. Serguei Alex. Oushakine, "The Terrifying Mimicry of Samizdat," *Public Culture* 13, no. 2 (2001): 192.

126. "Bednye amerikantsy. Mne ikh tak zhalko," last modified August 18, 2018, https://www.youtube.com/watch?v=Bb1OF47Zs9k.

127. Ivan Kurilla, *Zakliatye druz'ia: Istoriia mnenii, fantazii, kontaktov, vzaimo(ne) ponimaniia Rossii i SShA* (Moscow: Novoe Literaturnoe Obozrenie, 2018).

128. Dominic Boyer and Alexei Yurchak, "American Stiob: Or, What Late-Socialist Aesthetics of Parody Reveal about Contemporary Political Culture in the West," *Cultural Anthropology* 25, no. 2 (2010): 179–221; Alexei Yurchak, *Everything Was Forever, Until It Was No More: The Last Soviet Generation* (Princeton, NJ: Princeton University Press, 2006); Alexei Yurchak, "Gagarin and the Rave Kids: Transforming Power, Identity, and Aesthetics in the Post-Soviet Night Life," in *Consuming Russia: Popular Culture, Sex, and Society Since Gorbachev*, ed. Adele Barker (Durham, NC: Duke University Press, 1999), 76–109. Also Svetlana Boym, "Estrangement as Lifestyle: Shklovsky and Brodsky," *Poetics Today* 17 (1996): 511–30.

129. Iurii Saprykin, "Na slozhnykh shchakh," Afisha, accessed March 16, 2017, and "10 let khipsterskoi Rossii. Iurii Saprykin and Daniil Trabun o nachale i kontse epokhi," Afisha, accessed March 16, 2017, Daily.afisha.ru.

130. Boyer and Yurchak, "American Stiob," 186.

131. Boyer and Yurchak, 213.

132. Gabowitsch, "Are Copycats Subversive?," 6.

133. Vladislav Surkov, "Dolgoe gosudarstvo Putina. O tom, chto zdes' voobshche proiskhodit," *Nezavisimaia Gazeta*, February 11, 2019.

134. Valery Gerasimov, "Tsennost' nauki v predvidenii. Novye vyzovy trebuiut pereosmyslit' formy i sposoby vedeniia boevykh deistvii," *Voenno-Promyshlennyi Kur'er*, last modified February 26, 2013, https://www.vpk-news.ru/articles/14632; Mark Galeotti, "The 'Gerasimov Doctrine' and Russian Non-linear War," last modified July 6, 2014, https://Inmoscowsshadows.Wordpress.Com/2014/07/06/The-Gerasimov-Doctrine-And-Russian-Non-Linear-War/; Ofer Fridman, *Russian Hybrid Warfare: Resurgence and Politicisation* (New York: Oxford University Press, 2018).

135. Matthew A. Lauder, "'Wolves of the Russian Spring': An Examination of the Night Wolves as a Proxy for the Russian Government," *Canadian Military Journal* 18, no. 3 (Summer 2018): 5–16.

136. Maria Snegovaya, "Putin's Information Warfare in Ukraine: Soviet Origins of Russia's Hybrid Warfare," Russia Report I, *Institute for the Study of War*, September 2015.

137. Kakutani, *Death of Truth*, 158.

138. Alice Marwick and Rebecca Lewis, *Media Manipulation and Disinformation Online*, datasociety.net, last modified May 15, 2017, https://datasociety.net/library/media-manipulation-and-disinfo-online/.

139. Jan Plamper, "Abolishing Ambiguity: Soviet Censorship Practices in the 1930s," *Russian Review* 60 (October 2001): 526–44.

140. Katerina Clark, *The Soviet Novel: History as Ritual* (Chicago: University of Chicago Press, 1981).

141. Nikolai Starykh, "V podderzhku Putina," *Kommuna*, October 27, 2007.

142. "Den' narodnogo edinstva v Cheboksarakh," last modified November 4, 2019, https://www.youtube.com/watch?v=XCL-FP4Kyic.

143. Lisa Wedeen, *Ambiguities of Domination: Politics, Rhetoric, and Symbols in Contemporary Syria* (Chicago: University of Chicago Press, 1999).

Conclusion: A New Social Contract

1. Andrei Dolzhenkov, "6 iiulia Nikitinskii teatr provedet tealtral'nyi marafon," *Gorsovety Voronezh*, https://gorsovety.ru/recommended/6-iyulya-nikitinskij-teatr-provedet-teatralnyj-marafon, accessed October 22, 2019.

2. See "Budet li srok Putina poslednim, pytki antifashistov i sud nad SK," Leonid Volkov in *"Budet khuzhe" s Sergeem Smirnovym*, http://www.youtube.com/watch?v=AKY56QgnZus, last modified January 31, 2018.

3. Vladislav Surkov, "Dolgoe gosudarstvo Putina. O tom, chto zdes' voobshche proiskhodit," *Nezavisimaia gazeta*, February 11, 2019.

4. Valerie Sperling shows that gendered discourse likewise works as a mechanism of legitimation for both regime supporters and critics. Sperling, *Sex, Politics, and Putin: Political Legitimacy in Russia* (Oxford: Oxford University Press, 2014).

5. Yevgeny Gontmakher, "V Rossii poiavilas' novaia model' obshchestvennogo ustroistva: Feodalizm 2.0," MK RU, November 27, 2019, https://www.mk.ru/politics/2019/11/27/v-rossii-poyavilas-novaya-model-obshchestvennogo-ustroystva-feodalizm-20.html.

6. Oral Testimony (OT), Szentendre, Hungary, July 2017.

7. Serguei Oushakine, "In the State of Post-Soviet Aphasia: Symbolic Development in Contemporary Russia," *Europe-Asia Studies* 52, no. 6 (2000): 991–1016.

8. Bálint Magyar, *A Magyar Maffiaállam anatómiája* (Budapest: Noran Libro Kiadó, 2015).

9. Grigorii V. Golosov has argued that this has been the case in Russia, that contemporary authoritarianism at the national level represents an amalgamation of previous tendencies observable in the regions. Golosov, "Russia's Regional Legislative Elections, 2003–2007: Authoritarianism Incorporated," *Europe-Asia Studies* 63, no. 3 (May 2011): 397–414. In the United States, Robert Mickey, *Paths Out of Dixie: The Democratization of Authoritarian Enclaves in America's Deep South, 1944–1972* (Princeton, NJ: Princeton University Press, 2015).

10. Studies that examine electoral command performances through the lens of electoral fraud likewise find spatial variation. See Robert G. Moser and Allison C. White, "Does Electoral Fraud Spread? The Expansion of Electoral Manipulation in Russia," *Post-Soviet Affairs* 33, no. 2 (March 2017): 85–99.

11. Philip Abrams, "Notes on the Difficulty of Studying the State," *Journal of Historical Sociology* 1, no. 1 (March 1988 [1977]): 58–89. Reprinted in Aradhana Sharma and Akhil Gupta, eds., *The Anthropology of the State: A Reader* (Oxford: Blackwell, 2006), 112–30.

12. Loren Graham, *The Ghost of the Executed Engineer: Technology and the Fall of the Soviet Union* (Cambridge, MA: Harvard University Press, 1996).

13. Jessica Pisano, "Rethinking Regime Hybridity: Risk Shift and Economies of Compliance in Post-Soviet Space," paper presented at the annual meeting of the American Political Science Association, September 2013, and Jessica Allina-Pisano, "Social Contracts and Authoritarian Projects in Post-Soviet Space: The Use of Administrative Resource," *Communist and Post-Communist Studies* 43, no. 4 (2010).

14. See Max Fisher, "This One Map Helps Explain Ukraine's Protests," *Washington Post*, December 9, 2013.

15. Chrystia Freeland offered a helpful (if optimistic) corrective to some such interpretations, as posted by Thomas Young, "10 Maps That Explain Ukraine's Struggle for Independence," Brookings Institution, May 21, 2015, http://www.brookings.edu/blogs/brookings-now/posts/2015/05/21-ukraine-maps. On this variation in Russia see Henry Hale, "Explaining Machine Politics in Russia's Regions: Economy, Ethnicity, and Legacy," *Post-Soviet Affairs* 19, no. 3 (2003): 228–63.

16. Henry Hale, *Patronal Politics: Eurasian Regime Dynamics in Comparative Perspective* (Cambridge: Cambridge University Press, 2014); Dan Slater, "Democratic Careening," *World Politics* 65, no. 4 (October 2013): 729–63.

17. In the United States see Marc J. Hetherington and Jonathan D. Weiler, *Authoritarianism and Polarization in American Politics* (Cambridge: Cambridge University Press, 2009).

18. Natalia Zubarevich, "Four Russias: Rethinking the Post-Soviet Map," openDemocracy, March 29, 2012, https://www.opendemocracy.net/en/odr/four-russias-rethinking-post-soviet-map/.

19. Oleg Tkachuk, "Vybory—2019: Kak budut pokupat' golosa izbiratelei i v kakuiu summu eto oboidetsia," vesti.ua, last modified January 11, 2019.

20. Brian Taylor, *State Building in Putin's Russia: Policing and Coercion after Communism* (Cambridge: Cambridge University Press, 2011); Erica Marat, *The Politics of Police Reform: Society against the State in Post-Soviet Countries* (New York: Oxford University Press, 2018).

21. Stanislav Markus, *Property, Predation, and Protection: Piranha Capitalism in Russia and Ukraine* (Cambridge: Cambridge University Press, 2015).

22. Ukrainian media covered these events extensively: "V Odesi aktyvisty 'liustruvaly' nechesnoho suddiu na prizvyshche Bondar," ukr.media February 26, 2015; "'Smittieva' liustratsiia v Ternopil's'kii oblasti: U bak pislia sudu kynuly chynovnyka z lishospu," 112ua.tv, December 8, 2015. On lb.ua, "Deputata Odesskogo gorsoveta brosili v musornyi bak," July 29, 2015; "Nachal'nika iustitsii Ivano-Frankovskoi oblasti brosili v musornyi bak," April 9, 2015; "Khar'kovskogo deputata, kotorogo 'liustrirovali' v musornom bake, gospitalizirovali. Vladimir Skorobagach poluchil travmu golovy i ozhog rogovitsy glaza," December 24, 2014; "'Musornaia liustratsiia' dokatilas' do Chernovtsov. Po tsentru goroda v musornom bake prokatilsia glavvrach odnogo iz gospitalei," October 1, 2014; Prokuror Dnepropetrovskoi oblasti podvergsia 'musornoi' liustratsii. Genprokuror poobeshchal nakazat' obidchikov Romana Fedika," September 30, 2014; "V Cherkassakh dvoikh deputatov oblsoveta zasunuli v musornyi bak. Aktivisty proveli 'liustratsiiu' regionala i kommunista," September 25, 2014; "Pilipishin napisal zaiavlenie v militsiiu posle togo, kak ego brosili v musornik. Odin iz khuliganov zaderzhan," September 26, 2014; "Eshche odnogo nardepa okunuli v musornoe vedro. Aktivisty 'liustrirovali' eks-regionala Grushevskogo," September 23, 2014; "Tolpa pod Radoi zapikhnula 'regionala' Zhuravskogo v

musornyi bak (obnovleno). Politika poimali pod zdaniem Verkhovnoi Rady v Kieve," September 16, 2014.

23. "Narodna liustratsiia: Holovnoho likaria Terebovlians′koii likarni vykynuly u smitnyk," Channel 4 television, Ternopil′, https://tv4.te.ua/narodna-lyustratsiya-golovnogo-likarya-t/, last modified October 1, 2014.

24. "Liustratsiia po narodnomu holovnyi likar Terebovlia," https://www.youtube.com/watch?v=iPqTtkZKIuY, last modified October 1, 2014.

25. "Svoimi glazami—Vybory v Ukraine 26.10.2014," https://www.youtube.com/watch?v=NxIKVEtsOrs, accessed September 18, 2018.

26. "Chernovtsy. V musornom bake okazalsia Glavvrach voennogo gospitalia," https://www.youtube.com/watch?v=-9ys0KDf7WA, accessed September 18, 2018.

27. Oleg Kharkhordin, *The Collective and the Individual in Russia: A Study of Practices* (Berkeley: University of California Press, 1999).

28. Victor Zaslavsky and Robert Brym, "The Functions of Elections in the USSR," *Soviet Studies* 30, no. 3 (July 1978): 364, and Max E. Mote, *Soviet Local and Republic Elections* (Stanford, CA: Stanford University Press, 1965), 64.

29. Valerie Sperling, *Organizing Women in Contemporary Russia: Engendering Transition* (Cambridge: Cambridge University Press, 2009).

30. Shoshana Zuboff, *The Age of Surveillance Capitalism: The Fight for a Human Future at the New Frontier of Power* (New York: Public Affairs, 2019); Caroline Humphrey and Katherine Verdery, eds., *Property in Question: Value Transformation in the Global Economy* (New York: Berg, 2004).

31. Katherine Verdery, "Fuzzy Property: Rights, Power, and Identity in Transylvania's Decollectivization," in *Uncertain Transition: Ethnographies of Change in the Postsocialist World*, ed. Michael Burawoy and Katherine Verdery (Lanham, MD: Rowman & Littlefield, 1999), 53–82.

32. Timothy Mitchell, "The Limits of the State: Beyond Statist Approaches and Their Critics," *American Political Science Review* 85, no. 1 (1991): 77–96.

33. Henry Hale, "Civil Society from Above? Statist and Liberal Models of State-Building in Russia," *Demokratizatsiya* 10, no. 3 (2002): 306.

34. Masha Gessen, *The Future Is History: How Totalitarianism Reclaimed Russia* (New York: Riverhead Books, 2017), 366.

35. Oleg Kharkhordin, *The Collective and the Individual in Russia: A Study of Practices* (Berkeley: University of California Press, 1999).

36. "Debaty Zelens′koho ta Poroshenka na NSK 'Olimpiis′kyi.' Zapys transliatsii," https://www.youtube.com/watch?v=ILvaYrmQZDw, accessed November 14, 2019.

37. F. A. Hayek, *The Road to Serfdom* (Chicago: University of Chicago Press, 1944).

38. Andrew Barnes, *Owning Russia: The Struggle over Factories, Farms, and Power* (Ithaca, NY: Cornell University Press, 2006); Jessica Allina-Pisano, *The Post-Soviet Potemkin Village: Politics and Property in the Black Earth* (Cambridge: Cambridge University Press, 2008); Katherine Verdery, *The Vanishing Hectare: Property and Value in Postsocialist Transylvania* (Ithaca, NY: Cornell University Press, 2003).

39. Mariela Szwarcberg, *Mobilizing Poor Voters: Machine Politics, Clientelism, and Social Networks in Argentina* (New York: Cambridge University Press, 2015); James A. Robinson and Thierry Verdier, "The Political Economy of Clientelism," *Scandinavian*

Journal of Economics 115, no. 2 (2013): 260–91; Susan C. Stokes, "Political Clientelism," in *The Oxford Handbook of Comparative Politics*, ed. Carles Boix and Susan C. Stokes (New York: Oxford University Press, 2007); Tariq Thachil, *Elite Parties, Poor Voters: How Social Services Win Votes in India* (New York: Cambridge University Press, 2014).

40. This situation can be viewed from different angles. Keith Darden has argued, conversely, that under certain conditions bribery can *reinforce* state administrative functions. Darden, "The Integrity of Corrupt States: Graft as an Informal State Institution," *Politics and Society* 36, no. 1 (March 2008): 35–59.

41. Gontmakher, "V Rossii poiavilas' novaia model' obshchestvennogo ustroistva."

42. See Elizabeth A. Wood, William E. Pomeranz, E. Wayne Merry, and Maxim Trudoliubov, *Roots of Russia's War in Ukraine* (Washington, DC: Woodrow Wilson Center and Columbia University Press, 2016), 104–5, and Elizabeth A. Wood, "Hypermasculinity as a Scenario of Power: Vladimir Putin's Iconic Rule, 1999–2008," *International Feminist Journal of Politics* 18, no. 3 (2016): 329–50. On gendered dimensions of performance across Russia's political spectrum see Sperling, *Sex, Politics, and Putin*.

43. Graham, *Ghost of the Executed Engineer*.

44. Alexei Yurchak, *Everything Was Forever, Until It Was No More: The Last Soviet Generation*. Princeton, NJ: Princeton University Press, 2005.

45. Edward T. Walker, *Grassroots for Hire: Public Affairs Consultants in American Democracy* (Cambridge: Cambridge University Press, 2014).

46. Dan Schneider, "1-800-HIRE A CROWD: The Business of Generating Fake Enthusiasm, from Flash Mobs to the Campaign Trail," *Atlantic*, July 22, 2015.

47. Beth DeFalco, "Weiner Paid for Phony Supporters at Campaign Events, Source Says," *New York Post*, August 28, 2013, http://nypost.com/2013/08/28/weiner-paid-for-phony-supporters-at-campaign-events-source-says/; "Anthony Weiner Paying Actors, Interns to Pose as Campaign Supporters: Report," *Huffington Post*, August 28, 2013, http://www.huffingtonpost.com/2013/08/28/anthony-weiner-paying-actors_n_3832141.html.

48. Hunter Walker, "Donald Trump Reportedly Paid Actors $50 to Cheer for Him at His 2016 Announcement," *Business Insider*, June 17, 2015, http://www.businessinsider.com/paid-actors-at-donald-trump-announcement-2015-6.

49. Aaron Couch and Emmet McDermott, "Donald Trump Campaign Offered Actors $50 to Cheer for Him at Presidential Announcement," *Hollywood Reporter*, June 17, 2015, http://www.hollywoodreporter.com/news/donald-trump-campaign-offered-actors-803161.

50. These included rallies titled "March for Trump NYC" (June 25, 2016), "Down with Hillary NYC" (July 23, 2016), and "Florida Goes Trump" (August 20, 2016). Indictment in *US v. Internet Research Agency et al.* (US District Court for the District of Columbia, February 16, 2018), as published in Peter Finn, ed., *The Mueller Report* (New York: Scribner, 2019), 571–78. Redacted descriptions of the activities of the Internet Research Agency may be found in the report, 74–95.

51. Walker, *Grassroots for Hire*, 189. Also see Walker, "Grass Roots Mobilization, by Corporate America," *New York Times*, August 10, 2012.

52. Lisa Wedeen, *Ambiguities of Domination: Politics, Rhetoric, and Symbols in Contemporary Syria* (Chicago: University of Chicago Press, 1999).

53. Alexander Hertel-Fernandez, *Politics at Work: How Companies Turn Their Workers into Lobbyists* (New York: Oxford University Press, 2018), 2.

54. Susan Berfield, "Why Time-Share King David Siegel Thinks He Got Bush Elected," Bloomberg Business Week, August 3, 2012, quoted in Hertel-Fernandez, *Politics at Work*, 189.

55. Noam Scheiber and Maggie Haberman, "Manafort's 2016 Gambit: A Back Channel from Trump Camp to Labor," *New York Times*, November 13, 2019.

56. "Trump Makes Migrant Caravan a Campaign Issue," CBC News, October 23, 2018, at 2:00/4:54, https://www.youtube.com/watch?v=bVZOfi-51KA.

57. Craig Timberg and Drew Harwell, "Parkland Shooting 'Crisis Actor' Videos Lead Users to a 'Conspiracy Ecosystem' on YouTube, New Research Shows," *Washington Post*, February 25, 2018. In the United States, this discourse appears to have its origins with the conspiracy theorist and founder of media site InfoWars Alex Jones, who suggested in 2012 that the murdered first graders at Sandy Hook Elementary School in Connecticut were mere performers. "Sandy Hook Parents Sue Conspiracy Theorist Alex Jones for Defamation," Reuters, April 17, 2018, https://www.reuters.com/article/us-texas-lawsuit-alexjones/sandy-hook-parents-sue-conspiracy-theorist-alex-jones-for-defamation-idUSKBN1HO2FU.

58. Jason Wilson, "Crisis Actors, Deep State, False Flag: The Rise of Conspiracy Theory Code Words," *Guardian*, last modified February 21, 2018, https://www.theguardian.com/us-news/2018/feb/21/crisis-actors-deep-state-false-flag-the-rise-of-conspiracy-theory-code-words.

59. Wilson, "Crisis Actors, Deep State, False Flag."

60. Gregory S. Schneider, Laura Vozzella, Patricia Sullivan, and Michael E. Miller, "Weapons, Flags, No Violence: Massive Pro-Gun Rally in Virginia Capital," *Washington Post*, last modified January 20, 2020, https://www.washingtonpost.com/local/virginia-politics/2020/01/20/4b36852c-3baa-11ea-8872-5df698785a4e_story.html.

61. Jonathan Albright, "Welcome to the Era of Fake News," *Media and Communication* 5, no. 2 (2017): 87–89.

62. Edward Walker estimates that approximately 40 percent of Fortune 500 companies are clients of companies providing "grassroots for hire" services. Kieron Monks, "The Lucrative Business of Crowds for Hire," CNN Business, October 20, 2015, last modified January 21, 2018, http://edition.cnn.com/2015/10/16/business/crowds-for-hire/.

63. Juan Linz and Alfred C. Stepan, "Toward Consolidated Democracies," *Journal of Democracy* 7, no. 2 (1996): 14–33.

64. House Committee on Oversight and Reform, "Violations of Hatch Act under the Trump Administration," last modified June 26, 2019, https://oversight.house.gov/legislation/hearings/violations-of-the-hatch-act-under-the-trump-administration.

# Acknowledgments

Many people contributed to this book, but I owe special thanks to two mentors for their encouragement and support early in the project. This book draws inspiration from the work of James C. Scott, under whose direction I had the great fortune to work as a graduate student. Scott shepherded his students the hard and responsible way, rejecting the hermaphroditic intellectual reproduction so common in the academy and instead encouraging his students' autonomy. The influence of his early work on clientelism and later studies of subaltern performance may be found throughout this book. Years ago, while I was researching another book, Harvard political scientist and Russia specialist Timothy J. Colton suggested I write this one. I am grateful for his support and encouragement.

I was lucky to benefit from several residencies and fellowships that provided intellectually stimulating and collegial environments to think while I wrote. I am grateful to colleagues and students at the École des hautes études en sciences sociales in Paris for their conviviality and lively debate as I presented a French cycle of lectures on the manuscript in 2017. The creative energy and camaraderie of fellows at the Institute for Advanced Study at Central European University in Budapest in 2015–2016 helped drive the project forward and pushed me to think across disciplines. Many conversations with colleagues and students at New York University's Jordan Center for the Advanced Study of Russia sharpened the argument. Early in the project, research seminars at Harvard's Davis Center for Russian and Eurasian Studies, the Harvard Ukrainian Research Institute, and the Kennan Institute and Woodrow Wilson International Center for Scholars shaped the project's design. This book draws on research supported by the Social Sciences and Humanities Research Council of Canada and the National Council for Eurasian and East European Research.

Colleagues and students at a number of institutions read and engaged with draft chapters of this book. Seminar participants at Columbia University, CUNY Graduate Center, the École Normale Supérieure, Georgetown University, Harvard University, King's College London, the Moscow School of Social and Economic Sciences, New York University, Princeton University, Sciences Po, the University of Toronto, the Slavic Research Center of Hokkaido University, and Tufts University offered their time, attention, and thoughtful comments and questions. Colleagues at a PONARS workshop in Saint Petersburg offered particularly helpful feedback.

I owe special thanks to the people who feed the perpetual intellectual ferment of my institutional home, the New School for Social Research in New York City. Participants in the Heilbroner Center for Capitalism Studies fellows' seminars and the General Seminar contributed to the project. Thanks also to faculty and staff colleagues of the Politics Department and Dean's Office for their support and interest. For the last seven years and especially in 2020–2021, the fellowship of the Decolonizing Eastern European Studies research group has been a consistent source of intellectual respite, trenchant and thoughtful criticism, and inspiration. At the University of Ottawa, where I conducted initial work on this project, special thanks are due to François Houle; Marcel Mérette, the chair of Ukrainian Studies; and colleagues of the École d'Études Politiques.

A number of people gave generously of their time to read and comment on the manuscript in whole or in part, at various stages of the project. They include Ying Chen, Mayra Cotta, Mark Frazier, Samuel Greene, Vicky Hattam, Max Head, Charles King, Clara Mattei, James Miller, Viacheslav Morozov, Alexander Nikulin, Julia Ott, Sanjay Ruparelia, Mark Setterfield, Gulnaz Sharafutdinova, Olga Shevchenko, Oxana Shevel, Irina Soboleva, Ioana Vrabiescu, Grigory Yudin, and Amanda Zadorian. I am particularly grateful to Amanda Zadorian for guidance on theater practice and terminology. The unflinching critique of doctoral students at the New School for Social Research who read the entire manuscript twice made this a better book: Ihor Andriichuk, Dina Antonacci Shvetsov, Anastasia Kalk, Karolina Koziura, Orsolya Lehotai, Lala Pop, Mariia Shynkarenko, Agnés Szányi, and Malkhaz Toria. NIU series editor Christine Worobec and anonymous readers at the press read attentively and provided thoughtful comments and suggestions. I am most grateful to Amy Ferranto for deftly shepherding the manuscript and providing helpful advice throughout, and to Karen Laun for overseeing the production process.

Conversations with many colleagues helped the project develop at various stages. I offer particular thanks to Alex Aleinikoff, Andrew Barnes, Mark Beissinger, Kate Brown, Valerie Bunce, David Cameron, Paul D'Anieri, Keith Darden, Françoise Daucé, Henry Drobbin, Ben Fountain, Nancy Fraser, Timothy Frye, Mischa Gabowitsch, Scott Gelbach, Bruce Grant, Anna Grzymała-Busse, Henry Hale, Halyna Hryn, Nina L. Khrushcheva, Sergei Kukharenko,

ACKNOWLEDGMENTS

Ivan Kurilla, Alena Ledeneva, Arien Mack, Elzbieta Matynia, Andrew G. McCabe, Dmitri Nikulin, Scott Radnitz, Maria Repnikova, Graeme Robertson, Peter Rutland, Ekaterina Schulmann, Ioulia Shukan, Rogers Smith, Timothy Snyder, Peter Solomon, Valerie Sperling, David Stark, Ann Stoler, Sherrill Stroschein, Joshua Tucker, Katherine Verdery, Joris Wauman, and Lucan Way. Shortcomings are my responsibility alone.

Anton Agrofonov, Ihor Andriichuk, Orsolya Lehotai, Joseph Livesey, Dina Antonacci Shvetsov, Mariia Shynkarenko, and Amanda Zadorian contributed to the research for this book and to its preparation for publication. I am grateful to Cambridge University Press for granting me permission to use material previously published in my 2014 chapter "Pokazukha and Cardiologist Khrenov: Soviet Legacies, Legacy Theater, and a Usable Past," in *The Historical Legacies of Communism in Russia and Eastern Europe*, edited by Mark Beissinger and Stephen Kotkin. This material appears in chapter 2. I am likewise grateful to Johns Hopkins University Press and the Woodrow Wilson International Center for Scholars for permission to reprint several paragraphs from my 2010 book chapter, "Legitimizing Facades: Civil Society in Post-Orange Ukraine," in *Orange Revolution and Aftermath: Mobilization, Apathy, and the State in Ukraine*, edited by Paul D'Anieri. This material appears in chapter 7.

In Russia and Ukraine, scores of people across both countries generously gave of their time, shared their stories, tolerated my endless questions, responded to my missteps with good humor, challenged my assumptions, and taught me much more than their politics. I wish I could thank them by name. Friends and colleagues who at different times contributed their ideas and expertise and smoothed the way include Vil Bakirov, Viktor Belinskii, Lilia Kim, Vitalii L'vov, Natalya Osipova, Lyudmyla Pavlyuk, and Svitlana Slava.

I could not have completed this project without the patience and support of friends and family, including Adil Baizhumanov, Sergei Markov, Jane Burbank, Frederick Cooper, Elaine Goldenberg, Phoebe Moore, Liam Pisano, Landon Reid, Jean-Paul Rodrigue, and Anne-Marie Stabile. I am indebted to Reyna Zarate and Dóri Ajtay for the care they extended to my family while I worked. I am grateful for the love of Zsófia Nagy, who should still be with us, of Sasha, Alex, and Cédrik, whom I am so lucky to love in return, and of Oscar, whose childhood this project accompanied. André, my companion in all things and most challenging intellectual critic, was present throughout and read the manuscript more times than I can count. Without him, this would have been a very different book.

INDEX

1990s, *likhie*, 53

Abakunova, Anna, 82
activism. *See* associational life
administrative resource. *See* pressure
AFL-CIO, 177
Afghanistan, veterans of, 27, 169
Africa, 7, 130
"against all," 66
agitation, 82, 123, 168, 170
agriculture: 9, 16, 24, 35, 70–71, 84; conditions for smallholders, 95–99, 102; labor needs of homesteads, 59–60, 107; livestock slaughter, 58, 60; monopsonic control of local labor markets, 108–109; oversight of, 76; as site of political theater, 9, 35, 58, 66, 72–79, 85, 87, 90, 103, 108, 110, 164–165; smallholder dependence on large enterprises, 58, 61, 86–87, 99–100; theft of farm machinery, 61; threats against wages and land rents, 85; use of land rents in vote buying, 66. *See also* enclosure
Aksakov, Ivan, 40
alcohol, 25, 77, 93, 104, 110, 138
algorithms, 168
Almaty, 124
Alushta, 27
Amanpour, Christiane, 114, 116
ambiguity, 14, 17, 136, 137, 144, 155–159, 178. See also *mnogoznachnost'*; doubt
Amur, 27, 139
Another Russia, 157
Argumenty i Fakty (newspaper), 49
Arlington National Cemetery, 137
Aristotelian theater, 4, 119, 134–135
army, 106–107, 137, 138, 140, 142, 158. *See also* Immortal Regiment; soldiers
arson, 9, 104, 141
associational life: 17, 144–148; dues base of NGOs, 149, 150; neo-Tocquevillian traditions, 148; private-sector funding, 102; state attacks on and harassment of, 84, 150, 151; state co-option of, 144–148; state influence on, 79, 137, 148, 149; state support for, 91, 96, 101, 150, 151. *See also* street demonstrations; religion
Auschwitz, 104
austerity, 57, 64, 67. *See also* structural adjustment
automobiles: 24, 25, 57, 63, 109; parts, 23, 107; tires, 145
Austro-Hungary, 104
authoritarianism: xi–xii, 10, 13, 34, 51, 111, 120, 122, 126, 163, 164, 167, 178; appearance of xii, 6–7, 54, 132, 153; challenges of research in, 126; spectacle in, 16, 160; subnational, 164, 220n9. *See also* regime type; signaling mechanisms
Avtoradio, 41
Azhaev, Vasilii, 18

Bakhchysarai, 27
Bakhtin, Mikhail, 44
Balandier, Georges, 4
Baloha, Viktor, 91, 107, 108
Barkhunova, Tatiana, 144
Baudrillard, Jean, 13
Bayart, Jean-François, 130
Belgorod, 19, 56
belonging, 122, 133, 140, 170
Berehove (Beregszász), 27, 80
berkut, 114
Berlin, 140
bespredel, 52–53, 68
biscuit politics, 114–118, 130–135
blackmail, xii, 82
"black PR," 129
Black Sea, 141, 175
Blagoveshchensk (Amur *oblast'*), 19, 27, 56, 139, 164
blat, 134

229

INDEX

Bloomberg, Michael, 177
Bolotnaya demonstrations, 172
borders and borderlands: xii, 16–17, 51–52, 56–59, 67; checkpoints and crossings, 24, 25, 96, 98; demarcation of, 56, 97; local impact of border security, 28, 92, 95–97, 101; within political communities, 5, 6, 164, 167; research in, 19, 22, 24–25, 27–28; Russia-Ukraine border, xii, 6, 16, 19, 24, 28, 51, 58, 74, 139, 145; Sino-Russian border, 19, 27, 139; Ukraine-EU border, xii, 16, 22, 25, 27, 95–103, 106–107, 111, 164. *See also* Donbas; Kharkiv; war against Ukraine; Zakarpattia
boredom, 114, 159, 178
boyars: 37, 38; *chinovniki* as, 37
Boyer, Dominic, 157
bread: threats against deliveries, 69, 84, 87
Brecht, Bertolt, 11–12, 54–55, 134
Brest, 123
Brezhnev, Leonid, 36
bribery, 34, 134
Brussels, 96, 99
Bryansk: 53; Bryansk *oblast'*, 52
Brym, Robert J., 123
Budapest, 91
Bulgaria, 46
bureaucrats: conversations with, 23–25; discretion of, 15, 33–37, 65, 103, 106–107, 142, 150; politicization of, 7, 14–15, 37, 65, 88, 148, 168, 170, 174. *See also* Hatch Act
Bush, George W., 177

cadres. *See* bureaucrats
call-in shows, 29, 31–34, 36, 37, 41–46, 48–50. *See also* Khrenov, Ivan
Canada, 93
capitalism, 4, 16, 17, 50, 51, 162, 172–175, 179
care, in contrast to rights-based frames, 131
categories of analysis and practice, 132, 163
catharsis, 11–12, 134
Catherine II (Catherine the Great), 39, 153
censorship (Soviet-era), 73, 159
Center for Political Technologies, 50
Central Asia, 140
Chaigneau, Aurore, 133, 192n23
Chaplyga, Mykhailo, 168
Cheboksary, 159
Chekhov, Anton, 18, 54, 167
children: meaning of their participation in demonstrations, 44, 109, 138, 139, 142; targeted to pressure parents, 3, 5, 21, 22, 46, 65, 67, 74, 80, 88, 99, 105, 125

China, 19, 22, 27, 56, 98, 100, 139, 163
choice: illusion of, 5, 66, 121, 124, 127, 129, 161, 162, 179; meanings of, 30, 54, 55, 87, 113, 118, 121–124, 127, 130, 133, 161, 167, 178. *See also* democracy: meaning of elections in
Chop, 79
Chuhuiv, 75
churches: and parties of power, 101, 204n34; role in political theater, 79, 92, 93, 95, 101, 127; as social service providers, 79, 101; village priests, 101, 102
civic duty, 56, 77, 119, 123–127, 129, 130, 134
civil society. *See* associational life
clientelism: brokers, 11, 69, 84, 117, 177–178; meaning of positive and negative inducements in, xii, 10, 65, 67, 84, 87, 118, 129, 174; patronalism, xii, 73, 87, 116, 130; relationship to Soviet-era patrimonialism, 199n74
CNN, 114, 177
Cobain, Kurt, 1
coercion, 5, 17, 19, 21–22, 29, 77, 83–84, 88, 91, 94, 105, 110–111, 131, 153–155, 165–166, 170
Colbert Report, 157
collective farms (former): as social service providers, 27, 59–62, 87, 95, 100–101. *See also* agriculture
collective punishment, 16, 84–89, 90–91, 132
color revolutions, 116, 145. *See also* Orange Revolution
Committee of Voters of Ukraine, 23, 110. *See also* elections: organizations monitoring
company towns, 84–85, 90, 105, 165, 175
concepts: 183n32; emic, 7, 122
consent, meanings of, 175
contempt, 159
Cooper, Anderson, 177
corruption, 42, 65, 125, 129, 175, 179
La Cosa Nostra, 61
covfefe. *See* kayfabe
Cramer, Katherine J., 29
Crimea, 19, 22, 24, 27, 39, 61, 92, 94, 123, 140, 142, 153
crisis actors, 177
currency devaluation, 93. *See also* hyperinflation

Dahl, Robert, xi
decentralization, 91, 107, 165, 178

INDEX 231

de Custine, Marquis, 40
defamiliarization. *See ostranenie*
democracy: consolidated, xi, 6, 127, 128, 176; frustration with, 124, 127, 128, 162, 179; meaning of elections in, 118, 119, 124–125, 130, 178
derision, 32, 43, 47, 52
Desmond, Matthew, 23
dictatorship. *See* authoritarianism
disinformation, 114, 177, 178
disorder. See *bespredel*
dissimulation: 11, 13, 120–122, 132; "as if," 13, 40, 47, 88, 120, 160. *See also* authoritarianism; Homo Sovieticus
Dnipropetrovs'k (Dnipro), 82, 146
dogs, 93, 97–98
domination-resistance paradigm. *See* resistance
Donbas, 19, 90, 94, 106, 140
Donetsk, 28, 72
doubt, 17, 137, 144, 155–159
Dzerkalo Tyzhnia (newspaper), 80

economic insecurity: local elites' response to, 67, 92, 99, 102–103, 167, 170
economic hardships, 63, 97
economic loss, 29, 52, 64, 103, 107
economic risk: 5, 8, 15, 29, 56, 59, 83, 86, 95, 104–106; individuation of, 7, 64, 91
education. *See* schools; universities
elections: attempts to discredit legitimacy of, 117, 129, 131, 158; as choice (*vybory*), 118, 119, 121–125, 127, 129, 161–162, 173, 178, 208n44; competition in, 1, 71, 103, 118–119; early voting in, 74–75; foreign intervention in, 117, 131, 147, 158, 176; local, 84, 103, 110, 123, 166; meanings of, 3, 10, 118–119, 121–124, 126–127, 129, 132, 161; as obligation (*golosovanie*), 118– 119, 121–127, 129–130, 134, 178; organizations monitoring, 23, 110. *See also* Soviet Union, elections; democracy
electoral manipulation: interpretations of, 118, 122; local knowledge of, 95, 99, 105, 122, 123, 169; refusal to participate in, 80, 111; tailored to individual households, 77, 88, 93, 99, 107, 111; use of carousels in, 84, 110, 122. *See also* vote buying
electricity: access to, 27, 58, 86, 102, 108; outages as electoral payback, 87
Ekho Moskvy, 143
emic concepts, 7, 8, 122, 132

emotions: 53–55, 77, 152–153, 156, 159; in Aristotelian theater, 11–12, 134; in politics, 29–30
enclosure, 4, 25, 52, 64, 66, 89, 92, 93, 102, 128, 132, 168, 171, 173, 175. *See also* land alienation
England, 2, 19
entitlements, 5, 65, 66, 88, 94, 170. *See also* social welfare
entrepreneurs, 61, 99
epic theater, 11, 12, 134
epistemological silos, 36, 113, 147, 155
Epstein, Mikhail, 13, 40
Esquith, Stephen, 55
Euromaidan. *See* Maidan
European Union, xii, 16, 19, 20, 22, 25, 27, 78, 90, 95–100, 106, 111, 140, 164, 165; enlargement of, 95–99
eviction, 23, 60

fakery, accusations of, 31, 141–142, 178
fascism, accusations of, xi, 140
Fatherland bloc, 92, 146
fear: 29, 49, 53, 75–77, 99–100, 167
fealty. *See* loyalty
Fesenko, Volodymyr, 168
Finland, 139
fire code inspections, 5, 88, 201n109
Florida, 104, 176, 177
freedoms, 164, 50, 63; experience of, 5, 112, 147; meanings of, 7, 10, 35, 50, 161; perceptions of, 2, 166
FSB, 32, 44
fuel: natural gas, 5, 69, 83, 86, 100, 108, 111, 125, 128. *See also* gasoline
funerary services, 101

Gabowitsch, Mischa, 135, 137, 143–145, 154, 157
Gaidar, Yegor, 2
Gamzatov, Rasul, 138
garbage lustrations, 168–169
gasoline, 24–25, 58, 66, 99. *See also* fuel
Gazprom, 82
Geertz, Clifford, 4
Gerasimov, Roman, 43
Gerasimov, Valery, 158. *See also* hybrid warfare
Germany, 2, 76
Gessen, Masha, 172
Goffman, Erving, 13
Gogol, Nikolai, 39–40
Goloborodko, Vasily, 79
Gontmakher, Evgeny, 162, 175

INDEX

graffiti, 1–2, 9, 12, 118
grazhdanskii dolg. See civic duty
Great Patriotic War. *See* World War II
Great Recession, 23
Grebenshchikov, Boris, 68
GreenJolly, 152
Gubin, Andrei, 95
Gudkov, Lev, 122

hagiography, 55
Hale, Henry, xii, 167
Hanukai, Maksim, 137
Hatch Act, 179
Havel, Václav, vii, 46–47, 50
Hayek, Friedrich, 17, 173
health care. *See* hospitals
Heihe, 27
Heilongjiang. *See* Amur
Hertel-Fernandez, Alexander, 8, 177
Hiroshima, 138
Holodomor, 92
Homo Sovieticus, 120
Horace, 54
hospitals: access to, 65, 88–89, 112, 174; deteriorating conditions in, 48–49, 68; head doctors in political theater, 78, 169, 170; threats against staff, 73, 77, 86; as site of political theater, 31–36, 45, 48, 71, 76, 85, 164, 173
humor, 2, 29, 47, 73
Hungary: 77, 92, 98, 162; Fidesz, 101, 106; Magyars in Ukraine, 26, 91, 96, 101, 106, 108–109, 111; Status Laws, 78, 96
hybrid regimes, xi, 9–11, 163. *See also* patronalism
hybrid warfare, 158. *See also* Gerasimov, Valery; Mueller Report
hyperinflation, 52. *See also* currency devaluation

identity: ambiguity and multiplicity, 14, 170; boundaries within the polity, 167; created by political theater, 118; after dissolution of Soviet Union, 68; ethnic, 91; gender, 13, 26; irrelevance for staging performances, 5; linguistic, 92; national, xii, 39, 132, 138; perceptions of connection to voting behavior, 165; Soviet, 146; 163
ideology: relationship to loyalty, 46, 150, 163; vacuum of, 63, 127
illiberalism, 5, 6, 29, 38, 162, 163, 175
illusion, 13, 32–39, 42, 50, 162
imitation, 4, 7, 36–37, 40, 50, 133, 143, 153

Immortal Regiment: 17, 136–144, 147–148, 152–154, 158; evidence of state capture of, 136, 140, 141–144, 147–149, 152–153; Putin's participation in, 141, 144, 152, 154; virtual commemoration, 139, 142
inflation. *See* hyperinflation
informal institutions, 183n31.
  See also telephones: *telefonnoe* pravo; "understandings"
irony, 17, 43, 47, 137, 156–159, 169
Ivanovo, 31–34, 36, 42–45, 47–50
Izvestiia (newspaper), 33, 50

jail, 96–97, 144. *See also* prison

Kakutani, Michiko, 159
Kaliningrad, 139
Karelia, 139
Kárpátaljai Magyar Kulturális Szövetség (KMKSZ), 91. *See also* Hungary
Katyusha, 139, 140
kayfabe, 8
Kazakhstan, 56, 124
Kennedy, John F., 156
Khabarovsk, 140, 142
Kharkhordin, Oleg, 126
Kharkiv: 19, 24, 52, 56, 74–77, 150; Kharkiv *oblast'*, 19, 52, 75–76
Kherson, 78, 82, 84
Khrenov, Ivan, 31–34, 37–38, 41–46, 48–50
Khrushchev, Nikita, 169
kinship, role of, 38, 52, 103. *See also* reciprocity
Kiselev, Evgenii, 143
kolkhoz. See collective farms
Kollman, Nancy Shields, 38
kolorady, 140
Kommuna (newspaper), 124–129
Komsomol, 44
Komsomol'skaia pravda (newspaper), 42, 48
Kotkin, Stephen, 154
Kremlin, xii, 50, 127, 156, 169; local efforts to please, 143; narratives about the 1990s, 52–53. *See also* Immortal Regiment, evidence of state capture of
Krokodil, 73
krugovaia poruka. See collective punishment
Krylova, Anna, 36, 155
Kuchma, Leonid: attacks on civic organizations, 150; political theater under, 56, 165–166. *See also* referendum
Kyiv, 19, 72, 74, 77, 78, 91, 113, 116, 124, 140, 146–147, 170; Kyiv *oblast'*, 82

INDEX 233

land alienation: consequences of, 90, 92, 95–99, 103–105, 108–109, 128, 171; threats of, 79, 103, 104; use of eminent domain, 66, 96. *See also* agriculture
landlessness, 56, 79, 96, 103, 107
land privatization. *See* enclosure
Landsknecht, 117
Larina, Ksenia, 143
Latvia, 115
laughter, role of, 29, 44–45, 47, 73, 94, 159. *See also* irony
Lavrov, Sergei, 106
Lebed, Alexander, 1
Ledeneva, Alena, 73
legitimacy, 15, 37, 39, 48, 53, 65, 123, 126, 130–131, 149, 151. *See also* elections: attempts to discredit
Lemon, Alaina, 55
Leningrad. *See* Saint Petersburg
Lepore, Jill, 19
Leskov, Nikolai, 18
Levitsky, Steven, xi
Lewis, Rebecca, 159
liberalism: xii, 3, 6, 13, 20, 119, 127, 132–135, 146, 163; liberal subjects, 120, 155; in Russia, 34, 123–126
life expectancy, declines in, 67
Ligachev, Yegor, 2
Linz, Juan, xi
Lipetsk, 28
local knowledge, 7, 110–112
Los Angeles, 176
Lounsbery, Anne, 18
loyalty, 5, 43, 65, 122–127, 130, 132, 135, 167; defining boundaries of political community, 5, 163, 167; elections as opportunity to express local fealty, 58, 64, 88, 99, 118, 122, 163–165, 168, 179; perceptions of loyalty to a foreign power, 116–117
Luhansk, 19

machine politics. *See* clientelism
Magyar, Bálint, 163
Maidan: 17, 23, 82, 113–118, 120, 131; "Blue Maidan," 144–146; kitchen brigades on, 116; use of the Ukrainian language following, 26; violence against peaceful protesters, xi, 113–114. *See also* Orange Revolution
Makarkin, Alexei, 50
Makeiev, Oleksii, 115
Manafort, Paul, 177

market economy. *See* capitalism
Marwick, Alice, 159
massovka, 142, 153
Matthews, Owen, 50
Meyerhold, Vsevolod, 55
Michigan, 177
middle income countries, 7, 175
Mikhalkov, Nikita, 139
military service, avoidance of, 26, 106–107. *See also* army; soldiers
Milwaukee, 23
mimicry. *See* imitation
misrecognition, 35, 173
misrepresentation, 35, 122
Mitchell, Timothy, 14
mnogoznachnost' (multiplicity of meaning): 4, 17, 47, 113, 118, 121, 126, 140, 159–160; as a tool of destabilization, 137, 158
monogorodok. *See* company towns
Morozov, Pavlik, 42–43
Moscow, xi, 34, 35, 50, 62, 124, 125, 129; appeals to, 38; demonstrations and parades, 136–137, 139–141, 143, 152; distance from, 18–19, 170; economic ties to Donbas in early 2000, 91; performances for, 45, 48, 49; unproven assumptions about loyalty to, 165
Moskovskii komsomolets (newspaper), 34
Mueller Report, 223fn50. *See also* hybrid warfare
Mukachevo, 80
Murzilki International, 41–42
Muscovy, 38, 41

Navalny, Alexei, 159
Nashi, 117
National Bolshevik Party, 157
Neschastnyi sluchai, 41
Nevada, 177
Nemtsova, Anna, 50
New York, xi, 19, 140, 176
Nezavisimaia gazeta (newspaper), 162
NGOs. *See* associational life
nostalgia, 37, 45
Novyny Zakarpatiia (newspaper), 78, 80
Nuland, Victoria, 114–118, 130

Obama, Barack, 177
obligation. *See* civic duty
Odesa, 72, 141
odnoznachnost' (singularity of meaning), 159
Ogonek, 123

INDEX

Ohio, 2, 177
Okean Elzy, 114
oligarchs, 117, 172, 175
Olympic Stadium (Kyiv), 172
Orange Revolution: 81, 91, 94, 146–147, 150, 152; civil society and, 150; temporary disappearance of political theater, 23, 83; varying interpretations of, 116–117, 131
Orbán, Viktor, 96, 101, 162
Ost, David, 29
ostranenie (defamiliarization, *Verfremdungseffekt*), 12
Ottawa, 140
Ottoman Empire, 153
Oushakine, Serguei, 138, 140, 155, 163
"overwhelming majority," 8

palimpsest, 34, 36, 37, 39
Parkland, Florida, 177
parliament: 64; dissolution of Ukrainian, 146; shelling of Russian, 125; Ukrainian deputies' immunity from prosecution, 71, 80; weakened legislatures, 79, 126, 179
parties of power, 7. *See also* clientelism; political theater
Party of Regions, 91–93, 101, 104, 109, 111, 127, 146, 169; as social service provider, 101, 109
Parubiy, Andriy, 94
patronalism. *See* clientelism
patron-client relationships. *See* clientelism
Pelevin, Viktor, 11, 35
Pennsylvania, 104, 176
pensions, 3, 8, 27, 57, 64, 82, 86, 89, 93, 102, 168, 171, 173
Peskov, Dmitrii, 36
Petrine era, 38, 39
Petrov, Nikolai, 135, 153
Plamper, Jan, 159
Plato, 4, 12
plebiscite. *See* referendum
Poe, Marshall, 38
pokazukha, 7, 31
Poland, 19, 29, 61, 77
polarization, xii, 89, 165
police: 81, 109, 172; absence of, 100–101; traffic, 24–25
political ethnography, 7, 23, 29–30, 54, 92
political participation: in 1990s, 124–126; in 2000s, 127–130; disaffection with, 127–128, 179; diverging interpretations, 113–122, 130–135; meanings of, 3, 5, 9–11, 17, 20–22, 41, 45, 54, 146, 152, 159–160, 167, 171, 174; reasons for, 4–9, 11, 15,

21–22, 26, 30, 49–50, 65–66, 69, 71–81, 82–89, 92–107, 110–111, 115–117, 131–133, 134, 138, 141–142, 146–148, 150–153, 155, 163–170, 173; Soviet-era, 123–124
political technologists, 11, 20, 50, 127
political theater: advantages for political incumbents, 5, 12, 15, 65, 83, 88–90, 100, 106, 136, 145, 148, 168, 173, 178, 179; audience for, 3, 4, 6, 8–9, 11–12, 20, 32, 39, 45, 73, 83, 155, 158; boundary conditions, 6; consequences of, 3–5, 9, 16, 17, 47, 66–67, 71, 74–77, 79, 80–89, 99–100, 110–112, 129–135, 148–158, 161–168, 171; dangers of even a little, 17, 158–160, 163, 164, 168, 175–179; exit from, 9, 127, 167; as a middle-class phenomenon, 7, 174–175; motivation of players in (*see* political participation, reasons for); preconditions for, 4–6, 10, 17, 21, 30, 83, 127–128, 148, 165, 175, 179; presidential participation in, 8–9, 31–34, 48, 94, 158, 175, 177; and regime change, 163–164; roles in, 8–9, 11, 169–171, 175; spatial politics of, 20, 164–167; as a total system, 91, 164, 172; transparency in, 158, 168; variation in practice of, 17, 19–21, 81, 105, 110, 119, 134, 164–166; in the United States, 8, 176–178; use by opposition parties, 6, 12, 20, 145, 146
Poltava, 75, 83, 87, 150
Pomerantsev, Peter, 11
populism, 5, 6, 12, 52, 71, 135, 162–164
Poroshenko, Petro, 94, 172, 173
postsocialism, 7, 14, 20, 120, 148, 170, 173
post-truth, 119, 159. *See also* disinformation
Potemkin villages, 7, 39, 50, 154
precarity, 17, 49, 64, 69
pressure: administrative and economic, xii, 4, 6, 15, 21–22, 26, 29, 60, 62, 71–89, 90, 92–95, 99, 101–112, 117–119, 123–124, 131–132, 143, 148, 152–153, 164–177; climate pressure, 179; market pressure, 119, 137; societal valves, 126; spatial variation, 164–167
prison, 36, 42, 72, 107, 152, 172. *See also* jail
privatization. *See* enclosure
propaganda, xi, 2, 41, 63, 81, 119, 156
property: rents on, 52, 61, 66, 86, 96, 103, 108, 174; rights, 77, 173. *See also* enclosure
protests. *See* street demonstrations
Pugacheva, Alla, 41
Pushkin, Alexander, 39
Putin, Vladimir: xii, 6, 66, 71, 128, 131, 140, 144, 158, 162; as actor in political

theater, 175; "Brezhnevization," 36; characterizations of Russia, 11, 14, 126, 129, 172; and dissolution of Soviet Union, 69; as dramaturge, 8, 145; imperial repertoires (*tsar' dast*), 37–38, 156; as participant in Immortal Regiment, 141, 152–154; reasons for support for, 52–53, 120, 122, 153. *See also* call-in shows
"Putings," 145
Pyatt, Geoffrey, 114

quid pro quo, 24, 65–66, 84, 115, 134, 164

Radio Mayak, 44–45
Radnitz, Scott, 145
raids, 5
reciprocity, 51, 52
referenda, 8, 70–81, 84, 95, 119, 127
reflexive control, 156
regime type, 6–7, 9–10, 162–164, 167
religion. *See* churches
remittances, 92, 95, 100, 165
resistance, 2, 42, 82, 84, 120, 132, 154
resentment, 29
"revolving doors," 170. *See also* clientelism
Revolution of Dignity. *See* Maidan
RIA Novosti, 115
The Rich Also Cry, 63
ridicule, 42, 157, 176
Right Sector, 169
Rimskii, Vladimir, 119
Robertson, Graeme, 145
Rokkan, Stein, 19
Romani communities, 28, 104, 108–110
Rosenfeld, Bryn, 15
Rudakova, Natalia, 119
rule of law, 7, 19, 134
"rules of the game," 33, 45, 47. *See also* "understandings"
rumors, 33, 62, 105, 107, 147
Russian Internet Research Agency, 176

Sacks, Paul Martin, 87
Saint George's ribbons, 139–140
Saint Petersburg, 19, 27, 39
salaries: threats to withhold, 69, 73, 86; unpaid, 57, 64, 67
Saratov, Georgii, 122
satire, role of: 29, 35, 73, 94. *See also* humor
Schaffer, Frederic, 118
schools: 138; civic education, 126; condition of infrastructure, 101–102; false accusations of political theater, 177; research in, 23–24, 26; role in political theater, 9, 65, 73, 74, 76, 79–83, 85, 86, 88–89, 115, 107, 139, 142, 144, 162, 164, 170, 173; role in Soviet-era performance, 35; as site of debate, 52–53; teacher layoffs, 91–92
Schulmann, Ekaterina, 4
Scott, James C., 120
Seifrid, Thomas, 13, 38, 39
Sevastopol, 27
Sharafutdinova, Gulnaz, 53
shortages, 35, 49
Siberia, 18, 56, 136, 137, 144, 175
signaling mechanisms, 80, 126, 131, 135, 153, 160. *See also* authoritarianism
siloviki, 114
Simonyi, André, 92, 100
sistema, 14, 38, 42, 47, 88, 91, 111, 172
Sittel', Maria, 31–32
Slovakia, 19, 77, 80, 96–98, 103, 104, 107, 111, 164
Smyth, Regina, 122
Soboleva, Irina, 122
social capital, 148
social contract, 5, 7, 16, 65, 69, 88, 95, 113, 121, 161, 163, 179. *See also* welfare
Social Democratic Party of Ukraine, 81
socialism, 2, 4, 56, 151, 157. *See also* Soviet Union
social movements: 17, 136–137, 152–154, 157; coordination of, 147; elite-directed, 3–4, 8, 117, 139, 141–145, 176. *See also* associational life
society. *See* associational life; social movements; state-society relationships
soldiers, 85, 97, 106, 107, 114, 116, 136, 138, 139, 141–144
Solov'ev, Vladimir, 139
só para inglês ver, 7
soundscapes, 97
Soviet Union: central planning, 35, 67, 74, 105, 165; constitution, 35; culture, 11, 35, 41, 73, 119, 140, 146, 157, 159; discursive repertoires in, 119–121, 143, 175; dissolution of, 1, 6, 27, 71, 79, 86, 121, 123, 124, 132, 144; economic institutions of, 35, 60, 74, 90, 168, 175; elections, 121, 123–124; everyday life after, 51–53, 55, 57, 60, 67–69, 95, 98, 119, 148, 168, 170; industrial policies in, 74, 165, 171, 175, 179; legacies of, 37, 95, 138, 144, 165, 175, 176; liberal politics in, 3, 13, 120, 157; Ukrainian SSR, 91
spectacle. *See* political theater
stage: view from, 20, 23

Stalin, Joseph, 4, 18, 43, 92, 155, 159
Stanislavsky, Konstantin, 55
state: agents, 15–16, 65, 67, 90, 92–94, 99–107, 110, 112, 136, 148, 154, 162, 163, 166, 169–171, 173; as assemblage, 15; capture of, 14, 141, 143, 163, 168, 174–175; celebrations (see World War II, commemorations of); economic dependence on, 51, 58, 65, 173; immanence of, 172; obligations to, 119, 130–131, 133; as palimpsest, 185n59; regulatory offices, 61, 86, 88; relationship with business, 14, 70, 163, 168, 174; role of, 5, 7, 14–17, 65, 82–84, 88–89, 91, 96, 101, 111–112, 130–134, 137, 147–151, 159, 163, 168–175; state-society relationships, 5, 10, 13–15, 17, 48, 50, 91, 119, 121, 130, 136, 143, 145, 151–154, 168, 170–172; Weberian definitions of, 14; withdrawal, 16, 67–68, 70, 89
statism, 132, 133, 171
Stes'kiv, Taras, 147
stiob, 157–160. *See also* satire
Strategy-31, 157
street demonstrations: Astroturf, 8, 176, 178; financial support for, 142, 145–148, 176; grassroots, 3, 8, 21, 131, 136–138, 142–144, 145, 147–148, 152–153, 158, 176, 178; *massovka*, 142, 153; meanings of, 3, 8, 10, 16, 113, 116–117, 122, 131–135, 142–146, 152; motivations of participants, 5, 21, 56, 69, 72, 84, 117, 135, 152–153, 157; operational planning, 56, 83, 147, 176; payment for, 56, 84, 152, 176; perceptions of payment for, 116, 117, 133, 147, 142, 152, 178; by political opposition, xi, 117, 146, 172. *See also* Bolotnaya demonstrations; Maidan
structural adjustment: demographic change and, 68; prostitution and, 67
Studio Kvartal-95, 29, 94
subjectivization, 13
sunflower seeds, meanings of, 146
supply chains: disruption of, 16, 35, 51, 52, 62, 68, 70, 124; global, 98; Soviet era, 35
Suprycheva, Evgeniia, 42, 43
Surkov, Vladislav, 158, 162
Swan Lake, 125
Symonenko, Petro, 72

Tagirova, Alsu, 124
taxation: 40, 67, 79, 86, 149; avoidance of, 103; burden of, 59, 61; incentives, 15, 65; 173; perceived as coercive, 131; used to target private enterprises, 88
telephones: role in political theater, 8, 31–33, 41–46, 49, 50, 85, 176; *telefonnoe pravo*, 81
television, xii, 8, 16, 29, 31–34, 36, 43, 47, 50, 63–64, 87, 127, 156–157; as site of political critique, 36–37, 72–73, 79, 94; state, 31–33, 125, 139, 141–142. *See also* call-in shows
Ternopil', 169
theatron: view from, 8, 54
threats: collective, 16, 65, 69, 74, 83–87, 90–91, 104, 177; credibility of, 52, 65, 69, 88, 99, 103, 107; individual, 21, 46, 69, 74, 82, 93, 105, 110, 112. *See also* coercion; collective punishment
Tomsk, 82, 137, 143
Toronto, 140
Total Dictations, 144
totalitarianism, 120, 122, 154–155, 172
trade unions, 78, 149
traffic police. *See* police
transportation: xi, 28, 57, 68, 76, 96, 109, 174; buses, 40, 56; 60, 84, 97, 110; cost of, 93, 111; invitations to political theater on, 77; as research site, 24, 25, 27, 77; threats against access, 69, 76, 87, 89
Trianon settlement (World War I), 96. *See also* Hungary
Trump, Donald, 175–177, 179
"two Ukraines": narrative of, xii, 72, 146
Tymoshenko, Yulia, 92

Ukrainian language: instruction, 80, 92; speakers of, 26, 56, 72, 92, 165; Ukrainianization, 92
Ukrains'ka Pravda (online newspaper), 146
uncertainty, 46, 57, 61–62, 137, 158, 178. *See also* ambiguity; doubt
"understandings" (*poniatiia, poniattia*), 22, 81–82, 94
unfunded mandates, 25, 92, 106, 164
United Russia, 37, 52, 82, 84–85, 117, 128, 140, 153
United States, 8, 29, 104, 114–116, 122, 131, 176–178
universities: dormitories in political theater, 72, 84; mobilization of students, 2, 56, 74, 79, 88, 159; role of rectors in political theater, 74, 80–81, 88; threats of closure, 69, 74, 86; threats to eliminate tuition stipends, 34, 74, 80, 86
Urals, 84, 85

INDEX 237

usable pasts, 43
utilities, 59, 73, 128. *See also* electricity; fuel
Uzhhorod, 80–81, 108, 111, 164

valenki, 116–117
Vedomosti (newspaper), 4
"victim of the regime," 20
Victory Day celebrations. *See* World War II, commemorations of
Vinnytsia *oblast'*, 77, 83, 86
Virginia, 177
"voluntary-obligatory," 73
Voronezh: 1, 2, 9, 12, 19, 25, 27–28, 52, 55–57, 63, 82, 118, 119, 124–125, 130, 139, 159, 161; Voronezh *oblast'*, 19, 28, 129, 141
vote-buying: amounts paid, 93, 110; morality of, 95, 129, 134; reasons for participating in, 66–67, 84–87, 92, 105, 107, 168
VTsIOM, 137

Walker, Edward, 8, 176
war: 93; aftermath of, 68, 91, 104, 128, 162; against Ukraine, 22, 85, 94, 106–107, 140. *See also* World War II, commemorations of
Washington, DC, 114, 140
water: loss of access to, 27, 55, 57, 59, 171; Romani communities and, 108–109; in rural areas, 23, 60, 100–102, 128; threats to block access to, 86
Way, Lucan A., xi
wealth, 96, 103, 108, 131, 175, 179, 194n49
Wedeen, Lisa, 13, 176
welfare: 64, 82; in liberalism, 130; local discretion over, 102; loyalty-based, 4, 84, 130–131, 168, 174–175, 179; in neoliberalism, 7, 51, 175; postwar, 48, 168; waning of, 4, 64; welfare state, 7, 48, 84; workplace-based, 52

Wilson, Andrew, 11
Wisconsin, 29, 177
workplaces: role in political theater, 8, 21, 166, 178; as systems of support, 52, 62
World War II: commemorations of, 17, 136–143; memory of, 53, 68, 138, 143. *See also* Immortal Regiment

Yalta, 27
Yanukovych, Viktor: command performances under, 56, 83, 93, 107, 165–166; and Euromaidan, 113, 145; party organization, 91, 109; personality and speech, 72, 116, 152; supporters, 117. *See also* "understandings"
Yazyk do Kyieva dovede, 72
Yekaterinburg, 85
Yeltsin, Boris, 1–3, 62, 64, 118, 125
Yevpatoria, 27
Young Pioneers, 36, 37, 42
Yudin, Grigorii, 118
Yugoslavia, 35
Yurchak, Alexei, 2, 11, 44, 120–121, 157
Yushchenko, Viktor: absence of performances under, 83, 166; alienation of Magyar Ukrainians, 91–92; dissolution of parliament, 146

Zadornov, Mikhail, 35, 36
Zakarpattia, 19, 77–81, 90–93, 95–112
Zaslavsky, Victor, 123
zelenka, 169
Zelensky, Volodymyr: use of Aristotelian theater, 12, 134, 184n43; critiques of command performances, 29, 79, 94; policies of, 71, 173; as populist, 172–173; relations with Russia, 6
Zhuravli, 138
zombification, 54, 133
Zubarevich, Natalya, 167
Zyuganov, Gennady, 1, 3

www.ingramcontent.com/pod-product-compliance
Lightning Source LLC
Chambersburg PA
CBHW021854230426
43671CB00006B/387